The Irish Way

RANDOM HOUSE

NEW YORK

The Irish Way

..

A WALK THROUGH IRELAND'S

PAST AND PRESENT

Robert Emmett Ginna

SKETCHES BY THE AUTHOR

Grateful acknowledgment is made to the following for permission
to reprint previously published material:

Cherry Lane Music Company, Inc.: Excerpt from "Leaving on a Jet Plane," words and
music by John Denver, copyright © 1967 and copyright renewed 1995 by Cherry
Lane Music Publishing Company, Inc. (ASCAP) and DreamWorks Songs (ASCAP).
Rights for DreamWorks Songs administered by Cherry Lane Music Publishing
Company. International copyright secured. All rights reserved. Reprinted by
permission of Cherry Lane Music Company, Inc.

Pete St. John: Twelve lines from "The Fields of Athenry."
Reprinted by permission of Pete St. John.

LIBRARY OF CONGRESS CATALOGING-IN-PUBLICATION DATA

Ginna, Robert Emmett.
The Irish way : a walk through Ireland's past and present /
Robert Emmett Ginna.
p.   cm.
ISBN 0-375-50430-3
1. Ireland—Description and travel.   2. Ginna, Robert Emmett—Journeys—
Ireland.   3. Historic sites—Ireland.   4. Walking—Ireland.   I. Title.
DA978.2 .G56 2003
941.7—dc21   2002031759

For Margaret

and

for the Irish

I am of Ireland
And of the holy land
Of Ireland
Good Sir, pray I thee
For of sainte charité
Come and dance with me
In Ireland.

ANONYMOUS,
fourteenth century, translated by Frank O'Connor

. .

And after the commanded journey, what?
Nothing magnificent, nothing unknown.
A gazing out from far away, alone.

SEAMUS HEANEY, *Seeing Things*

Contents

. .

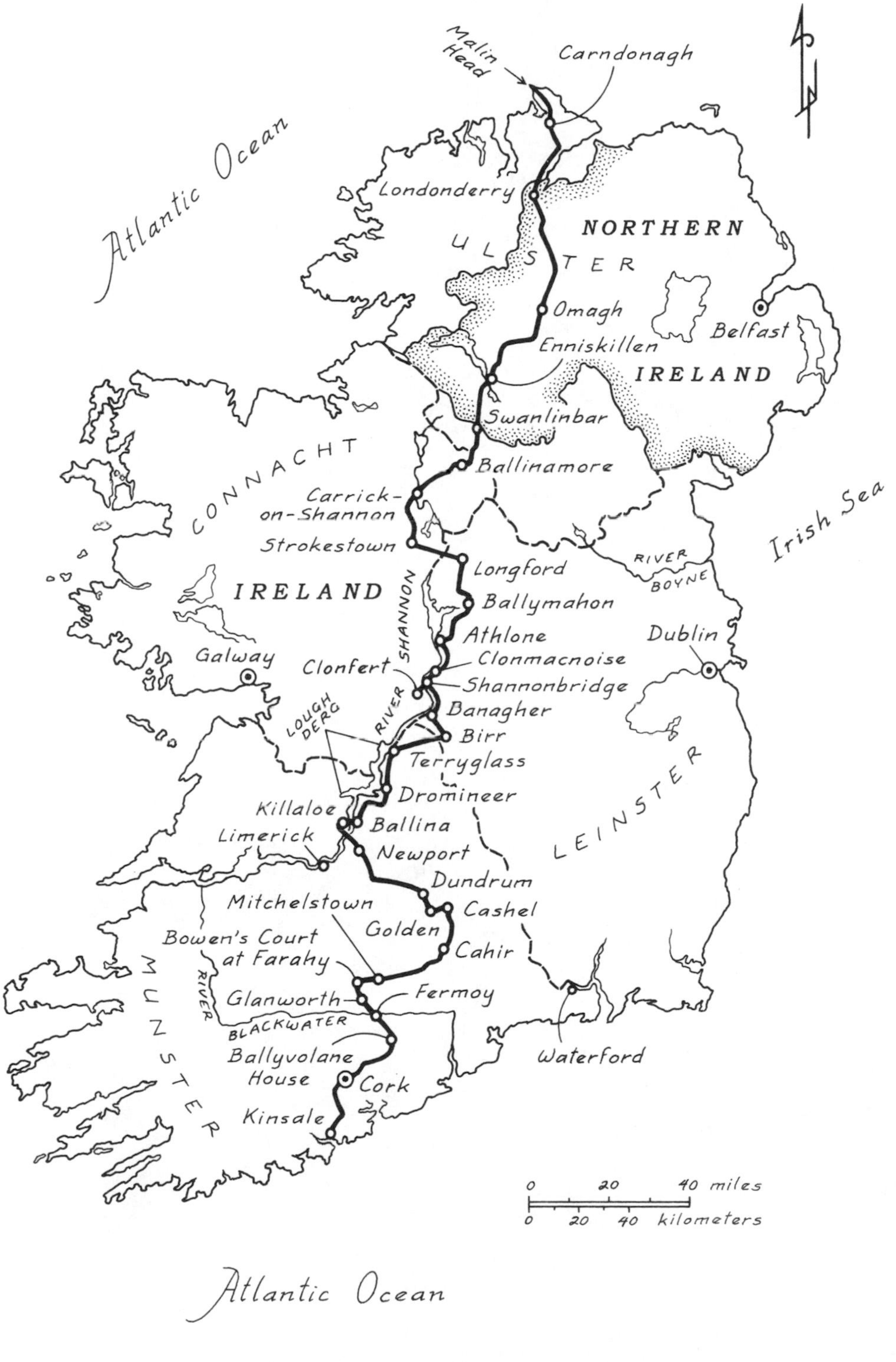

ROBERT EMMETT GINNA'S JOURNEY

PART ONE

Old Ulster and New

Lookout at Malin Head.

From Malin Head

NEVER IN MY DREAMS HAD I QUITE FORESEEN THE WILD BEAUTY of Malin Head, not as I saw it that September day. I was standing at the most northerly point of Ireland, a high promontory jutting into the North Atlantic Ocean. Rain pelted down; curtains of it raced across the cobalt sea rolling toward the jagged rocks just offshore and bursting over them in cascades of emerald.

Though I was waterproofed head to toe, I took shelter in a crumbling lookout post erected during the Second World War as Ireland was guarding its vaunted neutrality. The rain dripped through every fissure in the ruin and made blots in my journal. A tiny fireplace in the corner of the hut would have given scant comfort to a sentry enduring a winter storm here.

Below me, the headland fell away over slabs and crags and grassy patches to the surf beating against the shore. At its rocky lip a little cross marked the place where a youth, heedless of Plato's warning that the sea makes a dangerous neighbor, had been snatched away by a great wave. On a green plot the word EIRE was picked out in white stones, perhaps so the pilot of a transatlantic airplane descending toward Britain might sight it on a clear day, a welcome landfall.

Behind me rose the signal tower built in the nineteenth century by the British Admiralty on Malin Head, or Banba's Crown, as it is also known, after one of the several mythological names for Ireland. The tower was long manned by Lloyd's of London, the dauntless insurers. The approach of ships bound for Britain would be semaphored to the tower from the now deserted islet of Inishtrahull, six miles offshore, then telegraphed to expectant shipowners in British ports. Shipborne radio changed all that.

Intermittent shafts of sunlight slashed through the rain, illuminating distant hills and fields. Far to the west, beyond the great gash of Lough Swilly opening to the sea, Donegal's Derryveagh Mountains were a purple backdrop. In the near distance verdant fields were interspersed with heather-covered bog, the green patches dappled with sheep and cattle, and here and there was a white cottage.

As the rain lightened, I stepped out into a pool of sunlight beneath the tower and caught sight of two small fishing boats, perhaps a mile offshore. Suddenly, they were haloed by a double rainbow. A happy portent for the journey I was about to begin—a walk through the heart of Ireland, the length of the country, north to south, from Malin Head in Donegal to Kinsale in Cork.

I HAD FIRST COME to Ireland decades ago and found a country much like the posters that invited tourists. Thatch-roofed cottages of whitewashed stone nestled in the green bosoms of its hills; donkeys carried wicker baskets piled with bricks of peat cut for farmhouse fires; tinkers, later called itinerants and now, formally, Travellers, plied the roads in their painted wagons; and sheep and cattle were driven along Dublin's North Circular Road to the docks. To be sure, there were some industries; Ireland's universities continued to be centers of learning; the Abbey Theatre and the Gate Theatre were world renowned, as was Dublin's Institute of Advanced Study; the country produced playwrights, poets, and artists. But until the 1970s, Ireland remained a distant, backward cousin of Europe—largely rural, agricultural, and poor. By the dawning of the millennium, however, inventive government policies leading to vast investments by international high-technology companies, the infusion of funds by the European Community, which Ireland joined in 1973, and Ireland's ardent membership in the European Union, which succeeded it in 1993, had wrought astonishing prosperity. By 1999, this republic of some 3.75 million people was achieving the highest economic growth rate in Europe,

7 percent, and was touted by economists as the Celtic tiger; it was the apogee of Ireland's prosperity before the information technology bubble burst. I wanted to learn in just what ways this new affluence had affected the land and the people I'd long known. What better way than to view Ireland at eye level? I was eager to see what the Irish had accomplished, what they had gained for themselves and perhaps had lost, and what they had preserved from a rich and tumultuous past.

SO, IN MY seventy-fourth year, I had come to Malin Head, in Donegal, to begin my journey. Paradoxically, the northernmost point of Ireland is said to be in the "South." For Donegal is one of the twenty-six counties constituting the Republic of Ireland, or Éire in Irish, commonly called the South especially by those in the six counties of Northern Ireland, which others casually call the North. From time immemorial, Ireland has been divided into four provinces: Ulster, Leinster, Munster, and Connacht. In 1921, the Anglo-Irish Treaty, creating the Irish Free State, gerrymandered off six counties from the nine that had made up the province of Ulster (including Donegal, Cavan, and Monaghan) to form Northern Ireland and remain part of the United Kingdom. In 1937, the Irish Parliament (Oireachtas) enacted a new constitution, which declared that the twenty-six counties constitute a sovereign, independent republic and that "The national territory consists of the whole island of Ireland, its islands and the territorial seas" and claimed jurisdiction over the whole. However, in 1993, the British and Irish governments jointly acknowledged that reunification of the six counties of Northern Ireland and the twenty-six counties of the Republic "must be achieved and exercised with and subject to the consent of a majority of the people in Northern Ireland." Not until the Republic of Ireland's constitution was emended as part of the Good Friday Agreement of 1998, which was ratified by an overwhelming vote of the peoples of North and South, did it give up the claim to jurisdiction over the North.

AS A FRESH TORRENT of rain swept in from the sea, I turned away and started off from Malin Head toward the nearby hamlet of Ballygorman. A friendly sergeant of the Garda Síochána, as the police are known in Irish, whom I'd met on my way here, had suggested that I not miss the Seaview Tavern of "Vera Dock"—properly Vera Doherty—in Ballygorman.

The Seaview Tavern is a pub–cum–grocery and filling station overlooking a little harbor, where several fishing boats sheltered behind a high stone breakwater. On shelves behind the small wooden bar were assorted bottles and such dusty goods as batteries in several sizes, locks and keys, Wellington boots, dip for sheep, and nostrums for ridding cattle of worms.

I took one of the few wooden stools and ordered a Powers whiskey. A young couple who had scooted in from the rain ahead of me asked for Guinness. After sipping appreciatively, they remarked that the brew in Ireland was superior to what they drank in London, where both worked. We were the only customers, and after we'd each offered a round, they introduced themselves as Seamus and Patricia. Although she had long lived in London, where she had met Belfast-bred Seamus, it transpired that Patricia was from the area. She and the buxom blond barmaid were catching up on mutual acquaintances when the door opened and out of the rain stepped a character from a Synge one-acter. Lean as a rake, he wore muddy Wellingtons, a shabby tweed jacket, and a conical hat of the shape and size favored by Chico Marx. He asked to see the proprietor, the redoubtable Vera Doherty, but the barmaid adroitly put him off. Undaunted, he launched into a catalogue of the things he could provide the Seaview Tavern at bargain prices. A rapid-fire dialogue of feints and sallies ensued, in which I recall five planks and other building supplies offered and declined before the defeated salesman took his leave.

"A traveling man?" asked Seamus.

"A Traveller, surely," said the barmaid. "I hope the doors of your car are locked. And I hope our stores are secured, as well as the petrol pumps."

By her comment, I was reminded of the long-seated prejudice of the regularly employed and settled against the people now called Travellers. Just then the proprietor and local doyenne, Vera Doherty, appeared and was filled in on the departed peddler.

"God help us! You did well to be shut of him," said Vera Dock.

I would have liked to hear more from the proprietor, and the couple offered another round, but it was midafternoon, and although the sun would not set until late evening in this latitude, with the rain still falling, I wanted to move on before dark. So, I bid all a good-bye, pulled up my hood, and set off, squishing along in my Gore-Tex togs.

Ahead I saw a cluster of white buildings and the tall radio masts of one of the Irish government's three land, sea, and air rescue stations. Curious, I sloshed the half mile or so there, hoping to be admitted. I was fairly sure that if you wanted to check out one of the government's key communications facilities in the United States, you'd have to go through channels and, in this age of terrorism, possibly be checked out by the FBI. But this was Ireland. I walked up to the principal building and knocked on the door.

A slender chap with thinning hair and a ready smile opened, and I introduced myself. Mike Mullins, for so he was, ushered me in to a large room on the ground floor, said that he was one of two radio officers on watch—they stand twelve-hour tricks—and introduced me to the other, Jack Kenny, a burly man with a grand red beard and twinkly eyes behind metal-rimmed glasses. He sat before a panoply of receiver, transmitter, computer, printer, and other instruments to the right of a similar setup, which was Mike Mullins's post.

Jack Kenny was responsible for the "emergency channel," transmissions from and to aircraft, vessels, and those on land in need of emergency aid. At the adjacent console it was Mike Mullins's duty to communicate by the "working channel" with the services that must deliver that aid by land, sea, or air, calling for ambulance, lifeboat, helicopter, or other aircraft as required.

On one wall of the room was a huge map of Ireland, dotted with disks representing the locations of helicopters, fixed-wing aircraft, ambulances, and other medical and rescue facilities. Other markers placed around the many-fingered coast of Ireland indicated the positions of the government's rescue craft. Mike Mullins explained the sequence of operations that follows receipt of a distress call and showed me the forms on which are recorded particulars of each call and its disposition. He handed me a log for the years 1947–1997, in which were entered the distress calls from ships and aircraft. Most seemed to have been either sinking or afire, and I found chilling the frequent terse notations "sank," "ditched," and "crashed."

Just then, the station's commanding officer—crisp in white shirt and black tie—appeared, and Mullins introduced me to Regional Controller Mike McGarry. He headed a crew of fourteen men, each of whom must have served at least two years at sea as a radio operator. Jack Kenny told me that he had served more than twenty years afloat in the merchant service.

"Do you prefer being ashore?" I asked.

Kenny thought for a moment, stroking his beard. "I do now, but when I was young, no."

Showing me to the door, Mike Mullins told me that he had been a radio operator for four years at sea aboard the *M. V. Doulos,* as part of Operation Mobilization, a Christian missionary organization. "I was a missionary," he said.

As he opened the door and I stepped out, Mullins spoke the words of an old Irish toast: "May the road rise up to meet you . . ."

I chimed in with "May the wind be always at your back . . ."

"May the sun shine warm upon your face . . ." he continued; then, as he shook my hand, he altered the usual closing, saying simply, "God bless you."

I knew Mike Mullins meant it.

THE RAIN HAD eased to a dense mist when I struck off in the dim light of late afternoon for the village of Malin, some six miles south of Malin Head on Donegal's great peninsula of Inishowen (from the Irish Inis Eóghan, or Owen's Island), named for a son of the great High King Niall of the Nine Hostages. Referring to the detailed Ordnance Survey map for this section—its scale one centimeter to one kilometer—I chose a little byway, a bohereen, or *bóthairín.* Although the rain still fell steadily, the wind had slackened, and I made good time across a treeless landscape, passing the occasional cottage and one derelict farmhouse, which enjoyed a grand prospect. My map indicated "standing stones," ancient megaliths, off to my right—the country roundabout on Inishowen is sprinkled with megalithic tombs, ancient single standing stones, promontory forts, and ring forts—and I trudged across a sodden field in a fruitless search for the two close by. Then, after one gradual ascent and a somewhat steeper descent, I arrived in Malin, a little village laid out around a triangular common, typical of the plantation settlements of the seventeenth century, when King James I of England and VI of Scotland planted loyal Scottish and English subjects on lands seized from the refractory Irish. At the apex of the common was a pretty Church of Ireland (Anglican) chapel, and on the east side was the small, old Malin Hotel, recently renovated, the family-run establishment of Martin and Bridie McLaughlin.

After a scrub, I dined very well in the hotel's cozy dining room. A lively waitress recommended the chowder, and it was memorable, rich with plump mussels. In a benign mood, I sallied forth for a stroll around the little village. Malin boasted three pubs, besides the hotel's attractive bar, and I dropped in to McGonagle's. No lights showed from without, the curtains were drawn, and within the one public room ten people—eight men, two women—were playing cards, matchsticks for chips. The play was swift, conversation sparse. When one player came to the bar, a kibitzer took his place.

"What's the game?" I asked the cardplayer.

"Thirty-five," he said, glancing back at the play. "In thirty-five, with only two cards out, you pretty well know."

I didn't know thirty-five and was none the wiser but ordered a whiskey and regarded the gold stud in the barmaid's right nostril. Besides the cardplayer and me, only an old-timer, nursing a Coke and puffing on a full-bend pipe, occupied the little bar. He and the barmaid had been conversing in Irish, and the odd man out joined in; their Irish was hardly more impenetrable than their brogues in speaking English with me.

Above the bar, which was finished in bright new pine, hung a clock whose face, with Roman numerals, bore the legend J. A. JOHNSTON, CARNDONAGH and was set in a handsome marquetry case.

"Would Mr. Johnston have made both case and works?" I wondered aloud, indicating the clock with my pipe.

"I'd say so," answered the barmaid.

"There aren't many clockmakers nowadays," I said, impressed by the craftsmanship.

Removing his pipe, the old man contributed, "That would be a hundred years old."

EARLY ON A FAIR, bright day, I made for Carndonagh, not to look for a clockmaker but keen to see a wonder far older than Mr. Johnston's clock: one of the earliest of Ireland's carved stone crosses. On the bridge over the Ballyboe River, which debouches into Trawbreaga Bay, I mused on sea trout, become scarce in recent years, and followed a straight, fairly busy road that skirted the bay for a mile or more.

Carndonagh was a bustling town, with a new county building going up, a square thronged with cars, and a bank where the ATM was out of order but an obliging teller honored my card with cash. At the west end of town, by the Protestant church of St. Patrick, which incorporates parts of a medieval Christian edifice, I came upon the cross, called St. Patrick's Cross, which has been the object of much study. Only St. Mura's Cross, at Fahan, near Buncrana, Donegal, is considered by some scholars to be of a slightly earlier date, sixth or seventh century.

St. Patrick's Cross at Carndonagh, perhaps nine feet high, stands between two short pillars, beneath a simple wooden canopy. The stubby arms of the cross do not make sharp right angles to the shaft but are slightly uplifted and rounded at their ends. Like the cross at Fahan, this one at Carndonagh seems to represent an evolutionary stage between the typical early-Irish grave slabs, which were often incised with a rudimentary cross, and the later deeply carved Irish high crosses, with arms extending at right angles through a central ring, or nimbus.

On one face of St. Patrick's Cross, a design of intertwined ribbons is incised above a crude, moon-faced figure with arms outstretched in a gesture of invocation or benediction. Below, three large-eyed cowled figures in profile, perhaps worshiping monks, fill a panel. In the arms of the cross, small birds may be discerned. On the opposite face of the cross and on the sides, interlaced designs and human figures appear. On the pillars on each side there are large simplified human figures, shown frontally and in profile.

The simplicity of St. Patrick's Cross was affecting; one was conscious that it had been carved by devout hands more than twelve centuries ago and that, surviving storms and warfare, it has stood here since, an object of veneration. I recalled watching the great sculptor Jacques Lipchitz many years ago as he ran his hand along the curve of a Gothic statue of the Virgin in his collection, saying, "When I touch this stone, I shake the hand of the sculptor." I felt the urge to do that here but resisted, for despite having endured the Donegal weather over the centuries, even stone is perishable.

FROM CARNDONAGH TO Londonderry, or Derry, as the second city of Northern Ireland is usually called, the most direct route would have been the main regional road, the R240; instead, I chose another, less trafficked and somewhat longer. However, I knew of no B&B or other hostelry along my way. Bord Fáilte, the Irish Tourist Board, used to publish a directory of every establishment it had inspected and approved, from four-star hotel to simple B&B, indicating the amenities and rates of each. In recent years it ceased to do so; to find lodging along one's route, a tourist or professional traveler was obliged to consult some half dozen directories published by competing trade associations. Several of these publications contributed to the thirty-eight pounds my rucksack weighed. While I had found the Malin Hotel in the Irish Hotel Association's directory, I'd noted no other accommodation on my route between Carndonagh and Derry in any of the guides I carried. I had a reservation in Derry, but Derry was eighteen miles farther. Just a few weeks before, I'd been a sedentary university teacher, and despite being a veteran of a number of walks, I had not been training for this one. Still, I had better get moving.

After retying my bootlaces, I set off. Once past a few houses on the outskirts of Carndonagh, I did not see a soul for the next five miles. The road ran southeast, following the Glenngannon River for the first couple of miles and climbing gently. Bogs stretched away on either side of the narrow road, and turf cutters had been at work on them. The peat bricks were piled along the road. Overhead the clouds were fleets of galleons, their shadows racing over the heathery bogs and fields of malachite green across the river. The light was silvery, magical. After a while a rising wind came whistling down the glen, and the sky became swags of purple and black. A little squall. I bent against it, munching on an apple. The Ordnance Survey map indicated a megalithic tomb and stone circle to my left, but somehow I missed them. However, near lonely little Lough Inn, as the road was rising more steeply, I sighted an ancient circle of stones to my right, not far from the road and higher. It was not shown on my map. I trudged up and inspected the hoary stones, most about my height, some broken, others tilting crazily. The treeless landscape was as desolate as any I'd ever seen in Ireland, and this place rather eery. I hunkered down and wondered about the builders of such circles, millennia ago, and their purpose. Religious? Astronomical? Scholars are uncertain. While in one way, I would have liked to know, I took a certain pleasure in the mystery.

After regaining the road, no more than a narrow track now, and tramping slowly, I stepped to the side on hearing a vehicle overtaking me. Coming abreast, a van slowed and stopped. "Care to ride?" the driver asked.

"I'd be grateful," I said, somewhat winded.

A remark may be due here. This was not a thumb-tripping journey. I liked walking and was resolved not to ask for lifts unless I found my-self desperate. But if an unsolicited ride were offered, I told myself I'd feel free to accept if circumstances—weather, distance, or misery—warranted. Just then I didn't know if I'd make it to Derry by dark. I climbed into the van.

The driver introduced himself as Padraig, a housepainter. He was amused at my answer to his question about what I was up to, humping a pack about the hills of Donegal.

"Enjoying yourself, is it?" He chortled. "I had enough of that lark in the army." His good humor was infectious.

Padraig carried me over the steepest part of the route and set me down at Vance's Point, on the nastily busy road along Lough Foyle, the great sea lough leading to Derry. About seven miles on I came to Muff, still in Donegal.

Just ahead was the border of Northern Ireland. Crossing it, I was in County Londonderry and expected to see a watchtower and fortified checkpoint of the British Army or the Royal Ulster Constabulary. For County Londonderry and Derry itself had been the scenes of violent events during the recent Troubles between unionists and nationalists. I noted no checkpoint, but I was pressing on. Soon I was in the built-up sub-urbs of the city, and the close-of-day traffic was heavy. Walking was no joy. At a stop ahead I saw a bus, hurried, tottered aboard, and was shortly in Derry's center.

Derry Resistant

· ❁ ·

I HAD LONG WANTED TO KNOW THE CITY. WITH NINETY THOUSAND inhabitants, 60 percent Catholic, Derry is the largest city in Northern Ireland after Belfast, and its history has profound significance for all Ireland, North and South, not to speak of Britain. On January 30, 1972, soldiers of Britain's crack Parachute Regiment opened fire on a parade of Catholics protesting civil rights abuses, particularly the internment of suspected terrorists without trial. Thirteen were killed that day, another died later of wounds, and others were wounded.

The British claimed that IRA terrorists had fired at their soldiers first. The IRA insisted that the organizers of the march had asked them to stay away and that they had complied. Although no weapons were found on or about those shot by the Paras, an initial judicial inquiry found the British Army without fault. A public outcry of whitewash by Catholics and nationalists, North and South, and pressure by the Irish government led to a renewed investigation and subsequent judicial inquiry. It commenced in Derry's Guildhall in the fall of 1999 and later sessions were transferred to London, to protect the security of soldiers called to testify; the inquiry is still in progress as I write. Bloody Sunday, as the day instantly was known, became a rallying cry for continuing protest by the Catholic population of the North and, indeed, a red flag to many in the Republic, including the government and the Dáil, the elected lower house of Parliament, to which the government must answer.

Bloody Sunday united many Catholics in the North behind the IRA, which they saw as their only line of defense against the several unionist paramilitary organizations, the armed and overwhelmingly Protestant Royal Ulster Constabulary, and the British Army. After Bloody Sunday, for some time the breach widened between Catholic and Protestant, nationalist and unionist, with appalling consequences in human life and property. Derry was long a war zone before the first breath of peace was felt in the city.

I made my way to the Saddler's House on Great James Street, a B&B just a block away from William Street, where the fateful events of Bloody Sunday had unfolded. It is a Georgian rowhouse operated by Joan Pyne, an engaging bluestocking in tweed and horn-rims, and her affable husband, a retired university professor. She showed me to a small room overlooking the garden, recommended some books and restaurants, and called me a taxi to take me to Oysters, some distance across the wide river Foyle. As the cab approached Craigavon Bridge, we could see cars ahead being waved down and stopped by a few armed RUC men.

"What's this?" I asked the cabbie.

"Random check by the coppers."

We were glanced at and waved through; I noted a policewoman with a machine gun standing well to one side. Real peace was still only a hope in the North. I dined well at Oysters, an intimate place, taxied back, then collapsed into bed.

ON A SUN-WASHED DAY, I sauntered out to explore a fascinating city, where the seeds of discord had been sown centuries before. Derry takes its name from the Irish *doire*, an oak wood. St. Columcille, or Columba, founded a monastery here in 546. For over a thousand years the monastic settlement was successively attacked, destroyed, and reedified by Viking, Irish, and English forces. In 1613, King James I of England and VI of Scotland granted Derry and much surrounding territory to the City of London's trade guilds, whereupon the new charter styled the city Londonderry, from which the county took its name.

In the previous century, in the brutal Elizabethan wars, the queen's forces had grievously harassed the old Irish aristocracy, dispossessing them and granting their estates to English soldiers, adventurers, and administrators like Sir Walter Raleigh and the poet Edmund Spenser. King James I continued the process with English and Scots Protestant plantations in Ulster. Between 1614 and 1619, formidable walls with strong gates and great bastions were erected to defend the city of Londonderry from the hostile Irish. They survive still, twenty feet or more in height, up to thirty feet in breadth, leaving Derry the only intact walled city in Britain or Ireland. The walls afford a promenade of about a mile around. I strolled over it, ruminating about Derry's tempestuous history, which has so informed the Troubles of our time.

In 1649, after the execution of King Charles I, Oliver Cromwell led a great parliamentarian army to punish the vexatious Irish Catholics who had risen in 1641 and with great savagery exacted vengeance for the wrongs—repression of their religion and usurpation of their lands—inflicted by such Elizabethans as Sir George Carew and Raleigh and their Protestant successors. With his superior troops and firepower, Cromwell campaigned with a ferocity that has made him a bogeyman in Ireland to this day, slaying hordes, laying waste the land, and offering resistant Catholic landholders the choice of being dispatched "to hell or to Connacht," Connacht being the province west of the river Shannon whose mountains, bogs, and rocky soil were far inferior to the fertile lands to the east, from which the Irish Catholic landholders were displaced.

Some eleven million acres were granted to the officers, soldiers, and creditors of England's armies. Thousands of Irish peasants were transported to England's colonies in the West Indies in conditions of virtual slavery. By Cromwell's death, in 1658, three quarters of Ireland was in the hands of English and Scots Protestants, the Catholic church had been rigorously suppressed, and denial of civil liberties to Catholics was being enforced.

With the restoration of King Charles II, some Irish Catholics enjoyed the restitution of their lands and titles, and there was some relaxation of the anti-Catholic laws. With the accession of Charles's brother as King James II, an avowed Catholic, the Catholic population of Ireland, still the vast majority, revived its hopes for full restoration of ancient liberties.

When King James appointed Richard Talbot, the Catholic Earl of Tyrconnell, as his Lord Lieutenant in Ireland, Tyrconnell moved to re-

store civil rights to Catholics, open the profession of law to them, permit
their service in the army, and confer commissions on many. Alarm spread
through the Protestant plantations in Ireland, not least in Londonderry.

In the fall of 1688, Tyrconnell ordered the commander of the Protestant garrison of Derry, Lord Mountjoy, to withdraw his force to Dublin, to
be replaced by the Catholic Earl of Antrim and his troops. On December
18, as the first of the Catholic soldiers approached the Ferryquay Gate to
the city, expecting to be admitted, a parcel of young apprentices locked the
gate against them; the three other gates were also barred. It was a day
never to be forgotten in Derry.

Negotiations followed, with the upshot that Lieutenant Colonel
Robert Lundy, as governor and commander, and a Protestant garrison
were established in Derry. Meanwhile the so-called Glorious Revolution
had taken place in England. Tories, Whigs, Anglican prelates, and many
others had been angered at King James's favoritism toward Catholics and
his assertion of royal prerogatives over the interests of Parliament; moreover, they were fearful of what the succession of another Catholic, the
young Prince of Wales, would bring. A group of powerful Englishmen invited William, Prince of Orange, grandson of King Charles I and son-in-
law of King James II, to come from Holland to England and claim the
throne. William landed in England at the head of a strong force. Much of
the nobility and Parliament and the largely Protestant populace rallied to
William and Mary, both Protestants. King James was allowed to escape to
France.

The people of Derry resolved to hold their city for William and Mary,
newly proclaimed King and Queen of England, Scotland, and Ireland, and
William dispatched a supply ship to them. Early in 1689, a Catholic, Jacobite force, soldiery loyal to James, advanced toward Derry. Robert Lundy
moved to confront it some miles upriver from Derry with every man he
could raise but was roundly defeated and retreated to the city. His loyalty
to the cause of William was suspect, and the citizens of Derry were outraged with him. Lundy found it prudent to flee. (The burning of Lundy's
effigy by the Apprentice Boys of Derry Club became an annual event, on
December 18, to celebrate their forebears' barring of the gates.) Thereupon, the Reverend George Walker and Henry Baker, a prominent citizen,
were chosen as joint governors, and the able-bodied were formed into regiments charged with guarding the walls.

In March 1689, James II, accompanied by French generals and the ambassador of King Louis XIV, long a foe of William of Orange in Continental wars, landed at Kinsale, on the south coast of Cork. James proceeded to Dublin, convened a Parliament, attainted a number of Protestants—depriving them of rights, holdings, and offices—and proceeded with a Catholic host to Derry. On April 18, with a small party, James presented himself at a little distance before the Bishop's Gate, the southwestern entrance to the city. He was greeted by gunfire, and some of his party fell. It must have been hard for James, a man with strong views about the sacred person of an anointed king, though he might have recalled that his own father, Charles I, had had his head chopped off by commoners. James waited in the rain through fruitless negotiations, then withdrew ignominiously. The great siege of Londonderry had begun.

A FRENCH COMMANDER tightened a noose about the city by erecting a boom across the river Foyle, downriver, to prevent supplies and reinforcements reaching Derry by ship. The normal population of the city, then about two thousand, swelled to some thirty thousand as the Protestants of the plantation poured in, fearful of the vengeance of a Catholic, Jacobite army. The multitude within the walls were reduced to eating cats, rats, and mice, and drinking horses' blood.

The Jacobite forces were not equipped with siege guns capable of breaching the walls, but they had cannon with which they showered hundreds of bombs on Derry. According to some accounts, the bombardment, disease, and starvation claimed thousands of lives. In heroic sallies the desperate defenders attacked besieging troops, killing several French generals. Derry held. The rallying cry was "No surrender!" In our time one could still hear it in unionist halls and see it splashed on the walls of Northern Ireland's Protestant enclaves. In Ireland, people of every persuasion have long memories.

On July 28, 1689, the ship *Mountjoy* and several others sailed up to the mouth of the Foyle. One dueled with the Jacobite gunners in the fort there, while the *Mountjoy* and the *Phoenix* made for the boom. In a daring action, they breached it. The captain of the *Mountjoy* was killed, but Londonderry was relieved. The siege was lifted, and the Jacobite army departed.

On July 1, 1690, William of Orange, with an army of Dutch and English troops, met James II, with his Irish, Scottish, and French forces, at the river Boyne, thirty miles north of Dublin. James—who as the young Stuart Duke of York seems to have been an able officer in the army of King Louis XIV, commended by the great Marshal Turenne—failed ignominiously at the Battle of Boyne. The Williamite army was superior in numbers and guns, experience and strategy, and it prevailed. The Jacobite army was forced to retreat, badly beaten. A few days later James II embarked from Kinsale, sailing to exile in France, never to return, the kingdoms of England, Scotland, and Ireland lost to him forever.

DERRY IS PERCHED on a low hill above the left, or west, bank of the river Foyle. As I strolled on the walls, I had a splendid view of the old town within and the modern city, which has spread far beyond them. The poor Catholic section called the Bogside lies just below the wall to the west; on the side of a building is painted the defiant YOU ARE NOW ENTERING FREE DERRY. The more prosperous, largely Protestant district known as the Waterside is across the river to the east; there, too, is the strongly fortified barracks of the British Army garrison. Just to the southwest of the old walled city lies the staunchly Protestant housing development called the Fountain, with its unionist graffiti saluting the British allegiance of the residents.

Within the city walls, Derry is laid out much as it was at the time of the great siege. Streets run from the central square, called the Diamond, a feature of a number of plantation towns, to the city's original four gates. Shipquay Street—leading steeply to the east gate of that name, which is closest to the river—is today the principal commercial thoroughfare.

I perambulated the walls, noting the heavily reinforced army checkpoint and watchtower, then deserted, at the Bishop's Gate; gazing at the cannon celebrated as Roaring Meg, which deafened Williamites and blasted Jacobites during the great siege and now frowns over the Bogside; lastly inspecting the seven guns atop the wall beside Shipquay Gate, one a gift of Queen Elizabeth I, the others presented by London guilds. This ordnance glowers over the Guildhall, a Victorian structure that was gutted by fire in 1908, rebuilt by 1912, and wrecked by a bomb in 1972. Beautifully restored, the Guildhall again became the focus of the city's civic and cultural life—the venue for the city council, concerts, dramatic presentations, and exhibitions—until the inquiry into perhaps the most infamous day in Derry's history, Bloody Sunday, was convened here.

After a good pub lunch at the Linenhall, hard by the much rebuilt Ferryquay Gate, I walked to St. Columb's Cathedral, near the Church Bastion on the city's walls. Erected in 1628–1633, rising nobly from its serene close, St. Columb's is said to be the first post-Reformation cathedral in Europe. In April 1688, its Anglican bishop, Ezekiel Hopkins, exhorted the citizens to remain loyal to James II, their rightful king, but he was ignored and chose to leave the city. During the siege that followed, the members of the Anglican communion shared their cathedral with the largely Presbyterian populace; the city's Catholics were banished. Cannon were mounted on the cathedral's tower, the original wooden steeple having been removed. Today a cut-stone spire rises heavenward. Within, the only visitor, I wandered about, looking into a museum room with documents and artifacts from the siege, and near the altar I viewed flags captured from French troops supporting James II. A few notables of the siege, such as the Reverend George Walker, are interred here, as are bishops of the diocese. Many of the monuments in St. Columb's commemorate young men who gave their lives on the fringes of empire and those men's faithful wives.

AMONG THOSE I WANTED to meet in Derry was Shauna Kelpie, newly appointed director of the Foyle Film Festival. When I telephoned, she suggested tea at a café and bakery called Boston Tea Party, in the Craft Village, a complex of workshops, retail stores, and living quarters in old buildings—among them a thatched cottage, which is a venue for performances of traditional Irish music—that catapults the visitor to long-ago Derry. It is off Shipquay Street, close by the Diamond, and walking there, I was struck by the liveliness of people in a city that has witnessed such strife—mothers, children in tow, shopping or strolling; men lingering over pints in the pubs; teenagers chatting gaily in fast-food places or hurrying about, wireless phones clamped to their ears. The Troubles seemed aeons ago.

Shauna Kelpie is a lissome, dark-haired young woman with an easy, open manner; I liked her instantly. If I had any doubt about the vitality of

Derry today, Shauna Kelpie would have dispelled it. She was not long married, and she and her husband, John, a structural engineer, had spent their honeymoon trekking through the Himalayas. She returned to launch herself into the demanding task of directing the Foyle Film Festival. It would present new and classic theatrical feature films, dramatic and documentary shorts, and animated films; it would also offer workshops and forum appearances by international notables like director Wim Wenders, actor Joseph Fiennes, and Irish writers and filmmakers Pat McCabe and Jim Sheridan. There were to be the Irish premieres of some five features, including John Sayles's *Limbo* and Roman Polanski's *The Ninth Gate*. Juggling all these elements to produce a rewarding, eclectic program requires the wizardry of a Merlin. Judging by the handsomely produced program, Shauna Kelpie would be making an impressive debut as the festival's director, and I was sorry that I'd be on the march, far away, when it was held.

I got an overview of Derry's arts scene from Shauna's perspective, and it was clear that raising money from the private sector to augment the slender fiscal support of the local and Northern Ireland governments was a struggle. (She was happy to report that Budweiser had become a major sponsor of the film festival. I noticed that its beer, brewed in Kilkenny, in the Republic, was being quaffed North and South.) She told me that the Nerve Centre had been the most imaginative arts initiative in Derry and that I should see it.

I supposed that Nerve was an acronym, but I was wrong.

"The Nerve Centre was the brainchild of Pierce Moore, an MBA and the Centre's CEO, and Martin Melarkey, its director," Shauna said. "They wanted to give the performing arts in Derry a home and to make a place for innovative filmmaking, multimedia production, music recording, video production, dance and theater workshops."

"So Nerve was conceived as a nexus?"

"Yes. They were determined to provide a focus for Derry and the region," said Shauna. "It was purpose built with a video-production facility, cutting rooms, and a small cinema. It opened in 1990."

The Nerve Centre, in which the Foyle Film Festival has its office, is on Magazine Street, just within the ramparts of the massive city wall overlooking the Catholic, republican Bogside.

"Moore and Melarkey were themselves Bogsiders," said Shauna. "They wanted to involve people of their own background in the arts, to bring them into the city's cultural life, because they had been so marginalized by the rigid sectarian structure of Derry."

When we got to the Nerve Centre, I looked at the young people bustling about and realized how remarkable was the achievement of Moore and Melarkey in a city as riven as Derry has been. The Nerve Centre hummed.

IN DONEGAL, about five miles west-northwest of Derry, crowning a hilltop, is the Grianán of Ailech. (Like other names in Ireland, there are various spellings in Irish and English; Grianán, pronounced "Greenan," means "sunny place," and Ailech, or Aileach, means a "stone building.") What one beholds, approaching along a track winding up from the Derry to Letterkenny road, is a massive, circular low stone fortress crowning the eminence. From at least the fifth century it was the royal seat of the northern Uí Néill (as the O'Neills they would dominate much of Ulster and, indeed, much of northern Ireland to the seventeenth century), descendants of Niall of the Nine Hostages, the titular High King of Ireland who died about A.D. 405. His son Eóghan (Owen) is reputed to have been baptized here by Saint Patrick in about 450. Folklore has it that the Great Hugh O'Neill—as he is usually styled, the extraordinary Irish champion of the Elizabethan wars—slumbers with his men beneath the Grianán's walls, to awaken magically when Ireland shall be free.

I found myself quite alone when I entered the single low doorway through the unmortared stone walls, some seventeen feet high, and peered around a grassy enclosure, which I paced off at seventy-five feet across. In ancient times there would have been wooden buildings within it. Stretching out my arms like Leonardo's figure, I reckoned the thickness of the walls to be fifteen feet at the base and noticed openings to two interior chambers. Then I ascended one of five stone stairways leading to three terraces, by which defenders could hasten to battle stations. From the parapet the liege men of the King of Ailech (comprising more or less what is Donegal) could hurl weapons upon an enemy who had the temerity to attack the citadel. Exhilarated by the superb panorama, I saw to the west much of Lough Swilly as an immense silver amoeba sprawling southward; farther west the Derryveagh Mountains of Donegal receded in transparent ranks, the cone of Errigal, Donegal's highest peak, faintly visible; to the north was spread out Inishowen, the vast territory that Eóghan could call his own; to the east was Derry; and to the southeast lush County Londonderry, through which I'd soon be marching. In the near distance the vast fields of green with patches of sepia bog were suddenly obscured by advancing veils of rain. Rapt, I gazed about, then tried to discern the remains of the three concentric earthworks that had guarded the fortress. It was hard to imagine a force successfully storming this lofty redoubt, yet in 1101, Muircheartach O'Brien, King of Munster, sacked the Grianán of Ailech after Donal MacLochlainn, King of Ailech, had laid waste the O'Brien seat at Kincora.

Regretfully, pulling on my rain gear, I went down the stairs, out the portal through which great chieftains and hosts of warriors had passed, and left the Grianán. Some way down the slope, I turned and stared back, imagining King Muircheartach and his warriors struggling up the hill, cutting their way through the men at the earthworks, dodging the missiles flung by the defenders, and flinging themselves at the Grianán's walls with wild cries.

TELLING ME THAT there was an interesting American connection with Beech Hill, an old mansion become a country-house hotel, Mae Beth Fenton of the Northern Ireland Tourist Board in New York had booked me in. It was about two miles south of Derry, right on my line of march. I was welcomed by Patsy O'Kane, who manages Beech Hill beside her brother Seamus Donnelly with engaging, low-key informality, then shown up to an enormous bedroom with canopied four-poster. A red velvet settee, lounge chairs, and a coffee table stood before a bay window looking over the garden. Adjoining was a bathroom of appropriate scale and decor. My bedroom was a place one could read and write. And I would discover that one dined extremely well.

Beech Hill had been the home of the Skiptons, a plantation family, who settled there in the seventeenth century. The present house was built in 1729 by Captain Thomas Skipton and enlarged and modified over time. Its appearance is curious: there is an odd entrance porch with bow windows in its second story (first floor in Irish and British usage), a chapel, many rooms furnished eclectically with antiques, and a new wing with state-of-the-art conference facilities. The pink, many-chimneyed house is set in a spacious demesne, with a stream coursing through it and a decorative pond whose waters rise and fall periodically; bosky pathways lead through towering trees.

Into this idyllic setting in May 1942 came a detachment of U.S. Marines. That February the U.S. Navy had established a base on the river Foyle, at Londonderry, to support U.S. operations in the North Atlantic and to prepare for the invasion of Europe in the Second World War. (The U.S. Navy maintained a base there until the 1970s.) A company from the First Provisional Marine Battalion was billeted at Beech Hill, charged with the security of an ammunition dump; other Marine detachments were stationed elsewhere about Londonderry. As allies in the war against Nazi Germany, the Marines and the locals struck up enduring friendships. In 1997, the U.S. Navy and Marine Corps Friendship Association was inaugurated, and a group of serving Marine officers arrived with Secretary of the Navy John H. Dalton and Lieutenant Colonel George O. Ludcke, USMC Retired, commanding officer of the Leathernecks at Beech Hill, 1942–1944, to dedicate a monument commemorating the Marines' wartime service there. It stands before the house.

Seven months before the Japanese attack on Pearl Harbor, after which the United States entered the Second World War, seventeen U.S. Navy pilots were sent to Northern Ireland on the orders of President Franklin D. Roosevelt—in an operation that remains little known—to train pilots of the Royal Air Force in the operation of the U.S.-built PBY Catalinas. The big, long-range flying boats, based at Lough Erne, were ideally suited to search for the German U-boats wreaking havoc on the ships sustaining Britain as, alone, she held off the Nazi might. Although it was a direct violation of the U.S. Neutrality Act for American military personnel to be engaged as combatants, on May 26, 1941, Ensign Leonard B. "Tuck" Smith of the U.S. Navy was at the controls of a Catalina, searching for the formidable German battleship *Bismarck*. The new, heavily armored German warship had sortied into the North Atlantic to destroy the shipping that was Britain's lifeline. On May 24, in the Denmark Strait, the *Bismarck* and the cruiser *Prinz Eugen* had been intercepted by a British force. In the ensuing battle, *Bismarck* sank the mighty *Hood*, long the pride of the British Navy, with a loss of fifteen hundred men, crippled the newly launched battle cruiser *Prince of Wales*, then slipped away from shadowing cruisers and vanished.

At 9:45 A.M. on May 26, some five hundred miles southwest of Ireland, copilot Ensign Smith, who had relieved the pilot, Flying Officer Dennis Briggs, gestured ahead and called out, "What's that?" He had found the *Bismarck*. Briggs ordered Smith to take them down for a closer look while he radioed the great quarry's position to the waiting British Navy. Smith brought the big, slow aircraft out of the clouds into a rain of AA flak from the giant battleship only five hundred feet below. The Catalina was riddled but made it back to base, mission accomplished. An armada of British ships, battleships, cruisers, aircraft carriers, and destroyers closed in on the *Bismarck,* which had been damaged in the Denmark Strait (the *Prinz Eugen* had escaped to Brest). Pounded by shells from British battleships and cruisers, blasted by torpedoes from ships and aircraft, at 10:40 A.M. on May 27, after taking extraordinary punishment, the *Bismarck,* until then the most powerful warship in the world, rolled over and went down with nearly two thousand German sailors; 115 were rescued. (In recent years, employing Russian minisubmarines to inspect the battleship's hull, American observers have concluded that the *Bismarck* was probably scuttled by its crew. However, using an undersea robot, British investigators have decided that naval gunfire and torpedoes doomed the *Bismarck,* even if her crew's scuttling may have hastened her end.)

ON A SUNDAY, when I came down to breakfast, Seamus Donnelly alerted me that the All-Ireland GAA football match was about to be played between Cork and Meath. The GAA is the Gaelic Athletic Association, under whose auspices the traditional Gaelic (Irish) sports are organized, and the year's final was to be played between Counties Cork and Meath in Dublin's Croke Park. While sport transcends the border, devotion to the traditional ancient Gaelic games, still ardently played North and South, tends to identify their players and supporters as nationalists.

When the time came, Seamus installed me in front of a big television set. Much of the match was played in heavy rain, and it was a corker, but the victory went to Meath. One after another of its athletes hoisted the huge silver tassie called the Sam Maguire Trophy—modeled after the eighth-century Ardagh chalice in the National Museum in Dublin—and they received the salute of Ireland's president, Mary McAleese. During the long, stirring game, several drinks had been served me, and when I saw Seamus Donnelly afterward, we were both merry. The proprietor had been celebrating the Meath victory and allowed, "It wasn't a bad game." When I expatiated on the athleticism of the players who had played thirty-five-minute halves on a ninety-meter field with no time-outs except for injuries, Seamus declared that he found European football, or soccer, boring compared to Gaelic football, which is closer to rugby, and, he added, apropos of American football, "Against our lads, your big fellas wouldn't have a clue."

I HAD BEEN GIVEN an introduction to Ian A. Young, managing director of an electrical engineering firm and a sort of unofficial PR man and booster for Derry. When I telephoned, asking to call on him, he graciously said he'd come to Beech Hill. We talked over coffee in the lounge, and I thought that if Derry needed an apostle, it had one in Ian Young. A handsome chap of middle years, with a buoyant, direct style, he was fervent about the spirit of renewal in Derry awakened by the peace initiatives. He credited much of this renewal and, indeed, much of the impetus for peace in the North to John Hume, MP, founder of the Social Democratic and Labour Party (and corecipient of the Nobel Peace Prize), whom Ian had known since they were youths.

"A marvelous man," he said. "We had twenty-two and a half percent unemployment in 1980. It's now eleven percent in this city and seven point three percent for all Northern Ireland."

When I asked what had brought this about, Ian spoke of the efforts Hume and others had made to encourage investment in Northern Ireland, where it had lagged behind the economic expansion in the South, as had tourism, because of the Troubles. Ian told me about a group called Derry-Boston Ventures, with which he was associated. Its Boston end was headed by Mike Donnelly, and with the backing of Boston's then mayor Ray Flynn, Derry-Boston Ventures had been instrumental in financing Derry's Foyleside Shopping Centre, which had been built below the old city wall by the riverside. (I'd already stopped by the stylishly designed Foyleside and wandered about the mutileveled space around the grand atrium. There were some forty shops—newsagents and stationers, shoe stores, wine merchants, boutiques offering filmy undies for women and modish leather jackets for young men, and the omnipresent McDonald's, in front of which tables and chairs were set out beneath the long, vaulted skylight.)

When I commented about other new building on bomb sites, Ian remarked, "Paddy Doherty, CEO of Derry's Inner City Trust, says, 'You're not likely to find kids who've built a place burning it down.' "

Ian mentioned that he traveled regularly to Washington, D.C., where Derry-Boston Ventures had established an office. "The area around Fairfax, Virginia, is a center for high-tech computer industry," he said. "We'd like to attract more of that here." Then, glancing at his watch, he arose, telling me that I should not fail to call on him for assistance. As we parted, Ian Young turned back and surprised me by a postscript: "I'm a unionist," he said, "but I consider reunification inevitable."

Soldiers of the Queen

·❀·

AS IAN YOUNG LEFT, SEAMUS DONNELLY CALLED ME OVER TO THE little bar, where he was polishing glasses, holding each to the light like a jeweler with a gem; there was a telephone call for me.

An upper-class English voice said, "Mr. Ginna?" (pronouncing my name *Jinn*-uh as "u" English people invariably do, like the name of Pakistan's governor general, while it is Ginn-*ah* in County Kerry and confoundingly has become Ginn-*nay* in the States).

"Yes," I answered. "Ginn-nay."

"Right!" he said. "CO of the First Battalion, Queen's Lancashires, here, Steve —" (He gave his full name, but security regulations prohibit publishing the names of British soldiers serving in Northern Ireland.) A few weeks before, I'd been in Scotland and lunched with a retired major general, a former colonel of The Queen's Lancashire Regiment. When I told him about the walk I planned, he exclaimed, "My Regiment is garrisoned in Omagh!" and straightaway he got up from the table and put in a call to the commanding officer there. On returning, he said, "They'll keep an eye out for you."

The colonel who telephoned me at Beech Hill said, "We're having a rather special evening here, Beating Retreat. The Duke of Abercorn will review what should be a good show, and there'll be a reception afterward. I'd like to invite you to attend and join us for dinner."

"That's extremely kind," I said. "Actually, I'm on a walking trip and was planning on tramping down to Omagh in the next couple of days."

"So I understood, but we'll send a car for you and get you back tonight. Do come."

"I'd love to. Dress?"

"You'll want a jacket and tie, but we could provide."

"If tweed will do, perhaps I'll pass."

"Good. A quarter to five, then?"

"Aye, aye!"

At a quarter to five, I was called to reception. A tall young man in mufti awaited me.

"You're a soldier, I presume?"

"Yes, sir. We don't wear uniform off the base."

I understood. In the dark days of Northern Ireland's Troubles, a lone British soldier had been a ready target for an IRA sniper. Since the Good Friday Agreement—to which Sinn Féin, the political party allied with the IRA, had acceded—the British Army had been keeping a low profile in Ireland. The corporal led me to a polished red sedan, as unidentifiable as he was, and we sped along the main road to Omagh, the county seat of Tyrone, thirty miles south of Derry. Omagh had been the scene of the single worst tragedy in Northern Ireland's Troubles, on August 15, 1998. A die-hard splinter group styling itself the Real IRA detonated a bomb that blew twenty-nine people to kingdom come, including a number of children. As I write, one man has been convicted as an accessory to the crime.

Like every other British Army or Royal Ulster Constabulary installation in Northern Ireland since early in the Troubles, Lisanelly Barracks was fortified with a high-perimeter fence, well lit, and surveyed by video cameras. At the main gate we were checked by armed soldiers in full combat gear. The corporal was known, and I was expected and identified. We drove past functional redbrick buildings on this long-established base to the Officers' Mess, where I was made welcome by my host, Colonel Steve, CO of the 1st Battalion of The Queen's Lancashires—spruce in pinstripes, a compact, dark-haired, youthful man with a military mustache and lively eyes. He gave me a ticket of admission and had me driven with several other guests to the adjacent St. Lucia Barracks. They were handsome old stone buildings housing the 4th Battalion of The Royal Irish Regiment, on whose parade ground Beating Retreat would take place.

Beating Retreat is a venerable ceremony in the British Army and has its origin in a military maneuver. I read on my ticket that proceeds from admissions (a ticket cost five pounds) were to go to the Disabled Police Officers Association to aid men and women of the Royal Ulster Constabulary disabled by terrorist attacks and invalided out of the service, of which there were about two hundred. (As of November 2002, 303 have been killed.) It was a beautiful evening in Omagh; the Union flag waved on its flagstaff against a sapphire sky, but a precautionary marquee had been erected for the numerous guests. I found myself seated in the front row, next to the lieutenant colonel commanding the 4th Battalion of The Royal Irish Regiment, smartly turned out in tweed beside his stylish wife.

Alone on the small reviewing stand before the marquee stood His Grace the Duke of Abercorn, KG, looking every inch ducal, and as he had been a Grenadier Guardsman he carried his many inches nobly, standing erect and hatless, attired in dark mufti, as the Band of The Royal Irish Regiment marched on from his left, playing "Arnhem." I had looked forward to seeing the duke, being interested in his stately home, Baronscourt, not far away in County Tyrone—of which he is Lord Lieutenant—which he does not open to the public. I had been fascinated by accounts of his forebear, the first Marquess of Abercorn, known as Don Magnifico, an exquisite of such sensibility that he required a senior member of his household to fumigate the rooms where servants had worked. A Knight of the Garter, like the present duke, the marquess traveled always with his regalia and was said to be the most arrogant man in Europe.

The Band of The Royal Irish Regiment marched in complex formations while playing a variety of tunes, from old regimental marches to such Irish showstoppers as "Riverdance" and the "Kerry March." It was followed by the Corps of Drums of the 1st Battalion, the Grenadier Guards. The Grenadiers marched in complicated evolutions, the drummers producing fifes from time to time as they dazzled with a startling treatment of "Brazil" or the thunderous march "The British Grenadiers," a recording of which I have found effective in rousing slugabeds. Then the Band and the Corps, led by their respective drum majors, both stocky soldiers who commanded with parade-ground voices, joined in intricate maneuvers—all resplendent in parade fig, boots polished to a fare-thee-well, thumping in perfect cadence, instruments gleaming—climaxing with the "Sunset Salute," the lowering of the colors, and the playing of the national anthem. The massed Band and Corps then performed a stirring medley of regimental marches and Irish airs before marching off as the Duke of Abercorn took the salute. As promised, it was a grand show.

The reception afterward for guests at Beating Retreat was an informal affair, and the Duke of Abercorn proved more affable than his predecessor Don Magnifico was reputed to have been. Later, in the Officers' Mess of The Queen's Lancashires, the Mayor and the Mayoress of Burnley in Lancashire—the recruiting area of the Regiment—were honored at a dinner.

The dining room was hung with portraits of Colonels of the Regiment, including my friend in Scotland. (In peacetime a British Army regiment usually has one battalion on active service, commanded by a lieutenant colonel, who is always addressed as Colonel. The Colonel of the Regiment is a senior officer who may well hold a general's rank. The Colonel-in-Chief of the Regiment is a distinguished person, usually of royal rank, who is effectively its patron. Queen Elizabeth II is Colonel-in-Chief of the Lancashires, and they have the status of a Royal Regiment.)

We took our places around a long table dressed with the regimental silver and enjoyed a fine dinner—nicely poached fish, excellent Irish lamb, the inevitable pudding—which concluded with a noble Stilton and the passing of the port. To my left was the battalion's second in command, a major who revealed that he was the author of a forthcoming mystery novel with a military setting, and we chatted about publishing. We also spoke of Northern Ireland, and the major remarked that he was married to a woman from Belfast who makes a point of asserting that she is British.

After dinner my host, the CO, presented me to other officers—all but the colonel are addressed by first names in the mess—and showed me about, not excepting the pine-paneled bar beyond the billiard room, where he introduced the barman as the soldier of longest service in the regiment. It seemed as if every inch of wall on each of three floors displayed paintings, prints, photographs, and vitrines of medals commemorating battles, heroes, hallowed events, and the valorous deeds of the Regiment and its predecessors.

The Regimental Color of The Queen's Lancashires has on it a laurel wreath embroidered with forty-one selected Battle Honors earned before 1914. As the present Regiment is an amalgamation of several forebears going back to the 30th Foot, raised in 1689 to fight for William of Orange as King William III, it is entitled to claim 203 Battle Honors, more than any other regiment in the British Army. The Victoria Cross, Britain's highest decoration for valor on the field of battle, has been awarded to nineteen officers and other ranks of the Regiment and its predecessors, all of whom are represented on the walls of the Officers' Mess.

Until gazing around this intimate museum, I hadn't realized how the esprit de corps of British Army regiments is nourished by the trophies, pictures, and other mementos they preserve. As the amiable Colonel Steve, with a nonetheless easy air of authority, showed me through the principal rooms of the brick building, which might have been a motel in Indiana, I was conscious that the handsomely furnished sitting rooms, dining room, billiard room, and entrance hall suggested an English country house, in which officers and gentlemen might feel at home. When a regiment moves from one post to another, its fine antique furniture, carpets, pictures, and treasures are carefully packed and moved as well. Like a tortoise of splendid carapace, the regiment or battalion, as the case may be, travels with its household on its back. The Queen's Lancashires were the last British garrison in Berlin, moving with their lares and penates in 1994 from the fine barracks of the pre–Second World War Wehrmacht in Spandau, Berlin, to Tidworth, in southern England. A photograph of the officers and sergeants commemorates the occasion.

The most arresting treasure of the Regiment is the half-life-size silver statue by Sir William Reid Dick that honors the sacrifice of brother officers who fell in the First World War. The model was Second Lieutenant S. W. "Sam" Boast of the South Lancashires. It depicts him pistol in hand as he advanced on an enemy position near Arrowhead Copse in France, August 8, 1916. The statue is never polished, its dark surface suggesting the mud of Flanders, but the helmet is shiny from the touch of regimental officers who would emulate the spirit of Sam Boast, one of three brothers who won the Military Cross in the Great War.

At the appointed hour the corporal was at the door with his car. On bidding me good-bye, the colonel urged me to return as the battalion's guest when I passed through Omagh on my march. Then the corporal drove me back to Beech Hill.

AFTER BREAKFAST next morning, Crawford McIlwaine, the offgoing night receptionist, watched me studying the Ordnance Survey map to pick my route and said, "I'll put you on the Trench Road." He did just that, sparing me dreary turns through new housing on Derry's southeast edge.

What started as a fair day, making for lovely views over the valley of the Foyle toward Donegal, soon changed. A steady rain began to fall, and I stopped and pulled on my rain gear. Near where County Londonderry borders County Tyrone, in a region of small farms, I came upon automated stop-go lights controlling one-lane traffic. Men were working on the drainage on one side of the road. As the light turned green and I started forward, a navvy put down his long-tailed shovel and came over, curious about the solo hiker. He asked if I was on holiday, and as the rain fell and the day shortened, I agreed that I was.

"I took the wife and four children to Florida last year," he said. "We visited Disney World and Tampa, and we particularly liked an island near there." He glanced up at the lowering skies and added, "The wife and I hope we can afford to take the two youngest children to Disney World this year. They ought to see it, and the people in Florida are so friendly and the hotels are so reasonable."

Pondering this good father's views, I slogged on to the village of Dunnamanagh, arriving as it was growing dark. The Village Inn cast a welcome glow. After I had slung down my rucksack and ordered a Smithwick's ale, the publican asked, "Where are you going to spend the night?"

"I was about to ask you that," I said. For although I had the name of a couple of B&Bs near Plumbridge, it was seven miles or so farther, and I didn't fancy doing that in the darkness on a wet night.

Thereupon, Cyril Donnelly, the publican, had a word with the young man at the other end of the bar, the only other patron, then stepped away. He returned shortly to say, "You're all set at a B and B about two and a half miles away. It's a farm, the people are lovely, and Mrs. Gamble will pick you up in about forty-five minutes."

I nipped next door and got some fish and chips from a bright, barebones takeout. Cyril Donnelly provided plate, utensils, salt, vinegar, and coffee. When Mrs. Gamble's car drew up, I wished the helpful publican well and dashed to it through the slashing rain.

As we drove off, after introductions, Helen Gamble said, "While I was driving to Derry today, I saw you walking toward Dunnamanagh, and I said, 'Maybe he'll stay with us tonight.'"

At the Gamble farmhouse, I was introduced to young John, who was about to start his homework, and shown to a comfortable lounge with a big TV, then to a small bedroom and the nice, carpeted bathroom opposite.

Before a hearty breakfast, I met Billy Gamble, Helen's husband. They raise beef and dairy cattle, milking forty-five. Billy is also a contractor of farm machinery. The day before, he was at another farm, making silage. "It wasn't the weather for it," Billy said. "Too wet. Some farmers aren't motivated enough to get the work done when they should."

Helen added, "You might leave it"—the hay or corn—"cut for one day when the weather is fine." She shook her head. I was to hear much of the travails of farmers on my journey.

BETWEEN DUNNAMANAGH and Plumbridge, about a mile and a half past the hamlet of Ballynamallaght, where I bought an apple and banana in the only shop, I happened upon a small circle of standing stones in a dell, another of the hundreds of megalithic circles that abound in Ireland. An old beech towered above the stones, many mossy, others lichen encrusted. I sat for a while, reflecting on the toil it took to raise this circle before the dawn of history. I found the remote site haunting.

The day was alternately bright and dark, and I swung along in good heart through a lush, undulating country, occasionally recalling bits of poetry or singing snatches of old marching songs. Cows came to the gates of stone-walled fields to stare curiously at this passerby, and I obliged by addressing them: "Well, Great Maeve! How goes the day?" or some such nonsense. The mind grows happily unfettered when tramping.

By one long green field that fell away from the road, a few sheep grazed near a gate while perhaps a hundred more were scattered down the slope. As I came abreast of the gate, the nearest ewe fixed me with a baleful eye, turned, and bolted. As if a trumpet had sounded, the whole flock turned in unison and fled after that woolly dam as if the devil were after them. Sheep.

I was skirting the western edge of the Sperrin Mountains as I entered Plumbridge, a pretty village through which the Glenelly River flows en route to the Foyle. I sat on a bank and enjoyed my fruit, thinking that the river looked invitingly fishy. However, Peter McCullagh of the Glenelly Bar pronounced the fishing so-so just then. "We need some rain to move the fish," he said, and I wondered what had been wetting me.

Having learned that Ethel Beattie's B&B was close by, I telephoned.

Although Mrs. Beattie was away, her son Charlie, just home from cutting barley, thought they could put me up. The Beatties' Crosh Lodge was a twenty-year-old brick house, comfortable and surgically clean. After sprucing up, I went down to a parlor furnished with heavily overstuffed pieces, framed scriptural exhortations, family photographs, and romantic landscapes. I was browsing in some books and considering a stroll into Plumbridge for some pub food when Jim Beattie, Charles's father, appeared. A short, sturdy man with the strong blunt hands of a farmer and a cheerful face, dressed in a dark-blue suit, he said that he was off to a Grange meeting in Newtownstewart. He offered to drop me off and pick me up at a restaurant near there.

The Mellon Country Inn was a considerable establishment. When I came in, a fashion show was in progress in the banquet room adjoining the restaurant and pub. The decor was pleasantly rustic, and I enjoyed a relaxed meal by the open fire. The inn takes its name from the Mellon homestead, which stands on its original site in what is now the Ulster-American Folk Park, just across the road. From this modest farmhouse, Judge Thomas Mellon immigrated to the United States in the early nineteenth century to found the dynasty in Pittsburgh that amassed a great fortune and made such great benefactions as the National Gallery of Art. The folk park, between Newtonstewart and Omagh, is an assemblage of original and replica buildings in which authentically garbed guides and artisans present a picture of life for Irish immigrants to the United States and Canada in the eighteenth and nineteenth centuries.

Jim Beattie drove me back to his home, and we had a stimulating conversation. A well-read man of strong opinions, he remarked, "The landlords and the church were the death of this country; the landlords kept the people in tenure, and the church tithed them, whether they liked it or not."

We discovered a mutual interest in history and archaeology, and Jim Beattie talked knowledgeably about O'Neill castles, the Flight of the Earls (when the two most formidable of the Irish chieftains chose exile rather than life under the English heel), and the dolmen in one of his fields. Getting out a scrapbook, he showed me some newspaper cuttings about the recent discovery of a Bronze Age burial in Newtonstewart. A team of archaeologists from the Environment and Heritage Service had been excavating a ruined castle built by Sir Robert Newcomen during the plantation of Ulster and wrecked by order of James II on his retreat from Derry. Led by Ruari O Baoill (anglicized as Rory O'Boyle), they were removing the concrete floor of a derelict grocery in front of the castle when they discovered the capstone of a cist grave, a Bronze Age stone burial chamber. "We expected to uncover evidence about life here some four hundred years ago, but not about death here some four thousand years ago," O Baoill told the reporter for the *Belfast News Letter*. Jim Beattie offered to take me to the site next morning.

The castle ruin is on the main street of the town, and we found Ruari O Baoill working near a ponytailed young woman manning a jackhammer. Jim Beattie introduced me, and the archaeologist affably showed me about, indicating where his crew had uncovered the original foundations of the castle and the positions of original walls, windows, and stairs, and what they had done so far to preserve them. Then he led me to the cist grave. I gazed at a small, rectangular enclosure formed of stone slabs, just below the former floor level. There were two chambers, in each of which was a clay pot of identical design, one larger than the other. These urns had held what were presumed to be human remains.

When Dr. Eileen Kelly, an osteoarchaeologist, had come to examine the burial, she confirmed that the urns contained cremated human remains, which she removed to the laboratory for study. Ruari O Baoill said that he was later informed that the bone fragments found in one of the urns had not yet fused, indicating that the remains were those of a juvenile. The age and sex of the individuals had not yet been determined. There was some speculation that the grave might have been that of mother and child.

Although a veteran of many digs, the burly, reddish-bearded O Baoill was excited about this find. "There are only seven hundred Bronze Age burials in all Ireland," he said. "Less than twenty cist graves have been found; the last was unearthed in 1973, near Strabane." Smiling, the archaeologist said he was sure the occupants of the shop that had stood there knew of the grave just beneath their floor: "Superstition is often a potent force in Ireland."

JIM BEATTIE POINTED me toward the road to Gortin, and shortly I came to a bridge over the Owenkillew River. A sign apprised me that the fishing rights for salmon, sea trout, and brown trout were reserved by the Beltrim Estate and that fly-fishing only was permitted. Another sign pro-

claimed: RIVER WORKS HAVE BEEN FUNDED BY THE SALMONID ENHANCE-
MENT PROGRAMME FOR PEACE AND RECONCILIATION, and it bore the seal of
the Ministry of Agriculture of Northern Ireland and the circle of golden
stars on a blue field that is the symbol of the European Union.

As I leaned over the parapet of the bridge, watching an angler casting
in the Owenkillew, which coursed swiftly from the Sperrin Mountains, a
Lexus parked near the bridge abutment. A gentlemanly chap joined me,
and we spoke of the river and the fishing. Then he asked me where I was
walking, and when I said through Gortin Glen to Omagh, he told me
about an odd phenomenon he'd experienced in Gortin Glen Forest Park.
He said, "I would park my car, leave it in neutral, and watch it roll about
fifty yards uphill." Leaving me cogitating, he went back to his car, suited
up in waders, took his rod, and descended to the river. I had not gone
much farther when the rains came.

At Gortin, I passed the forbidding Royal Ulster Constabulary post;
like the one at Dunnamanagh, it was surrounded by high steel walls
bristling with lights and surveillance cameras. On the tidy main street of
the town, I was happy to escape the sodden day into the warm ambience of
Peter and Kate McKenna's Badoney Tavern. A good bowl of soup, a
toasted ham, cheese, tomato, and onion sandwich—almost unfailingly dependable in an Irish pub—and a beer refueled me.

When I was the last lunchtime customer, Peter McKenna joined me,
his interest piqued by a Yankee wanderer in County Tyrone. He was an
engaging man who told me that he'd had a managerial position in a clothing company that took him to big cities, but he'd come back here to his
roots and bought the pub. "Really because I like the company and the
chat," he said. "Though don't tell my wife that." He had grown up in a
cottage in the Sperrin Mountains, was full of lore about the district, and
generously presented me with a publication of the local historical society,
Meetings and Memories in Lower Badoney. From it I learned that the pub
had taken its name from the parish name (in Ireland, counties used to be
made up of baronies, which were constituted of parishes that accorded
generally with the original ecclesiastical precincts) and much else about
the town and district. In times not far past, flax had been grown, there was
distilling, legal and illegal, and Gortin had had a flourishing market day.

From Gortin the road rose steeply through the Gortin Gap and then
took me through the glen. The bosky landscape, doubtless enchanting,

was hidden from me by the rain; indeed, clouds seemed to drape the steep hills, some of which had the names of mountains. There was a long, gradual descent; then a fairly flat stretch brought me to Omagh.

I APPROACHED THE gate of Lisanelly Barracks gingerly; this time, I was not being driven there by a British soldier. I was mindful that a man in hooded green parka and pants, carrying a rucksack, might be an object of suspicion to the sentries of a British Army post in Northern Ireland. A number had been attacked by the IRA, and just a little over a year before, a breakaway group calling itself the Real IRA had wrought mayhem with a bomb in Omagh. To the challenge of the machine-gun-toting sentries, I gave my name and said that the CO of The Queen's Lancashires was expecting me. I was directed to the adjacent guardhouse, where I made the mistake of opening the door and stepping into a room where soldiers were observing TV monitors. I was ordered very sharply to stand outside. After I explained that I was expected, the adjutant was telephoned, a car was sent, and I was driven to the Officers' Mess. After dropping my gear in a bedroom, I was taken to Battalion Headquarters.

As the adjutant announced me, then showed me into the CO's office, he was conferring with the CO of the 1st Battalion, The Worcestershire and Sherwood Foresters Regiment (known familiarly in the British Army as the Woofers), which was to relieve The Queen's Lancashires about six weeks later. I saw the CO of the Worcester and Sherwood Foresters look at Colonel Steve of the Lancashires, who said, "It's all right, we can talk. We've had Bob checked out." I was amused to think that a fellow with my first and second names—those of a man hung and beheaded for rebellion against the Crown—walking about with a pack which could have held a bomb, had presumably been vetted by Army Intelligence and probably the Special Branch.

When coffee was served, I asked Colonel Steve about his experience with The Queen's Lancashires in Omagh. "This has been my fifth tour in Ireland—a tour is normally two years and four months—and first here," he said. "It's been very different from any other." Briefly he talked about the Battalion's patrols along the border with the Republic, to guard against unwelcome infiltrators. There had been a recent incident when a patrol had strayed inadvertently across the unmarked and tortuous line and found itself surrounded by a group of hostile though apparently unarmed men. "Almost certainly IRA," he said. "It was a potentially ugly confrontation. Perhaps serious trouble was avoided only because the Lancashires cocked their weapons and quickly retraced their steps."

Colonel Steve told the colonel of the Woofers and me that on the whole his own experience with his family in Omagh had been favorable. "Northern Ireland schools are superb," he said. "And my young daughter is into Irish dancing, taught by a very brave Catholic woman." He said that the Battalion had become much involved with community affairs since the terrible bomb blast of the year before: "We've raised ten thousand pounds for the Omagh Bomb Appeal, to assist people to rebuild shattered lives." He added that the Lancashires had given parties for families of the bereaved. "We'll be having a party for children of the community on Guy Fawkes night."

I couldn't help but reflect that the British national celebration, November 5, commemorates the torture and execution of a man who attempted to blow up the houses of Parliament as part of a Catholic conspiracy inspired by James I's unwillingness to repeal the onerous Penal Laws against Roman Catholics. Likely, when children all over Britain burn effigies of Guy Fawkes on their bonfires, the celebration's origin in religious strife is forgotten. But I wondered whether that was the case in Northern Ireland.

AFTER ANOTHER pleasurable dinner in the Officers' Mess, I enjoyed a spirited conversation with young officers of the Battalion around the fireplace in the lounge. All were well dressed in civvies, most wearing the regimental tie of black, maroon, and Lincoln-green stripes, the black commemorating the death of General James Wolfe in the moment of his victory at Quebec. *The Regimental Handbook*—which I read later—decrees hospitality to visitors, and it flowed. The Lancashires were equally keen explaining regimental lore and querying their Yankee guest about his experiences in the North, his own military history (as it happens, naval), and matters in the United States. I noted that the Battalion Intelligence Officer was well up on U.S. politicians, parties, and putative candidates in upcoming elections.

———

AS I WAS BREAKFASTING alone next morning, I was joined by a subaltern, who introduced himself as Joe. He told me that he had been raised in Switzerland and had not been long in the Army or in Northern Ireland. We got to talking about the political situation, which remained uncertain—the Good Friday Agreement to establish an Executive and an Assembly and return Home Rule to the North had not yet been implemented—and Joe expressed his pessimism. Doubtless it was informed by an experience that had shocked him. "Recently I was on patrol along the border," he said, "when I glanced toward a cottage and saw through a window a child, I'd guess about four. Suddenly he gave me the finger; then he ran around to the door of the cottage and loosed the family dog at me. It came for me, and I kicked out at it." Joe looked at me sadly. "Someday, when somebody asks that boy or man what he thinks of the British, I'll be remembered as that bastard who kicked his dog."

When I stopped at BHQ to bid good-bye to Colonel Steve, he said with warmth, "Stay as long as you like."

"Staying would be a pleasure," I said, "but as grandly as I've been welcomed by The Queen's Lancashires, I have many places to visit 'and miles to go . . .' "

Of Farmers and Belted Earls

VIRTUALLY ALL I KNEW OF OMAGH WAS FROM THE WORK OF Benedict Kiely, one of Ireland's most accomplished writers, who grew up there. I strolled along the High Street sloping up to the imposing courthouse, pausing to buy stamps at the PO, then for a newspaper. The site of the horrendous bombing, at the junction of Market Street and Drumragh Avenue, was marked by a cleared circular area with flower-filled planters and a few saplings. At the foot of one, someone had left a handwritten text about the healing power of prayer. On a hoarding was an illustration of the memorial center proposed for the site. Gloomily I walked to a bridge across the river Strule, formed by the junction of the Drumragh and the Camowen, and stared into its dark waters, swollen by days of rain, before starting off toward Enniskillen.

It would be a long slog. I had not found any byroads approximating my line of march, and on the route I took, big lorries whizzed by alarmingly. The rain, which had been light in the morning, came down more heavily. My worst day on the road. I put on a cyclist's belt and shoulder strap in fluorescent yellow with reflective panels. Somewhere between Dromore, with its picturesque ruined church, and Kilskeery, I stopped for a rest, slipped off my pack, and started to light my pipe. As I did so, a vehicle drew up across the road (I was facing the oncoming traffic on my side). The driver of a little blue van lowered the window; perhaps he thought I was thumbing. "Not a great afternoon for walking," he called out. "Where are you headed?"

"Toward Enniskillen."

"You might make it by dark, if you live. Get in."

I crossed the road and looked in; there was a passenger in the front seat. The back of the minivan was crammed with boxes. As I hesitated, the driver jumped out, opened the rear doors, and started jamming the boxes and some folded cartons together. "Push some of that lot back here," he directed. I complied, got my rucksack off, and slid into the space left. The driver, his white shirt soaked, hopped back in.

"Jerry," he said, as he accelerated.

"I'm Mick," announced his companion.

"Bob," I sang out.

"You must be daft," said Mick.

We all laughed. The usual questions followed; there was talk about sports and the States, where Mick had been and Jerry wanted to go; and they put me down in Enniskillen, at a pub by a roundabout. They wouldn't let me buy them a drink.

I got a room at the Ashberry Hotel, dined on a superb rack of a lamb in the candlelit dining room, and turned in.

ENNISKILLEN, THE COUNTY town of Fermanagh, is a much favored town. It is beautifully sited on an island in the river Erne, which connects Upper Lough Erne with Lower Lough Erne. That strategic position made the place frequently contested in the wars of the sixteenth and seventeenth centuries. The upper lough has so many islands that it appears like blue lace on the map; Lower Lough Erne has many, too, on several of which are notable prehistoric and early-Christian remains. Two of Ireland's grandest houses are close to the town; so, too, is a famous old school; Enniskillen's castle, the scene of so much strife, houses a military museum. I was bent on spending a few days prowling about. So on a morning to make the heart sing, I packed my rain gear against the odds and sauntered forth.

Enniskillen Castle stands on the west branch of the river. In the brilliant sunlight the azure water glistened like wrinkled foil. The castle's sixteenth-century Watergate, with its curious twin turrets, survives from the stronghold of the Maguires, great chieftains in the region. They alternately possessed the castle and were dispossessed during a series of struggles. In 1607, during the plantation of Ulster by James I, Captain William—later Sir William—Cole, first of a line of Coles who thrived here, became castellan.

In the castle grounds former barracks surround what remains of the original fortress, much modified over time. One has been made into the award-winning County Museum, which houses dioramas with striking, lifelike models and a theater in which the history and prehistory of Fermanagh is illuminated. I wanted particularly to visit the museum of The Royal Inniskilling Fusiliers (town and Regiment have had numerous spellings over centuries), which is housed in the castle's keep. The Inniskilling Fusiliers' martial history had long intrigued me, not least because of their sobriquet, The Skins. The story has it that The Skins won their name in Italy during the Napoleonic Wars: it seems that when soldiers of the Inniskilling Fusiliers were bathing in the sea, they were summoned because of an imminent enemy attack. They rushed from the sea, seized their arms, and mustered for combat, stark naked.

As I was to find, most museums, National Trust properties, and the like were closed by the end of September. But at the County Museum a comely young woman led me to the keep and called the custodian of the Regimental Museum of The Royal Inniskilling Fusiliers, who kindly admitted me. As I had loved toy soldiers as a lad, it was a treat to be allowed to wander happily and alone through several floors filled with well-lit, displayed, and described mementos of the Regiment. I stared at uniforms, presentation swords, captured weapons, trophies, medals, and pictures of heroes and battles.

Here was a record of many victories and rare defeats. I noted that the Battle Honors of The Skins included, among many others, Waterloo, the Relief of Ladysmith, the Somme, Gallipoli, Sicily, and Burma.

The Royal Inniskilling Fusiliers and the 6th Inniskilling Dragoons had their origins in a force of infantry and cavalry raised for the defense of Enniskillen in 1689. As Tiffin's Inniskilling Regiment the Fusiliers were in the army of William of Orange at the Battle of the Boyne in 1690. Opposed on that fateful day, in the army of James II, was a regiment commanded by The Maguire who was Baron Enniskillen. The Protestant, Williamite Inniskillings are remembered in the ballad called "The Boyne Water":

> But the brave Duke Schomberg he was shot
>   as he crossed over the water.
> When that King William did observe the
>   brave Duke Schomberg falling,
> He reined his horse with a heavy heart, on the
>   Enniskillens calling:
>
> "What will you do for me, brave boys—
>   see yonder men retreating?
> Our enemies encouraged are, and
>   English drums are beating."
> He says, "My boys, feel no dismay
>   at the losing of one commander,
> For God shall be our King today,
>   and I'll be general under."

In the amalgamation of Britain's forces after the Second World War, The Royal Inniskilling Fusiliers were disbanded as such and combined with battalions of the other two extant Northern Irish regiments as The Royal Irish Rangers in 1968. That regiment was united with the Ulster Defence Regiment in 1992 as The Royal Irish Regiment, whose band I heard and watched parade at Beating Retreat in Omagh.

The dust of distant battles seemed to have put a thirst on me. To slake it and perhaps to have an early lunch, I hied myself to Blake's public house on the High Street, which claims to be one of the oldest pubs in Ireland. The decor was persuasive, the interior dim and comforting but with light sufficient for several scholars to be consulting the racing pages of their newspapers. After a sound pub lunch, a walk was in order.

There is much in and about Enniskillen to charm anyone interested in archaeology, history, or architecture, not to speak of the miles of lake and river to entice boatman or angler. Close by is the Portora Royal School, founded by Charles I, which numbers among its graduates Oscar Wilde and Samuel Beckett. Its eighteenth-century buildings stand in beautiful grounds, where one may see the ruin of a castle built by William Cole on the site of a Maguire castle. About this edifice, in Lord Killanin and Michael V. Duignan's invaluable *Shell Guide to Ireland,* the authors dryly note, "It has suffered from schoolboy experiments with explosives." Portora must await another visit. I opted to visit Castle Coole, regarded by some as the most perfect classical house in Ireland, which is saying much, where many great country houses adorn the land.

The driveway through the demesne led past the small lough, with its resident flock of greylag geese, normally migratory but established here some three hundred years ago. At the front of Castle Coole, I stopped, stock-still, confronting the vast Palladian facade of dressed Portland stone (recently restored), gleaming white in the sunlight. Perhaps not as stunning as the Taj Mahal by moonlight but chaste, cold, splendid—fit for a princess. Indeed, Armar Lowry-Corry—successively Baron, Viscount, and Earl of Belmore—who built Castle Coole in the 1790s, took as his wife the daughter of the Earl of Buckinghamshire, of whom a contemporary noted that she was "a young lady possessed of youth, beauty, elegance of manner and a fortune of £30,000." A prudent marriage, for Lord Belmore, if he did not quite beggar himself in creating his palace, died owing £70,000.

I stared long at the facade of Castle Coole, with its pillared porch fronting the central block and the low colonnaded wings extending to each side, nearly the length of a football field. Then I rang a bell at the door within the east colonnade. Although Castle Coole, now a National Trust property, had recently closed, the custodian, Anne Kelly, agreed to admit one history-besotted writer. She conducted me from room to room, opening shutters that lit certain rooms dramatically, and lighting chandeliers and lamps in others.

The original drawings for the house—still there—were made by the Irish architect Richard Johnston in 1789. But the next year, having become Viscount Belmore, his lordship turned to James Wyatt, perhaps then the most fashionable of English architects, to complete the design. Wyatt retained Johnston's basic plan but eliminated certain embellishments, producing a final design in which the long, pure classical lines and proportions create the aesthetic impact. (Although Wyatt houses sometimes featured a bowfront section and corresponding interior rooms, which Castle Coole possesses at its rear, Johnston's earlier design had such a bowfront. It is interesting that the White House, in Washington, was designed by the Irishman James Hoban, who won a competition in 1792 for his plan of a classical building, complete with bowfront at the rear. It may owe much to an Irish predecessor.) Wyatt never visited the site, relying on Alexander Stewart as his clerk of works.

As we progressed through Castle Coole, I was as awed as Lord Belmore would have wished. In the entrance hall, I marveled at the tall Doric columns of wood coated in scagliola—a mixture of gypsum and marble or granite chippings that is polished to resemble porphyry—the work of the Italian Domenico Bartoli. The frieze of triglyphs and metopes, the latter decorated alternately with rosettes and urns, might have pleased Vitruvius. Beyond the hall a twin staircase with elaborate wrought-iron balusters soars to the upstairs sky-lit hall.

Platoons of joiners and plasterers from England labored on the house, not all joyfully. The plasterers grumbled about the dampness of their lodgings to the master stuccoist, Joseph Rose, who directed their work on the ceilings from his London workshop. As the cost mounted and Lord Belmore felt his exchequer draining, he tempered his craving for extravagance and requested Wyatt and Rose to modify certain of their designs. When they obliged by reducing the opulence of their conceptions, their employer desired them to restore some of the grandeur he missed.

Slowly the house took shape; the most lavish plasterwork was created in London, as were carved marble chimneypieces. Some of the furniture and the superb doors were created by the joiners in the house. In 1797, though much remained unfinished, the 1st Earl of Belmore occupied his new seat. Severely overextended fiscally, he died in 1802.

Somerset Lowry-Corry, 2nd Earl of Belmore, determined to see his father's dream realized. When I stood in the saloon, I realized that he had. The oval room, forty feet in length, with its majestic curved, paneled, and painted doors, scagliola pilasters, and great mirrors, was redecorated by John Preston of Dublin, as were other rooms, including the State Bedroom, intended to receive George IV. Preston fashioned the elaborately carved and gilded furniture and had the fabrics and hangings made. I imagined the great balls of long ago in this room, with beautifully gowned ladies, dashing peers, and gentry waltzing on the shining wooden floor.

In 1951, Castle Coole passed to the National Trust, which has spent millions of pounds to preserve it for those who may wish to marvel at a vision realized and to glimpse the life of the Anglo-Irish ascendancy, which is as much a part of Ireland's culture as the desolate, roofless cottages of the Irish peasants who toiled to support it and perished or emigrated in the years of the Great Famine. Grateful as I was to visit this austere palace, I would not care to dwell there.

———

TULLYHONA HOUSE (its name later changed to Arch Tullyhona House), set in green fields separated by hedgerows, is the white stuccoed guesthouse and farm home of Geoffrey and Rosemary Armstrong, just south of Enniskillen. They farm 360 acres, which is large for the region, near the hamlet of Florence Court. I was warmly welcomed, then dined in a wood-beamed dining room, which reminded me of a French country inn, though the rest of the house was typically Irish. Rosemary serves meals by reservation, and a few others and I savored good country food. I decided to spend a few days here while I reconnoitered several places nearby.

Over breakfast, I spoke with Geoffrey about the farm. A big, rugged man with thick, silvering, curly hair above a face that has seen much weather, and with an easy way, he could pass for the star of a Western. He told me that the farm had consisted of eighty acres when his father bought it for £1,500 forty years before. Geoffrey told me that "a farm was said to be a four-cow place or an eight-cow place and so on." This was an eight-cow place. His father, William, was the second oldest son of a farmer who became a storekeeper in Florence Court. "He was a grocer-undertaker," said Geoffrey. "His motto was 'from a nappy to a coffin.' "

In 1980, Geoffrey and Rosemary—whose father, Robert McFarland, was born in Philadelphia and brought to Ireland when he was four years old—renovated the old farmhouse. Chuckling, Geoffrey said, "I was always mad for farming. When I was just a lad, I bought four ewes," pronounced "yoes." "It's been a good life. Currently we have two hundred beef cattle and eighty ewes."

I knew that Irish farmers, North and South, like others elsewhere, operate on small margins, and I was curious about the economics. What about the European Union and subsidies? Articulate and patient, Geoffrey answered my queries.

"We get ninety pounds for a bull calf and twenty pounds for a ewe," he said. "Our cattle are a crossbreed, Charolais bulls bred to Limousin cows—French breeds—Charolais produce lean beef, which is in demand today, but don't produce enough milk for the calves.

"With beef, most of the profit goes to the butcher," Geoffrey told me.

"The abattoir pays the farmer four hundred fifty pounds for a beef, then sells it to the butcher for four hundred eighty pounds. The butcher sells the beef for twelve hundred fifty pounds."

As I would hear from every farmer I spoke with in Ireland—on both sides of the border—the market for Irish sheep was severely depressed. Lamb and wool from Australia, New Zealand, and Argentina, raised on immense spreads, costing less to produce than Ireland's or Britain's, are dominating the markets. "Our sheep go to the Republic now," said Geoffrey, "where they fetch a better price."

Despite the surge in high-tech industries, all Ireland remains heavily agricultural, as any traveler will see. Cattle and sheep thrive on the rich grass. "In Fermanagh we cut our grass in June," Geoffrey said. "Some land may permit a second cutting later. We cut one hundred fifty acres. The cut fields can be grazed in three weeks."

As satisfying as Geoffrey finds farming, it is not an easy life. Many small farmers barely hang on, and every few years their numbers grow fewer. Besides the long hours of toil, working with farm machinery and animals can be hazardous. Geoffrey remarked, "When a seven-hundred-fifty-pound bullock kicks you, there are consequences."

It seems that the Armstrong farm will remain in the family. Geoffrey and Rosemary's son James, eighteen years old in 1999, was a student at Greenmount Agricultural College in County Antrim. John-Ross, sixteen, was studying horticulture. Daughter Jayne, fifteen, in school at Enniskillen, was understandably undecided about her future. Geoffrey, eleven, would seem to take after his father, an athlete who excels at badminton, played football for the Enniskillen Rangers, and remains a devoted supporter. With quiet pride he said of his son, "Geoffrey is a groundsman for the club and a committed member."

AFTER ONE OF those serious Irish breakfasts, at which I rarely risked full indulgence, I set off to visit Belle Isle, an estate said to be remote and beautiful, some six miles from Enniskillen, belonging to the Duke of Abercorn. In 1991, he had acquired it for his second son, Lord Nicholas Hamilton. Perhaps confident that when peace came to Northern Ireland, so too would the tourists for whom it had much to offer, in a bravura bit of entrepreneurship the duke had transformed an old mansion and outbuildings into four-star holiday accommodations, with particular appeal for those keen on fishing or shooting.

On a bright, blustery day, I stopped to picnic at Carrybridge, where Upper Lough Erne funnels into the river Erne. When the wind became fiercer, I retreated to the modest Marina Hotel, had a coffee, and got directions to Belle Isle.

The estate actually consists of eight islands in Upper Lough Erne. No imposing gate announces the entrance to the main house. A drive winds through fields and woods to a bridge over a channel of the lough or a river entering it. Moored there was a handsome yacht, the *Trasna*, belonging to the Duke of Abercorn. Beyond I passed a large walled garden, a former coach house, and recently renovated stables and farm buildings around a courtyard, then came to the sprawling, gray stone mansion. A tall tower rose at the end, where the grounds sloped down to the lough.

I'd been given an introduction to the estate manager, Charles P. B. Plunket, whom I looked forward to meeting, not least because he bore the name of a family which had produced a number of distinguished Irishmen. (The most celebrated was Oliver Plunket, Archbishop of Armagh, who was accused in the Titus Oates plot, tried for treason, convicted on trumped-up charges, and hanged, drawn, and quartered in London in 1681. He was canonized in 1975. Saint Oliver's embalmed head is a grisly feature of St. Peter's Church in Drogheda.) Just a few weeks before, in a friend's house, I'd been browsing through *One Day in the Life of Ireland* and had come upon a photograph of Charles Plunket with two black Labradors, standing in front of another fine country house, which, the caption noted, had been a bequest to him from the Duchess of Westminster.

My knock at the stout door of Belle Isle's mansion brought the two welcoming black Labradors—the largest I'd ever seen—and Charles Plunket, red-haired, tall, and casual in cords and navy pullover; he had the look of a sometime soldier. He led me to the kitchen, brewed and served tea, and told me something of Belle Isle, its history, and the metamorphosis the duke had ordained here.

I learned that from the eleventh to the seventeenth century, Belle Isle was the territory of the MacManus family and was called Ballymacmanus. Cathal Og ("the Younger") MacManus, who died in 1498, was one of the compilers of the *Annals of Ulster*, now a treasure of Oxford's Bodleian Library. In 1607, during the plantation of Ulster, the Crown granted what became known as Belle Isle to Paul Gore, a prominent soldier. Successive Gores (one was created Earl of Ross), then Porters (descendants of an English cleric), possessed Belle Isle until the Duke of Abercorn purchased the estate.

Charles Plunket took me on a tour. In the mansion's Hamilton wing (after the family name of the Duke of Abercorn), we entered a grand banqueting hall, with arched beams and a minstrel gallery at one end. David Hicks, the eminent British designer with royal connections, was responsible for the decor, and with persimmon walls, light-ocher trim, antique furniture, and period portraits, he had created an eclectic, stylish ambience. The wing's eight bedrooms, five bathrooms, small dining room, modern kitchen, and drawing room offer accommodation for fourteen self-catering guests (though full food service can be arranged). Vibrant landscape and figurative paintings by artists from the Russian homeland of the Duchess of Abercorn enliven the commodious drawing room, pleasingly furnished with antique and contemporary pieces. When I remarked brochures on spiritual and holistic topics scattered about the drawing room, Charles told me that the Hamilton wing had been taken by followers of the Maharishi for a retreat. Perhaps they were off meditating somewhere; but imagining them eating lentils and yogurt in the ducal banqueting hall, my mind boggled.

Accompanied by the gamboling Labradors, we strolled in the demesne—two hundred acres are still farmed, and eighty cows are milked in new farm buildings—past a large walled garden in which a secluded cottage was available for guests. Charles led me to the coach house, with two apartments, and then to the complex of eight individual apartments in the former farm buildings around the courtyard. All had been converted into duplex apartments of one to three bedrooms; each was variously and charmingly decorated in a casual country style and had its patch of lawn and picnic table. There was an adjacent play area for children and a tennis court.

Northern Ireland hungers for tourists, has much to offer, and Belle Isle's development was a bold stroke to attract them. In the estate office, Charles tapped into his computer and printed out particulars of the coarse fishing to be had in Upper Lough Erne, the salmon and trout fishing in nearby waters, and the woodcock and snipe shooting to be had in season by guests at Belle Isle. I rather fancied returning with rod and gun one day.

IRELAND HAS MANY splendid country houses, most of them fruits of the wealth accruing to great landholders in the seventeenth and eighteenth centuries. Enniskillen is the rare country town with two of Ireland's noblest houses on its doorstep. I had seen Castle Coole and hoped to see Florence Court, seat of the Earls of Enniskillen, said to be one of the loveliest of Ireland's great Georgian country houses. Rosemary and Geoffrey Armstrong's farmhouse is close by Florence Court, now a property of the National Trust, and Rosemary knew James Chestnutt, the National Trust's manager at Florence Court, who kindly agreed to show me through the house.

A winding way through a forest park brought me to the house. Although the central block has low colonnades extending to pavilions at each end, as do other great Irish houses, Florence Court does not have the awesome effect, the startling whiteness of Castle Coole, even under a sapphire sky in brilliant sunshine. The scale of Florence Court is smaller, and its facade presents a concatenation of architectural detail—a Palladian window, pediments, rusticated window surrounds and colonnades—producing a play of light and shade and creating an effect more provincial and less intimidating than Castle Coole's stern beauty. James Chestnutt admitted me, and I was quickly captivated. Grand as it is, there is an intimacy and charm about Florence Court. Had God made me Earl of Enniskillen, I suspect I might have dwelled here quite happily.

Sir John Cole, great-grandson of Sir William Cole, who succeeded the Maguires at Enniskillen Castle, acquired the property that would become Florence Court about 1718 and began work on the house that he would name for his wife, Florence Bourchier Wrey of Cornwall. His son, John Cole, MP, completed the central block of the house one sees today and, elevated to the peerage in 1760, took the title 1st Baron Mount Florence. He died in 1767, and his son William Willoughby, brother-in-law of Lord Belmore of Castle Coole, completed the colonnades and the pavilions by about 1771. He was created 1st Earl of Enniskillen in 1784.

Despite the formality of the entrance hall, with its white Doric frieze and swags over doorways, against walls of celadon green, the scale is human and welcoming. A beautiful hanging staircase fashioned of three woods leads past stuccoed cornucopias of fruit on the stair walls to a spacious hall, flooded with light from the Palladian window, from which the bedrooms open.

On the main floor, I peered into reception rooms that preserve the air of a living house with appropriate period furniture and paintings, including portraits of the 1st and 3rd Earls of Enniskillen. One of the glories of Florence Court is the stuccowork, particularly that in the dining room. Its ceiling is a dazzle of acanthus leaves around a great oval, in the center of which Zeus, in the guise of an eagle, his talons clutching thunderbolts, is surrounded by the Four Winds blowing lustily. This must be close to the apogee of plasterwork in Ireland.

It was by a stroke of wit that this extraordinary ceiling survives. In 1954, the 5th Earl of Enniskillen's only son, Viscount Cole, gave Florence Court to the National Trust, and in March of the next year an electrical fault caused a fire, which ravaged the mansion. Quick-acting firefighters bored holes through the dining-room ceiling to drain the water being poured into the upper floors, which would have brought down the ceiling. The National Trust straightaway began a restoration of the house under the supervision of Sir Albert Richardson, famed for his reconstruction of bombed London churches after the Second World War.

In a small room on the main floor, my attention was caught by a group of photographs of the 6th Earl of Enniskillen and his very attractive countess at various times and places. The 6th Countess, née Nancy MacLennan, grew up in Washington, D.C., was a graduate of Cornell University, a sometime public-affairs attaché in the U.S. embassy at Cairo, and a correspondent for *The New York Times* when she interviewed Captain David Lowry Cole in Kenya (where some of the family had settled) on his succession as 6th Earl of Enniskillen in 1963. She became his bride.

The countess was smitten by the Coles' ancestral home, and in 1972 she published *Florence Court, My Irish House*. She and her husband lived here until 1973 and were active in improving the house and estate. Before his death, in 1989, the 6th Earl conveyed almost all that remained of his land—which in the late nineteenth century had amounted to thirty thousand acres—to the Northern Ireland Ministry of Agriculture, to be managed commercially as a forestry and a park for the pleasure of the public. The National Trust retains 350 acres. The 6th Earl's only son, who succeeded as 7th Earl of Enniskillen upon his father's death, lives in Kenya. In 1997, the year before she died, Nancy, Dowager Countess of Enniskillen, donated family furniture, silver, paintings, and memorabilia to the National Trust, for Florence Court.

MANY VISITORS TO Florence Court might find themselves as much pleasured without as within. I had no sooner strolled out to explore the grounds than perhaps fifty yards in front of the house I satisfied a curiosity as I came upon the ha-ha. I had encountered the word in numerous English novels, chiefly of the romantic sort, and imagined a bosky place for discreet courtship. The dictionary definition ("a sunk fence . . . not visible until one is close upon it," *Webster's Second*) had not disabused me of the idea. But no. At Florence Court, I got the picture: the ha-ha is a long, low, curving stone wall bordering the lawn before the mansion, about three feet higher than the pasture beyond it, thus keeping the grazing sheep from obtruding on the lawn. It was nice to know.

There are extensive walks at Florence Court, many designed by the 3rd Earl (1807–1887), who made such useful additions to the estate as a tilery and sawmill. He was an amateur scientist who collected some ten thousand specimens of fossil fish, which once adorned the south pavilion of his house and subsequently went to the British Museum. Among the delights of what the 3rd Earl called the Pleasure Ground is the enchanting little gazebo called the Summer House, a replica of the original nineteenth-century thatched structure. It was not hard to imagine the countess in flowing gown and great hat, parasol in hand, strolling out here to take tea with her husband. Doubtless favored guests were invited to this intimate abode and, like me, could enjoy the ravishing view over dells and knolls to the massifs of Benaughlin and Cuilcagh, which frame the horizon. On Cuilcagh, long ago, a tenant discovered the seedling that—when planted a half mile from the Summer House—grew into the mighty, upthrusting Irish yew that is a glory of Florence Court and from which every other true Irish yew is said to have been propagated. One was inclined to loll like an earl at the Summer House. Rarely have I spent more refreshing hours than at Florence Court.

———

IT WAS TIME to wander south. On another morning of inspiriting weather, Geoffrey Armstrong put me on the road for the border, the A32. Setting off at a good pace, I was "happy as Larry," as we say in Dublin (though I don't know why, for the song "The Night Before Larry Was Stretched" seems quite contrary). It was about five and one half miles to the border with the Republic. I tramped contentedly along, pausing now and again to sample the last fat blackberries to be found here and there along the ditches. Hardly a car appeared on the road, traveling in either direction; there were few animals in the fields, and I heard almost no birdsong.

Fairly high overhead, a British Army chopper accompanied me noisily. It seemed odd, when I came upon the heavily fortified British Army or RUC post just short of the border, to find it deserted. I knew the Army was keeping a low profile while the Ulster Unionist Party, Sinn Féin (the I.R.A.'s political wing), and the S.D.L.P., Social Democratic and Labour Party, were groping their respective ways toward realizing the Good Friday Agreement's intention to return the governance of Northern Ireland from the British Parliament to a representative Northern Ireland Assembly. Nonetheless, although the city of Derry had seemed so peaceful to me, every morning the newspapers brought reports of beatings, kneecappings, house bombings, or worse, inflicted by people of opposite political persuasions who wanted no part of the peace process.

The border fortification had barracks and two watchtowers, one overlooking the other, with narrow, darkened windows, probably bulletproof, and surrounded by heavy metal cages, to prevent explosives or Molotov cocktails being lobbed against them; around the perimeter was the familiar high steel wall, fitted with surveillance cameras. A mast festooned with antennae towered over all. The fortress was as silent as a cemetery when the Last Post has been sounded.

Not much farther, a sign in English and Irish welcomed me to County Cavan. I was in the Republic of Ireland. Soon I passed a man—the first human I'd seen for an hour—who was fastening a gate to a field, in which were five cows; then he swung up onto his tractor and passed me. He wore a natty new blue tweed jacket and smart checked shirt, and I thought how differently he looked from an American farmer at his chores.

Perhaps a mile farther on I came to Swanlinbar, where, by my count, villagers are served by six public houses on the short main street. I bought *The Irish Times* at a petrol station–cum–convenience store that might have been in Pennsylvania or Texas, except that it sold wine, then, beginning to feel a nasty pain in my right knee, I limped into The Welcome Inn. The cheerful barmaid produced a pot of tea and a ham and cheese sandwich, and I dawdled over my newspaper, the only customer until a man addressed as "Patrick" came in. Recognizing the farmer with the smart tweed jacket, I nodded. He did too, with a grin emphasized by several missing teeth, as he raised his whiskey, perhaps because he'd noticed me when I paused to upturn a rubber pylon on a section of road under repair.

When I rose and hoisted my rucksack, I knew I was in trouble. My right knee would barely take the strain of standing; the few steps out to the street were painful. Here was a rub. I had started off in great form this morning, indeed had felt in the pink since I left Malin Head. I wanted to reach Ballinamore, a good ten miles on, by evening, and I had gone lame.

What was my problem? I hadn't stumbled and twisted my knee, had never had more comfortable walking boots. But something was wrong, and I still had a journey of a couple hundred miles ahead of me by shank's mare. So I limped up the main street to the police station, to ask about finding some transport. To my surprise, like the Brits just across the border, the Garda Síochána were not manning their post. All quiet on the northern front. I found the station on the main street empty and in process of renovation, no workmen about either; it was lunchtime.

In Dublin, I had a friend, a doctor, who could advise me, and I telephoned him. "Get here," he counseled. In the petrol station, I learned that a bus from Enniskillen to Dublin would come through Swanlinbar at 12:10 P.M. When it did, I hailed it.

DR. DAVID NOWLAN, then a managing editor of *The Irish Times* and its drama critic, is a physician and the paper's former medical correspondent. He introduced me to Dr. James Sheehan, who is both a surgeon and an engineer and, as David informed me, Ireland's authority on the knee. Dr. Sheehan saw me in his Blackrock Clinic, kindly interested himself in my problem—old sailor run aground as it were—examined me, x-rayed the knee, pondered the swollen joint, and said, "I believe you have gout." No!

Except for the occasional whiskey and a modest daily wine intake, I thought I had been living like a mendicant friar. Could this be? "Probably. And gout does turn up in various joints, not just your big toe," said Dr. Sheehan, who prescribed an antiinflammatory time-release medication. Grateful, I repaired to a friend's house in Kerry to take my medicine, rest, and write up the notes in my journal until I was back in marching order.

Halloween and High Tech

I HAD PLANNED TO TAKE A BUS FROM KENMARE, IN KERRY, TO Swanlinbar, in Cavan, to resume my march, but I heard that Halloween had become a spectacular occasion in Derry, drawing thousands from far and wide, and was not to be missed. So I decided to bus somewhat farther back on my line of march, to see how folk there celebrate a festival that I thought was a peculiarly American phenomenon.

IN DERRY ON HALLOWEEN, a Sunday, I found a shop just off Waterloo Place that was crammed with Halloween gear and enjoying a lively trade. I bought a werewolf mask and shortly thereafter presented myself at the reception desk of the Beech Hill Country House Hotel. With raincoat pulled up around my hideous mask, in what I fancied was a monstrous voice, I intoned, "Have you a room available for a werewolf?" Patsy O'Kane replied, "We've got your room all ready for you, Robert." I was crushed.

I was prepared to believe that Derry would put on quite a Halloween party. The Derry City Council, with the Arts Council of Northern Ireland, various industries, and businesses, had supported a number of cultural enterprises in recent years. Earlier this month there had been the Two Cathedrals Festival (named for the Anglican St. Columb's and the Roman Catholic St. Eugene's), which had drawn acclaimed musicians from Ireland and abroad for a program of vespers and evensong in the cathedrals and opera, jazz, orchestral, chamber, and choral works in various other venues. Around the official program a Festival Fringe had sprung up in the Foyleside Shopping Centre.

The Banks of the Foyle Halloween Carnival promised a rock group, folksingers, a magician, street performers, a fireworks extravaganza, and a fancy-dress ball. Everyone was encouraged to turn out in masquerade.

By 6:00 P.M., I was in Guildhall Place, where a series of booths had been set up beneath the city wall and children were having their faces painted as ghouls or witches—or tigers or lions, which were particularly favored. A big mobile stage had been parked in Guildhall Square facing the city wall and Shipquay Gate, and by 6:30, when Sharon Shannon and Her Band cut loose, the square before the neo-Gothic Guildhall was thronged with people who had turned out for, and were turned on by, Sharon Shannon, three other young women fiddlers, two young men picking amplified guitars, and a fellow pounding out a resounding rhythm on the *bodhrán*, the traditional Irish single-sided drum. Sharon Shannon, who doubled effectively on fiddle and accordion and hails from County Clare, led her band in traditional reels and jigs mixed with more contemporary pieces. The music blasted from big amplifiers and bounced off the wall, which had withstood the great siege. I stood with my back against it, by Shipquay Gate, stamping my feet on the cold pavement.

The crowd of hundreds jammed in the square, swaying to the beat or tapping their feet, were mostly in fancy dress. There was the familiar Halloween assortment of ghosts, goblins, skeletons, and witches, but among them were more exotically costumed celebrants. Some who had created or acquired the most inspired, elaborate, or indeed astonishing costumes clearly felt they deserved to be admired and wandered through the crowd. I noted a saucy French maid; a fiercely mustachioed and bandoliered Mexican bandit; a merrymaker who appeared as a pint of Guinness, with the brew's trademark toucan perched on the rim; a reveler caparisoned as the mummy case and mask of Tutankhamen; a masked surgeon with blood-spattered gown and gory rubber gloves; and a number of fetching houris.

I was awed by the decapitated head of John the Baptist on a salver. A monstrous ghoul with hideous papier-mâché head strode about, groping with tremendous skeletal hands at squealing preteens, the huge apparition operated by a threesome within its voluminous white drapery.

The crowd was appreciative and orderly; throughout the evening, I witnessed no overindulgence or rowdyism. The only wrong note I thought struck was by one paragon of bad taste and worse judgment—considering Derry's tormented history—who swaggered around in the black balaclava and outfit of a paramilitary terrorist, brandishing a fake automatic weapon.

The program announced that the fireworks spectacular would commence at 7:30 P.M. Near that time a mass exodus from Guildhall Square began. I was one of the thousands who assembled on the Foyle Road, which runs along the river and is a dual carriageway for a short distance. It was closed to vehicles for the occasion, and on it many of the forty thousand visitors said to have poured into Derry for the Halloween gala joined many of the city's populace to view the spectacle. Another multitude was gathered along the Waterside on the far bank of the Foyle. A chill wind blew up the river, and the expectant audience waited patiently for the aerial show, the many tykes there as good as gold, for the first rocket was not launched till long after the appointed time. Just ahead of me a trio of willowy young fairies or perhaps angels—for they looked angelic, though they weren't wearing much more than they might on their bridal night—stamped their pretty feet as the wind stirred their gossamer wings.

When the first aerial bomb arced above the river to burst splendidly in starry constellations, a great pent-up *ahhh!* of satisfaction erupted from myriad throats. Rocket after rocket, singles and multiples, went up to explode in magisterial displays, each seemingly more elaborate than its predecessor and provoking successive exclamations of delight and, for particularly dazzling effects, cheers and applause. As pleased as everyone else by the mighty BOOMS! punctuating the procession of multicolored flares gyrating in the sky and illuminating both riverbanks, I watched until my feet, already icy from more than an hour on the Guildhall Square, urged me into flight. Then I had the happy thought of retiring to the nearby Peking Pagoda on Foyle Street, whose windows look over the low Ulsterbus bus station to the Foyle Road and the river. There, at a window table with a fine view, warmed by a large whiskey, I watched the grand finale of the fireworks and barely sampled the alleged and dreadful Peking duck in a gluey sauce, served by a sweet waitress. I counted Halloween in Derry memorable.

DERRY AND ITS ENVIRONS still glistened with the morning dew when I presented myself at the security gate to Seagate Technology, in the Springtown Industrial Estate, on Derry's northwestern outskirts, to meet Managing Director Gordon Hutchison. Seagate—a U.S. corporation that is the world's largest manufacturer of disc drives and recording heads for computers, with eighty-three thousand employees in eighteen countries and annual revenues of $7 billion—was exactly the kind of high-tech manufacturer both North and South were eager to lure to Ireland.

During the long years of the Troubles, while the Republic was experiencing its remarkable economic surge, Northern Ireland was finding it difficult to attract either tourists or new industry. Nonetheless, the Industrial Development Board for Northern Ireland and the Northern Ireland Tourist Board had striven to make a good case for all that the province had to offer the corporate investor as well as the traveler. Primarily, to address serious unemployment in the North, particularly among Catholics, the Industrial Development Board offered considerable inducements in tax relief, grants for capital expenditures, assistance in employee recruitment and training, and other enticements that foreign investors were finding seductive (as they had with the inducements of the Industrial Development Authority in the Republic). Seagate had commenced production in Derry in 1994.

The building to which I was directed was long and sleek, its glass and aluminum facade gleaming behind the woven steel security fence. I thought it suitable for a remake of Charlie Chaplin's *Modern Times* or perhaps René Clair's *À nous la liberté,* films of the 1930s whose creators made factories like this one seem dubious futuristic dreams. In a spacious reception area, severely stylish, I was directed to a seat and was barely in it before Gordon Hutchison appeared to welcome me. A short, bearded man, neat in shirtsleeves and tie, he led me to his front office, on the main floor, spare and functional, the lair of the engineer I found Hutchison to be.

In seeking the appointment, I had explained my journey and added that I was particularly interested in learning what had brought this big American corporation with worldwide clients to Derry and how that had worked out. Hutchison was affable and to the point in responding to my questions.

"Was proximity to the Continent a major factor in locating here?" I asked.

"Not really," said Hutchison. "The availability of skilled workers was a principal factor, and the Industrial Development Board for Northern Ireland provided significant incentives. As it happens, we're a vertically integrated company. The wafers fabricated in this plant go to the Seagate manufacturing plant in Penang, Malaysia, to be machined into the hard-drive recording heads which write the information onto, and read the information from, the recording disc in a computer's hard disc drive."

"Who are the people who make up your workforce?"

"Right now we have nine hundred fifty employees. About ninety percent are Northern Irish," he said. "The rest are from Britain and the Republic of Ireland."

"Any Americans?"

"One. He's going home in six months," said Hutchison. "My predecessor here was an American. Corporate headquarters are in Scotts Valley, California. The Recording Heads Group is centered in Minneapolis."

Because the products Seagate makes here are so technically sophisticated, I inquired where the company found the skilled people it needed.

"There is a very good educational system here, and we have strong linkages with universities and colleges in Northern Ireland," said Hutchison. "In the U.K. there is significant research in magnetics, which is important to us. We have two hundred and forty engineers and twenty-four Ph.D.'s just now and fifty people in R and D."

I asked how Seagate viewed its investment in Derry.

"I've just overseen the completion of a big new building here, adding two hundred forty thousand square feet to the original one-hundred-thousand-square-foot building," Hutchison said. "I'm the third managing director here, and each has seen productivity targets exceeded. Seagate has invested three hundred and fifty million dollars in this facility, and productivity has been so successful that the company began operations in a new plant in Limavady, near Derry, in 1997 and already employs eleven hundred there."

We talked about the recording heads that the Derry facility was set up to manufacture, and I asked whether there had been any change in the products.

"We're evolving into magnetoresistive wafers for our recording heads," said Hutchison. "The rate of change in our kind of technology is enormous, and it's why we have our R and D group. There's a great deal of retraining here. Also some sixteen percent of our employees are enrolled in advanced education courses in their fields, supported by the company's tuition-assisted plan."

"What's been the greatest problem Seagate has had to contend with here?"

"Dirt."

I don't know what I expected, possibly something social or political. "Dirt?" I said.

"Dirt," he repeated. "The kind of thin-film wafer we manufacture for our recording heads requires an absolutely clean environment; the atmosphere must be dirt free."

That explained why operatives in the Derry plant are clad in immaculate white gowns, hooded, masked, and gloved, when peering at a wafer through a microscope and examining its surface enlarged electronically on a computer monitor.

"There must surely be other problems on your plate," I suggested.

"The market for Seagate's products is highly price sensitive," the managing director said. "We are under orders to meet price sensitivity. As with many other companies, we are finding that price competitiveness and automation are trimming workforces."

Gordon Hutchison had previously managed a Seagate plant in Scotland that produced semiconductors and had been shut down. The Scottish engineer was put in charge of the operation at Derry's Springtown Industrial Estate some four months ago. Clearly a managing director's role had its pressures. I asked what his personal life was like in Derry.

"Our young children are still in school in Scotland," he said. "So I commute weekends to my family."

"And here, outside of this plant?"

"Well, I'm a golfer," the Scot said, smiling. "There's good golf here." (Hutchison subsequently has left Seagate and returned to Scotland.)

THAT EVENING I dined with a couple with an entrepreneurial connection to the celebration of Halloween in Derry. My friends Rita and Terry

George—he's a Northern Irish playwright, screenwriter, and director active in the United States—had said I must meet their friends Susan and Harry Friel and had alerted them that I would be in Derry. When I telephoned the Friels, I was promptly invited to their maisonette in a modern apartment complex in the Waterside district. I found them warm, instantly likable people. Harry is an executive of a company that recycles Lycra waste into a product used to build all-weather surfaces for racetracks and training arenas. As a sideline, Harry and his son Graham, who had twigged to the nascent addiction to Halloween in Derry, decided to take a flier and in 1995 invested $10,000 on fancy-dress costumes in the United States, where Graham was working. When the attire for ghouls, pirates, belly dancers, and other exotic types arrived in Derry, the Friels unloaded them at a comfortable profit, and they have continued the business, with annual growth in sales.

Over steaks grilled by Susan and wine produced from behind Harry's bar, conversation flowed. I discovered that Harry has a passion for the turf—quite aside from his role in its improvement—as the term refers to the Sport of Kings. I, too, had long enjoyed racing in Europe, especially in Ireland, where the splendid animals and gaily clad jockeys galloping over the greenest turf is a spectacle to stir the blood. But while almost everyone in Ireland knows more than a bit about horses, Harry is not the average punter. He is the scion of bookmakers and bloodstock dealers and can recall innumerable races—at The Curragh in Ireland or Epsom in England or Longchamp outside Paris—the winners, and the odds. These recollections are delivered with enthusiasm and enlivened with anecdote. Remembering the time just after the Second World War when Britain—desperately poor after the conflict she had so long endured—limited her subjects to forty pounds cash when traveling abroad, Harry told me of flying to Paris to attend the famous Prix de l'Arc de Triomphe at Longchamp. On the airplane with him were two Indian gentlemen whose fingers were adorned with a number of valuable rings. It transpired that they had been observing one entrant in the Prix, by no means the favorite, and were determined to back him. In the event, Harry backed the favorite and lost his packet; on the return flight the Indians were in grand good humor. In Paris they had pawned their precious stones for francs, bet the lot, and cleaned up when their mount won and paid very long odds. With the winnings they recovered their pawned rings and, laden with cash, returned to England having taken only forty pounds out of the country.

When I rose regretfully to leave, saying that I had an early-morning appointment, long sought, Harry said, "You cannot leave without knowing Derry's rarest bar." I was intrigued, of course, and shortly we were in the Glen Bar, which was no farther from Harry's domicile than you could sling a bottle cap.

Having written a tract on Dublin's pubs many years before, I had had occasion to visit numerous such Irish establishments, which are the venues for so much social life in Ireland, but none of such intimacy and few of such hoary ambience as the Glen Bar. It occupied a small two-story building, bar and building inherited from his mother by John Doherty, who was for forty-seven years an engine driver on the railroad. The place seemed virtually unchanged from its nineteenth-century origins in the decor and arrangements, consisting of two rooms, each perhaps fifteen by fifteen feet. The plain wooden bar, with some four stools, was in the front; the rear room, ostensibly the lounge and of very minimal appointments, was perhaps intended to accommodate ladies. From this rear room a door led to an outdoor privy. The amenities of the Glen Bar were scant, the character of the bar austere, yet it had a certain warmth. Something of this was surely owing to the publican, a small, balding man wearing a striped shirt and a florid tie, who sat quietly on a stool behind his bar, offering a comment now and then. Harry told me that the publican opens when he chooses, which is never before 8:00 P.M. He purveys no draft beer, only bottled. I was surprised to notice small bottles of wine, one-quarter-bottle-size, like those served on airplanes and now seen all over Ireland, ranked along the back bar. When I referred to them, Doherty shrugged and said, "I've had requests for them, so I thought I'd try them."

One other client appeared, a regular, it seemed from his greeting, who took a stool beside Harry and me. We all sat amiably, chatting, enjoying our drinks, and I my pipe. Samuel Johnson's apothegm on the virtues of the tavern came to mind.

"I've been offered a hundred thousand pounds for this place," said the publican. "I'll never sell. I like people. I like it here."

It occurred to me that someday a Northern Irish artist should make a simulacrum of the Glen Bar, with its elemental charm—bright lights;

pale, scruffy walls; the odd calendar; the clutter of bottles; a few regulars; the shrewdly observant publican—as Frank Kleinholz had memorialized Nate's Beanery in Hollywood. Meanwhile, as long as John Doherty presides, Derry has a treasure. Harry used the word *rare* for the Glen Bar; we will rarely look upon its like again.

ABOUT AS FAR from Seagate Technology's Derry plant as Tiger Woods could drive a golf ball is a small, flamboyant building in the Ulster Science and Technology Park, which, except for its scale, looks as if it might have been airlifted from Las Vegas. It is the Northern Ireland facility of Stream International, a pseudopod of a U.S. corporation headquartered in Canton, Massachusetts, which had been growing symbiotically with the proliferation of computers, information technology, and the Internet. (Stream was acquired by the Solectron Corporation in October 2001.) I was greeted by Kevin Houston, managing director of Stream's Derry facility. A compact, bustling chap, shirtsleeved and tieless, engaging and engagé, he took me on an orientation tour.

Houston told me that the two-story building had been built on speculation, that in 1996 Stream had moved in and was fast outgrowing it. Houston explained that Stream provided technical-support services to companies in information technology and related products. As I write, Stream has twenty-three call centers around the world: thirteen in North America, seven in Europe, and three in Japan. Stream has twelve thousand employees and offers global support twenty-four hours a day, every day of the year, in thirteen languages for some fifty client companies. Those companies found it more economical to focus on their principal products and "to outsource the servicing of those products to their consumers."

As Kevin Houston guided me from the plant-filled central atrium, with its stainless-steel staircase, through the open-plan floors, I watched many of the 350 employees in the Derry facility working in low-walled cubicles, each with telephone headset, eyes fixed on a computer's monitor. One hundred of them were providing technical support for Dell. There were large signs on the walls in various sections of the building, bearing the names of Stream's client companies serviced from this facility; besides Dell, I noted signs designating service areas for Hewlett-Packard and Microsoft (no longer a client in Derry).

If someone has difficulty using a product made by one of these man-ufacturers, he or she can call a telephone number designated by the manu-facturer—say, a man in Glasgow has a problem with his Dell computer; he calls the Dell support number and connects with a service representative in Derry who has been trained to help him overcome the difficulty.

Houston said that his workforce was predominantly young, 70 percent twenty to twenty-five years old. In dress and manner, Stream's employees in Derry appeared much like the young men and women using the com-puter center in the university I had recently left. Houston said that 20 per-cent of the employees were college graduates, although they were not necessarily educated in information technology when hired. Ten percent of his employees were long-term unemployed persons who had returned to the workforce. After telling me that his five top employees were in that group, Houston indicated one older woman: "She's my best employee, conscientious and a natural communicator." He said that the woman had returned to the workforce after raising a family; she did not have a college education. "By the way, neither do I," he remarked. "I'm from Derry, spent twenty years in corporate banking, then managed a call center in London before coming here."

Next we visited the canteen, where the atmosphere was palpably col-legial and everyone was on a first-name basis with the managing director, who bantered with one young man about the certification program he was in. Then Houston took me to his own large cubicle, and tapping into his computer, he pulled up and printed a number of tables and charts. They il-lustrated Stream International's global organization (European HQ is in Amsterdam); the services provided clients; Stream University, the incen-tive-driven continual-training and certification program; the proportional distribution of Stream's clients among hardware manufacturers, commu-nications companies, software publishers, and corporate help desks; and Stream International's revenues ($365 million in 2001).

Houston explained that Stream would design customized support ser-vices for a client: "For example, a bank is going on-line and has customer-relationship needs. We would go to the bank and train its people in serving their customers." He added, "My goal is to have a five-hundred-employee facility in Derry." (In 2002, there were 650.)

To keep his crew on their toes, Houston likes to call in as a distressed user of a product whose manufacturer Stream supports. Having myself been a desperate caller of both Apple's and Microsoft's "help" telephone numbers, I realized what a boon are the services that Stream provides in today's computer-driven world. In its Derry leader, I thought the company had a Pied Piper.

DURING MY TRAVELS in the Northwest of Ireland—County Donegal in the Republic and three counties of Northern Ireland—I had seen and learned much, but I realized that I had barely scratched the surface of Northern Ireland's six counties. While I was there, the slow process of peace and accommodation among the various parties who were unionist or nationalist, Protestant or Catholic, had led to devolution in accordance with the Good Friday Agreement of 1998. That meant the return of the governance of Northern Ireland from the British government in London to a power-sharing Executive and Assembly in Northern Ireland for the first time since 1974. However, as I write, the governance of Northern Ireland, from Belfast's Stormont Castle, remains a fragile thing, barely cemented by the common goal of all parties, self-government of the province, but threatened by the fierce determination of each of the parties represented in the Executive, that its vision for Northern Ireland should prevail. The several and rancorously divided parties of unionist allegiance are determined that Northern Ireland should remain forever part of the United Kingdom; the parties of Irish nationalist sympathies hold that one day Northern Ireland should be united with the Republic of Ireland—that is to say, reunited with the rest of the country from which it was separated in 1921. Radical extremists of both unionist and nationalist convictions continue to make violent attacks on others of opposing views. At several times since my walk through three of its counties, Britain has taken back direct governance of Northern Ireland, to prevent the total collapse of the Northern Ireland Executive and Assembly, due to continuing friction between unionist and republican members.

In ways I think of as typically Irish and paradoxical, devolution has made for uneasy bedfellows and continual jousting. Recall that the Irish and British governments' Joint Declaration of 1993 acknowledges that the people of Northern Ireland shall be free to "exercise their right of self-determination" and to "bring about a united Ireland . . . subject to the agreement and consent of a majority of the people in Northern Ireland."

Until that shall occur, if ever, Northern Ireland remains part of the United Kingdom. Meanwhile, Sinn Féin has been allotted two ministers in the devolved Executive for Northern Ireland. One of them, the Minister for Education, Martin McGuinness, is a former commander of the IRA in Derry. The two Sinn Féin ministers have refused to permit the flag of the United Kingdom to fly over their department offices on the seventeen days designated—by the Secretary for Northern Ireland in the government of the United Kingdom—for all government offices to display the flag. What the Sinn Féin ministers doubtless regard as standing on principle others may view as pettifoggery. To be sure, I was under no illusion that such unionist demagogues as the Reverend Ian Paisley would be more amenable to reason. I had to wonder how matters of real substance affecting the welfare of Northern Ireland's people would be resolved by an Executive with some ideologues ruled by prejudice, passion, and hubris. Yet tangible progress toward peace in Northern Ireland has been made. In accordance with the Good Friday Agreement, the British Army has been dismantling fortifications. An international commission has verified that the Irish Republican Army has "decommissioned"—that is, put beyond use—several of its arms dumps, if not all, as required by the Agreement. As I write, however, no unionist paramilitary organization has "decommissioned" any weapons.

DURING THE ANGUISHING years of the Troubles, the economy of Derry suffered significantly. The manufacture of clothing, once a mainstay of the local economy, declined; employment spiraled downward. However, native son John Hume campaigned in the United States, touting the advantages for investors in drawing upon Northern Ireland's English-speaking labor pool, its strong educational resources, the infrastructure, and incentives offered by the Industrial Development Board. Similarly inspired, a group of civic leaders formed the Derry Investment Initiative to address Derry's plight by vigorously seeking investment in the city and the region; targeting the United States, they focused on companies in the information-technology sector. Their Director of Operations, Dr. Barney Toal, wrote in the 1998–1999 annual report: "The local parliamentary constituency—Foyle—still has the largest actual number of unemployed of any of the parliamentary constituencies for Northern Ireland." Given the centuries-old division of the haves and have-nots in Northern Ireland, not to speak of the proportion of Catholics to Protestants in the Foyle constituency, it is probable that the preponderance of unemployed were Catholics.

Yet I could now bear witness to the burgeoning of hope for peace in Derry and its environs. There was a tangible feeling of rapprochement and revival in the air, despite episodic acts of violence by die-hard elements of differing allegiances. A number of cooperative cross-border initiatives were astir; one was an Integrated Plan for the Northwest, commissioned by groups in the Republic and Northern Ireland and financed by the European Union's Special Support Programmes to assist peace and reconciliation in border counties. The success of international companies like Seagate and Stream—equal-opportunity employers, who seek effective and dedicated employees regardless of religious, ethnic, or racial background—could mean a bright beginning to the millennium for a city and a region too long wasted by strife. Those companies were not alone. DuPont has had a major manufacturing facility outside Derry since 1960 and is now Europe's principal supplier of Lycra and Kevlar synthetics; Raytheon, the electronics and armaments behemoth, was establishing a software manufactory in Derry when I was there. And there were others.

I had seen less of the North than I would have liked on this journey, for I was following a more or less straight line north to south. Still, I had viewed much of old Ulster and new, from the citadel of the ancient Gaels at the Grianán of Ailech in Donegal to the walls of plantation Londonderry to the venerable Glen Bar and to the high-tech enterprises pumping lifesaving blood into the arteries of a beguiling city and region. Now onward!

..

PART TWO

The River Shannon's Reach

Temple Finghin, or "MacCarthy's Church," at Clonmacnoise.

Hazards and Serendipities

. ❧ .

SWANLINBAR SEEMED TO BE THE CHORUS OF A SONG THAT KEPT
rattling in my head as I took a bus there from Derry, looking from a high
window as we whizzed past towns and streams and cottages I had surveyed
from eye level. At the small town with its familiar main street, where I had
felt my knee give out, I debarked to resume my journey southward by shoe
leather. (Or, thankfully, marching in a high-tech substitute, ergonomically
designed and waterproofed, though I had hoofed many miles through Europe wearing stout all-leather boots bought in Ireland decades ago.) I was
now in the Republic of Ireland's County Cavan, whence my maternal
grandmother hailed.

After about six miles on a fairly quiet road through scraggy, undulating, little-settled country, I crossed into County Leitrim, one of Ireland's
smallest and poorest counties—and possibly the least known to outsiders.
Five miles on I came to Ballinamore, a town set prettily beside the Shannon-Erne Waterway, linking Upper Lough Erne in Northern Ireland to
the river Shannon, which courses through the heart of Ireland.

I put up at Riversdale, the commodious guesthouse and farm of Violet and Raymond Thomas; its faux half-timbered gables gave it the look of
a house in the English shires. A pair of Labradors, one black, one yellow,
were frisking on the lawn that ran down to the Thomases' dock on the wa-

terway. After I introduced myself to the welcoming Mrs. Thomas and shed my pack, the dogs accompanied me as I strolled through the farmyard to inspect the family's considerable fleet of canal boats for hire. Walking back to the house, I discovered the up-to-date fitness center, with its indoor heated pool and sauna, available to guests and operated as a membership club for locals.

Over tea in the conservatory, I said to Violet Thomas that I was startled to find Riversdale's mod fitness center in so rural a setting. With good humor, she reminded me that Ireland was quite au courant in many ways. Talking about Riversdale, Violet mentioned that she had met her husband in England, "where Raymond had read French and political science at Reading University, and I brought him back to Ireland to be a farmer."

When I said I had heard that Ballinamore had been a hotbed of IRA activity in the recent Troubles, Violet Thomas replied that too much had been made of the Troubles and that there was more harmony and cooperation among people of different backgrounds than was understood abroad.

"Despite what the world may think, the problem in Ireland is not religious but economic," she said. "Are you religious?"

"Reasonably," I allowed.

"I'm Church of Ireland, Anglican," Violet said, "and when our church here needed a new roof, the Catholic parish priest held a benefit concert in his church, with the Irish-Welsh Choir performing. It was a grand success. There is much more cross-border cooperation than people generally know of. The Shannon-Erne Waterway is one example."

THAT EVENING I dined in Ballinamore at the Sliab An Iarainn, a pub whose name means "iron mountain," after the massif that looms over the region and was mined for centuries. I ordered the "maxi-grill" featured on the menu. Informed that there was no lamb chop, I accepted the offered pork chop. Perhaps the "maxi-grill" is best forgotten, but I asked that the chop be wrapped for me, which was willingly done.

While I enjoyed a hearty breakfast in Riversdale's conservatory, I watched the occasional canal boat idling by and talked with the only other guest, a friendly young man named Cormac Healy. As we were discussing the remarkable economic and social changes Ireland was undergoing, Cormac remarked that his grandmother was "still sharp at one hundred years, when she was honored by visits from Ireland's President Mary McAleese and U.S. Ambassador Jean Kennedy Smith." His grandmother had lived through the First World War, the Easter Rising of 1916, the Troubles of the 1920s, the Irish Civil War, and the Second World War and had witnessed the proliferation of the telephone, automobile, radio, television, and computer.

Fascinating, if a good deal to digest after breakfast. I also learned that Cormac Healy was a consultant to the Shannon-Erne Waterway, which has its office in Ballinamore. He suggested that I stop by and said he could give me a good steer along the next stretch of the way.

After breakfast, Graham Thomas, Raymond and Violet's son, brought the *Deirdre*, a spanking-bright canal boat, alongside their dock, and I was invited for a trial voyage on the lovely Shannon-Erne Waterway. Raymond, unfailingly courteous, with an English reserve which complemented Violet's cheery Irish way, explained that their barges were specially designed for the waterway and, although built in England and called narrow boats, had a beam of ten feet, wider than those that ply the canals of England and Wales.

The *Deirdre*, on which we purred along at the maximum speed permitted—five knots, to prevent erosion of the banks—has a double-bedded cabin forward, a single amidships, a neat WC with shower, and seating in the capacious dining cabin–cum–galley, which could be converted to a double berth. The cabins have central heating, and there is a wood- or peat-burning stove in the dining area; pretty curtains and carpeting make for cozy accommodations. When I remarked on the tiller aft for steering, Raymond said, "This kind of craft isn't for everyone, but it's ideal for a family."

Graham added, "We also have a Dutch-style barge, which has two double berths and a wheelhouse."

That would suit me, I thought, and having already made three voyages on the Shannon with my family, I knew that I next wished to cruise the bucolic Shannon-Erne Waterway, which wends its way across a pastoral countryside for about thirty-nine miles, through four loughs and sixteen locks, before it joins the river Shannon.

———

RAYMOND THOMAS kindly dropped me off at the Waterway's office, where the enthusiastic Cormac Healy had maps and publications laid out for me. I learned that the present Shannon-Erne Waterway had begun as the Ballinamore-Ballyconnell Canal, built over fourteen years and opened in 1860. After only eight boats had made the passage in nine years, the canal was abandoned. The maintenance of the banks was exorbitant, and railroads were making canals redundant. Nonetheless, at the close of the twentieth century, visionaries on both sides of the border between Ireland and Northern Ireland had seen that a reconstructed and extended canal could bring peoples together in a cross-border enterprise to revitalize a long-depressed region. The gnomes of Brussels, in the guise of the European Regional Development Fund for Ireland, had seen the wisdom of an initiative that would provide employment during reconstruction and maintenance and thereafter should bring substantial income from tourism. The Irish and British governments and the Electricity Supply Board of Ireland joined in funding the reconstruction and development of the waterway. Subsequently the International Fund for Ireland and the Programme for Peace and Reconciliation were providing funds for marketing the waterway, a responsibility of Cormac Healy. Forces other than the terrorists and the spoilers—who wanted no Good Friday Agreement to bring peace to Northern Ireland—were acting to achieve just that.

Besides informing me about the Shanon-Erne Waterway, Cormac was as good as his word, pointing me on my way. He told me about the Kingfisher Cycle Trail, which passed his office door. Established in 1999, covering roughly 230 miles, mostly on secondary or even more minor roads, all clearly signposted, it traverses parts of Counties Leitrim, Cavan, Monaghan, and Donegal in the Republic and part of County Fermanagh in Northern Ireland. Giving me a map of the trail, Cormac pointed out that the route I'd planned was identical to the Kingfisher Trail from Ballinamore to Carrick-on-Shannon.

IN A CHEERFUL MOOD, under a firmament of an encouraging blue, I set off, armed with the Kingfisher Trail map, which was folded into eight sections, each covering approximately twenty-five miles and indicating points of interest and facilities as well as a route profile for that section, showing elevations. For the first mile and a half, the trail was a paved one-lane track, hugging the waterway to my left and leading to a nine-hole golf course. A note on the trail map read, "Clubs can be rented." The club-house, as modest as a youth hostel, was on my side; the course, across the water, was reached by a footbridge. As I approached it, a cyclist overtook me, a woman of some years, pedaling slowly and wrapped against the brisk breeze that had sprung up, and I called out, "Good morning!" but heard no response. Unusual. Perhaps a lone man, though burdened by a pack, was alarming to a lone woman, even near high noon on a brilliant day. I preferred to think that the elderly cyclist was deaf rather than that country manners in Ireland might be changing.

The waterway meandered in gentle bends beside the trail, and though it was late in the cruising season, the occasional craft passed and happy crews hallooed me. To reinforce the soft earth banks against erosion, at frequent intervals along this section, the rebuilders of the old canal had revetted the banks with riprap retained by stepped wooden forms, which comprised rough stairs. I stepped down one to the water's edge, slipped out of my rucksack, and sat on the lowest step. Huddling behind thick, heavily cut back willow shoots against the rising wind, I got out a quarter bottle of wine and last night's pork chop. With an apple it made an acceptable repast today. Saluting the odd passing craft, watching some mallards puddling at my feet, I was a man content.

All too soon the idyllic trail along the waterway intersected a busy secondary road. As I reached the top of a rise, I saw on my left a handsome stone Georgian house, beautifully sited, with fields sloping down toward a lock on the waterway. The stonework was fine, and I suspected that it had only recently been freed of the stuccoing—often with a pebble-dashed surface—so commonplace on Ireland's many stone-built Georgian houses and now, increasingly, being divested of the cladding. Having too briefly owned such a house, I felt a twinge of envy, admiring this fine building with its manicured lawn, well-kept outbuildings, and lovely prospect.

Musing thus but with eyes turned back to the road, I was cleaving to the ditch on my right as I climbed, facing the oncoming traffic at a sharp bend, when around it whizzed a car bearing down on me. I flung myself into the blackberry brambles to avoid being flattened. The driver's face was a rictus of horror, as she realized what she had nearly done. As she swerved outward too late, she honked furiously at me, apparently in outrage, though in this near miss neither of us seemed at fault.

Still, I had learned a lesson that would spare me at other times walking Ireland's narrow country roads, where drivers drive on the left. That is, when facing the traffic and approaching a bend in the road—one sharp enough to cut off my view of an approaching vehicle—I must cross to the other side of the road, from which I could see the oncoming traffic, until safely around the bend, even though for that short while I must have the near-side traffic at my back. That strategy would prevent my spouse's premature widowhood.

At Fenagh, I paused at Gannon's Abbey Bar. Though stools and chairs were upended and an electrician was working amid coils of wire and a litter of tools, installing a fire-alarm system, the publican gave the universal response of "no problem" to my inquiry about a cup of coffee. I had read that the gaunt abbey ruins, which one could view from the bar, were the scant remains of an ancient monastic establishment of St. Caillin. In the Middle Ages, the O'Roddys were the founder's successors, who caused to be copied, in 1516, the *Book of Fenagh*, which perpetuated the monastery's early records and the supposed wondrous acts of the saint, and is now preserved in the Royal Irish Academy.

Little remained of the monastery that once stood here. Centuries of warfare among the Irish themselves and between the Irish and their English invaders had reduced such establishments to vestiges. What enemies did not, local landholders and peasants did: the stones of abbeys and castles were carried off to build walls, cottages, or farm buildings. As I made my way around the two surviving shells of St. Caillin's foundation, I thought of what these walls had witnessed. The wind made a plainsong through a Gothic window while I gazed at the hoary tomb of an ancient family and glimpsed the shadow of mortality.

MY ROUTE ONWARD was by a very lightly traveled country road—still the Kingfisher Trail—past the occasional cottage and several small farms. The Shannon-Erne Waterway was again sometimes in view on my right. The sky had darkened, and the wind blew straight at me as I walked westward. Passing Castlefore Lough, I was surprised to see two tiny gorse bushes bravely showing brilliant yellow blooms, for the peak season for display was usually June, and all the other prickly gorse hedges I'd passed were a sullen autumn green. In fields spiked with marsh grass, bog cotton fluttered, and here and there a few remaining fiery fuchsia blossoms brightened my way.

Entering the outskirts of the village of Keshcarrigan, I saw a substantial modern house on a knoll overlooking the waterway, Canal View House, the B&B of Jeannette Conefrey. Both Violet Thomas and Cormac Healy had recommended Mrs. Conefrey's guesthouse and promised to call and ask her to take me in. A bit wearily I trudged up the driveway and rang the doorbell. No answer. I waited, then rang again. No response. There was a key in the front door, and with some misgiving, I turned it and stepped in, half expecting that a guardian with a loud bark might greet me. No one. I stood in the vestibule and called out. Silence. The house was toasty warm, and after my tramp on that windy day, I rather wanted a nap. Reluctantly, I went back out, hefted my pack again, and started down the drive, thinking I'd dawdle in a pub and call later. Just then a car turned into the drive and pulled up; from it emerged Jeanette Connefrey and the two daughters she had picked up from school, neat in their navy-blue uniforms. I was expected.

After a soothing hot shower and a nap, I found the capacious and pretty dining room at the agreed hour. Promptly Jeanette Connefrey appeared and put me at a prettily set table by a glowing hearth. In the boating season my hostess welcomes diners besides guests staying in her house, but this evening I dined alone, and very well, on potato and leek soup, poached salmon, and au gratin potatoes. With a glass of wine at hand, I made leisurely notes in my journal.

Darkness came early at fifty-four degrees north latitude, and strolling along the road to the village pub could be hazardous. So I took out my pocket flashlight, only to find the batteries dead. Still, I had my reflector belt, so I put it on and set off, passing the deserted marina. Keshcarrigan consists of a few houses at a road junction; three adjoining houses had been newly reconstructed and were for sale; there were a couple of shops and a post office. There was a pub on each side of the road; the first was Hillsbrook House, and I went in.

Like many such establishments in Ireland today, Hillsbrook House has been newly done up, and quite smartly. There was much warm wood paneling and pine bar fittings, a U-shaped bar, exposed brick wall, and a fireplace in which peat bricks burned fragrantly. A bizarre touch was the half-size effigies of Laurel and Hardy, regarding the scene from a niche. As it was still early in the evening when I came in, only the youthful barmaid was there, and she put down a book to serve me. I told her how agreeable I thought the pub was, and she said that it had been renovated only that year, by local craftsmen. Gradually a few friendly regulars drifted in, and the young barmaid was relieved by an older woman. From her I learned that the girl who had served me was a McKeown, as was Jeanette Connefrey.

Across the street was Gertie's Canal Stop, where I hove to for a night-cap. Gertie's had not been recently renovated and was richly cluttered. In the lounge section some young men were vociferously watching a football match on the telly. Beside me at the bar sat a German family—father, mother, and daughter—perhaps late-season cruisers, all nursing pints of Guinness. My whiskey was served by a shapely barmaid whose blue jeans seemed sprayed on. I savored my drink, scribbled a few notes, then headed back through the inky dark to Canal View House.

On a windy morning beneath a gray sky of fast-drifting scud, I swung on my pack and walked through Keshcarrigan, pausing beside a thatched cottage, trim as a doll's house, to read an inscription on a low granite slab. Between two silhouetted figures of men wielding pikes were graven these words in English and in Irish:

TO COMMEMORATE THE 1798 REBELLION.
GENERAL HUMBERT, HIS ARMY AND IRISH VOLUNTEERS
PASSED THROUGH KESHKERRIGAN—7TH SEPTEMBER, 1798
ON THEIR WAY TO BALLINAMUCK.
ERECTED 28TH AUGUST, 1998.

I sat on the low stone surround for a while and mused on the tragic history recalled by the stark inscription.

In 1791, a group of mainly Anglo-Irish Protestants in Belfast formed an organization called the United Irishmen. Inspired by the egalitarian and republican ideals of the French and the American revolutions and eager to throw off Britain's yoke, the United Irishmen made common cause with a widespread organization of Catholic dissidents called the Defenders, who had centuries of grievances to settle.

Seeing an opportunity to find an ally in England's ancient foe, an emissary of the United Irishmen, Theobald Wolfe Tone, a zealous young lawyer, went to Paris to seek military assistance in winning independence from Britain. Again at war with England, the French, then governed by the Directory, eventually agreed and dispatched a fleet of forty-three ships with some fourteen thousand soldiers under General Louis-Lazare Hoche. Before this armada reached Ireland, it was dispersed by bad weather. Reduced in number, on December 21, 1796, the French anchored in Bantry Bay in County Cork, where a severe gale prevented a landing and forced the ships to put to sea. The attempted invasion was a debacle.

In May 1798, an order for a general uprising went out from the United Irishmen's central committee to their organizations in various counties. Rebellion had been launched. Before it was over, there would be acts of terrible brutality on both sides, but the government in Dublin Castle, under the king's lord lieutenant in Ireland, was determined to take whatever steps necessary to put down the insurrection. With superior regular troops and loyal Irish yeomanry, they did just that, inflicting great slaughter on untrained peasants whose long pikes were no match for cannon and muskets. By midsummer the rising had been smashed; fleeing rebels were being hunted and exterminated.

Meanwhile, in Paris, Wolfe Tone persevered. He won from Napoléon Bonaparte the promise of another effort to land French troops and arms in support of the Irish struggle for independence; he also was given the rank of adjutant general in the French Army. A three-pronged expeditionary force was mounted.

On August 22, 1798, three French ships anchored in Killala Bay, in County Mayo, in Northwest Ireland. One thousand French soldiers, veterans of Napoléon's Italian campaign and commanded by General Jean-Joseph-Amable Humbert, disembarked. In short order the French overcame the local yeomanry and distributed arms and uniforms to the small number of Irish who rallied to them. Humbert then met and routed a superior British force under General Gerard Lake at Castlebar. The flight of the surviving British soldiers became enshrined in Irish lore as the Castlebar Races.

Humbert and the French Directory had been led to believe that the Irish peasantry would rise in great numbers to join their French allies in the cause of Irish freedom. Moreover, they had been assured that the yeomanry (predominantly Catholic, though usually commanded by Protestant Anglo-Irish landowners) would turn their coats and join the green revolutionary banner—with the legend *Erin go bragh,* "Ireland forever"—flown by the Irish irregulars who had gathered around Killala. Accordingly, Humbert marched toward Dublin, expecting that a great Irish host would join him.

At several points on his march, Humbert's hopes of numerous Irish rallying to him were raised, only to be dashed. After a march of 160 miles, at Ballinamuck, in County Longford, on September 8, 1798, Humbert and his force—by then some nine hundred French regulars and perhaps three hundred untrained Irishmen—were confronted by General the Marquis Cornwallis, Lord Lieutenant of Ireland and Commander in Chief, with some twenty thousand troops. Hopelessly outnumbered, the French, wise in war, made a token resistance and surrendered. According to a senior French officer, the Irish rebels "fought bravely to the last and were cut to pieces, selling their lives dearly."

The French soldiery were accorded the honors of war, transported to Dublin by coach and barge, and repatriated. General Cornwallis, vanquished at Yorktown and victor at Ballinamuck, was generally a humane man, by the customs of the times, and inclined to pardon the Irish rank and file as "deluded" people. But determined to deal rebellion a death blow, he acted summarily with the captured Irish leaders: ninety were executed, among them Wolfe Tone's brother, Matthew.

Wolfe Tone was aboard the *Hoche* in a French squadron when it was brought to battle by a British flotilla off Donegal on October 12, 1798. The *Hoche* fought bravely, with Tone commanding a battery; but outgunned, it yielded. Tone, in French uniform, was captured, transported to Dublin, tried, and condemned to death. As a French officer, he asked to be shot, but Cornwallis declined the request; Tone was to be hanged for treason. Instead, he managed to cut his own throat and died, just thirty-five years old, to become one of Ireland's most enduring martyrs.

CONTINUING MY MARCH southwest toward Carrick-on-Shannon, I reflected on the savagery of both sides in the great rebellion of 1798, of the terrible cost in blood and anguish of that revolt and all the others by which the Irish have striven to wrest their country from England's grip and how all those conflicts over centuries have branded themselves on the Irish soul, for good and for ill. While Ireland's struggles inspired so much of her poetry and her song, for too long her desperate wish for freedom encouraged the belief that it could only be won by the gun.

Walking encourages rumination. Tramping, looking, pausing; it's easier for the walker to light a pipe or sip from a water bottle than it is for the driver. One gets into a rhythm; the sense of the pack on the back, the heavy boots on the feet, fade away; the mind floats freely. I was unconscious of the rain that had begun to fall steadily, preoccupied by the somewhat melancholy thoughts prompted by the monument I'd seen. To cheer myself up, I began to whistle, then found myself singing, one of the best-known Irish songs, which springs from the '98:

> "Oh, then, tell me, Shawn O'Ferrall,
> Where the gath'rin' is to be?"
> "In the ould spot by the river,
> Right well known to you and me.
> One word more—for signal token
> Whistle up the marchin' tune,
> With your pike upon your shoulder,
> By the risin' of the moon."

Much cheered up, subliminally aware of marching to the old infantry pace of 120 steps to the minute, through gusts of rain I glimpsed a pile of stones in a rough pasture where bits of wool clung to scattered thistles—a dolmen, an ancient chamber grave. It wasn't indicated on the Kingfisher Trail map in my pocket, though it probably was on the Ordnance Survey map in my rucksack. A stile led into the field where the dolmen stood, some hundred yards from the shore of Lough Scur, which looked as bleak as Grendel's mere. No marker designated the site.

Dropping my pack, I went through the stile and down the slope from the road to the dolmen. Near it a solitary hawthorn bent in obsequy to the notability whose grave was marked by a few big stones capped by one great slab, which seemed to have broken. The passage between the uprights was clogged with brambles and nettles. An outlying stone or two suggested that there might once have been a stone circle around the sepulchre. It would originally have been heaped with smaller stones to form a cairn.

I retreated to the stile, crouched there, pulled out my journal, and, trying to shield it against the rain, noted my wonderment about whom this
monument commemorated—perhaps a chieftain slain in battle or an important woman who died in childbirth or mayhap an *ollamh*, an hereditary
poet and chronicler whose own story we would probably never know.
Without archaeologist or historian beside me, I knew only that, at great effort, these stones had been put in place, likely several thousand years ago,
by a people for whom memory and its perpetuation were important.

As I bent over my journal, I was conscious of a movement behind me
and glanced up to see the barrel of what proved to be a telescope thrust
from the window of a car that, unheard, had drawn up beside me. Surprised, I stood up and, despite the rain splashing on my glasses, made out
a dark, curly head looking up from the eyepiece. The observer said,
"Drawing the dolmen?"

"Making notes about it."

"Come around. Get in."

The rain was streaming down now, so, picking up my rucksack, I went
to the passenger's door, curious about this observer.

"Get in," the driver said again, pushing open the door.

I slipped off my rucksack and got in, introducing myself.

"Gerard Woods," the driver said. "I'm a salesman, cover much of Ireland." He put out his hand. He was a young man, thirtyish, wearing a
white shirt and a tie.

"What do you sell?"

"Hardware," he said. "I have a customer between here and Carrick."
He put his telescope in the backseat, shifted into gear, and started off,
adding, "Where are you going?"

"I hoped to be in Carrick-on-Shannon before nightfall. Anywhere
along the way would suit me," I said.

Gerard Woods seemed hungry for conversation, and we nattered
companionably to the beat of his windshield wipers. I asked about the telescope with which he had been examining the dolmen and learned that his
wife had given it to him for his birthday, and though he didn't speak of as-
tronomy, he expressed an interest in antiquities.

"Do you see that cairn there on that hilltop?" he asked, pointing.

I could just make it out beneath the rain clouds that grazed it.

"Leitrim is an interesting county. Not many tourists come here, but there are many old sites to be seen." Then, pulling into a grocery-pub–cum–filling station, he said, "I have a customer near here. This is Lynch's, a decent place."

"I don't think I'm quite ready for a jar," I said. "Maybe a pot of tea or a cup of coffee."

"Wait here," he said and shot out through the rain into the grocery. In a moment he waved me in.

"Here's the man for the tea!" cried the drummer and nipped out and away.

The woman behind the grocery counter led me into the public-house side of the establishment, which I was not surprised to find was another pub neatly retrofitted in new pine. I took a stool at one end of the short bar, and a pot of tea was promptly produced. The sole other client of Lynch's dispensary this morning sat on the farthest stool, a pint of stout before him, expertly rolling a cigarette. We exchanged perfunctory observations on the soggy day. He was slim as a splinter, with a grizzled beard, dressed in a paint-splattered blue pullover, black jeans, muddy Wellington boots, and a red stocking cap that would have suited a voyageur.

The headgear of the adept smoker was not inappropriate. For it transpired that Christopher Pennellier was the son of a French father and an Irish mother, had served with the French Army in Africa in the Second World War—"not a nice business"—and had adventured in Canada. I was struck immediately by his precise diction and easy discourse.

Having seen me drop my rucksack on the floor, he opened the conversation when he noticed me jotting in my notebook between sips of tea. Chris, as he wished to be called, confirmed his supposition that I was a wanderer and urged me to read a book by a friend of his, Anne Mustoe, who had resigned as headmistress of an English girls' school to bicycle around the world. Her journey produced *A Bike Ride,* in which she recounts her often curious experiences, such as accustoming herself to the stares of people in a remote Indian village who had never seen a white woman and assembled to observe her ablutions. Chris spoke, too, of other books he thought might interest me. One was *Woodbrook* by David Thomson, which I already knew and treasured. The title is the name of a Georgian house not far away, which I had succeeded in glimpsing when cruising the river Shannon. The book is the memoir of a Englishman who had gone to Woodbrook as the young tutor to the children of an Anglo-

Irish family and fell in love with the eldest of his charges. Beautifully written, it is one of the most poignant love stories I have ever known and recaptures an almost vanished world.

Chris mentioned that Anne Mustoe had been helpful to him with contacts when he took an Arabian horse to France and rode the length and breadth of the country, usually sleeping rough, as people here say of bedding down wherever one can, including the great outdoors, without paying for lodging. "A grand experience," Chris recalled.

It was no surprise to hear that he was a horseman; he had that wiry look and a visage that spoke of much exposure to the elements. He told me that he was expert with engines and that years before, he had been dispatched by a British contractor to an automotive factory in Canada, only to find that retrenchment made him a supernumerary. "Still under contract but with no work to do, I took a job as a horseman on the Alaskan pipeline," he said. "My job was to ride through the wilds of western Canada, ahead of the construction crew, marking particular trees or other obstructions for demolition."

His recall of his equestrian life led him to tell me that he came regularly from his farm near Carrick-on-Shannon to bring a horse to a farrier near Lynch's. "This chap may be the last great traditional blacksmith in Ireland," Chris said. "And unlike the blacksmith who is usually seen as a great brawny fellow, this chap is slight. About so high." He gestured with his hand about a foot above a barstool. "Very skilled. Very independent. The first time I took a horse to be shod, I started to tell the farrier what I wanted, saying, 'A bit lower on this shoe; the horse cants a bit, and . . .'

"He gave me a look. 'If you know so much, you shoe the fookin' horse.'

"I just handed him the reins. Now when I take a horse to him, he takes that horse and walks it up and down, looking at its gait, judging its weight. Very feisty he is. Difficult. A master."

I've listened to far stranger conversations in an Irish pub. Rarely one more pleasurable.

WHEN I REACHED Carrick-on-Shannon, about one hundred miles from Malin Head and a bit more by the snail's track I was making, I'd come about a third of the way along my planned route to Kinsale. Carrick is the county seat of Leitrim, which has about twenty-five thousand inhabitants and is the least populous of Ireland's counties. With a little over two thousand souls, Carrick is the smallest of Ireland's county seats, but it is the principal town on the upper river Shannon.

I ambled down long Bridge Street past the Bush Hotel; Mulvey's, a newsagent; and a fine old pub, P. Flynn's Corner House, which would have done nicely for a John Ford film, though it had acquired a battery of hi-fi gear and a ziggurat of tapes since I'd last sought respite in its dark old wood interior. Wedged between Flynn's emporium and the next shop front is one of Ireland's minor wonders, its smallest chapel and one Carrigians declare is the second smallest in the world—though who's to refute the claim?—an ostentatious Victorian thimble of a chapel-cum-mausoleum erected in 1877 by a wealthy merchant named Edward Costello in memory of his wife, Mary Josephine. The devoted husband had himself interred on the other side of the altar from his wife. This curious adornment to the town's main street is perhaps Carrick's most interesting building besides the eighteenth-century courthouse, which like so many other fine edifices in Ireland recalls what we might call the British Raj here.

Although I wasn't keen to add to my rucksack, I stopped to browse in a small but good bookstore near the bridge, then pulled myself away, unburdened. I crossed the Shannon by the seven-arched stone bridge, as long as a football field, that leads to County Roscommon in Connacht on the west bank. Midway an inscribed stone in the parapet informed me that the Earl of Bessborough had dedicated the present viaduct in 1836. A cool wind was picking up, whistling down the broad river, etching it with waves. I thought of the last lines of Joyce's story "The Dead," with its mysterious phrase about the snow falling softly "into the dark mutinous Shannon waves." Despite the rain, now a tiresome drizzle, I paused and looked north and south over the sprawling marinas of several companies that operate fleets of rental cruisers on the great river that bisects Ireland.

The Shannon is the longest river in Ireland—as well as in the British Isles, as many in Ireland are careful to articulate—and it looms large in Irish legend and history. According to an ancient myth that recalls the biblical story of Eve, some Salmon of Knowledge lived in a certain well. Desiring to acquire their wisdom, a woman named Sinann caught one of the wondrous fish, an act forbidden to her sex. When she began to eat it, the water surged up and carried her away to the river that now bears her name.

Arising in County Cavan, beneath 2,188-foot-high Cuilcagh Mountain, almost on the border with Northern Ireland, the Shannon flows some 230 miles to debouch into the Atlantic Ocean between Loop Head, in Clare, and Kerry Head, in Kerry. Its source is traditionally held to be the Shannon Pot, a small limestone basin in which water wells up from below. But like so much else in Ireland, this is a matter of disputation. Many years ago M. S. Wilkinson is said to have shown that a little lough close by was the true source, by dropping into it a bit of grass or straw that was carried to the Shannon Pot by an underground stream. Wherever born, the infant Shannon grows to a lordly river flowing through a series of lakes, among them island-studded Lough Ree, sixteen miles long and up to seven miles wide, and grand Lough Derg, twenty-five miles long and some six miles at its widest. At times this great artery through Ireland's green heart has run red with blood in the centuries of warfare: up it came the Vikings in their splendid longboats to pillage the monasteries that flourished on its islands and its banks; later the river served as a defensive line along which, at various times, the Irish fought to hold back the encroaching English: for long the Shannon was an avenue of commerce, until the railroads and motorways made that function obsolete; and in the 1920s the river's waters were harnessed to make electricity.

Today the Irish and holidaymakers from around the world cruise the storied river—past castles ruined or occupied, derelict abbeys, pleasant towns and villages—meandering with the river through lakes of unspoiled beauty and past rush-rimmed banks where great herons stand still as sentinels, interspersed here and there with anglers no less patient in the same pursuit, while overhead flights of swans creak by, and everywhere grebes dive and mallards dabble in the shallows.

My route would take me along the Shannon for many miles, but first I had friends to call on and sites I wished to visit roundabout Carrick. So, just across the bridge, I trudged up Liberty Hill to a handsome late-Georgian house called Hollywell, the home of Tom and Rosaleen Maher, who operate it as a B&B. Tom had been the proprietor of the Bush Hotel, an old family establishment in Carrick-on-Shannon, and he was a fount of knowledge about the countryside. I was installed in a vast bedroom with a view to the south over a wide bend in the river and offered a restorative drink. That evening, I dined agreeably in the fairly recently refurbished Bush Hotel, strolled about the quiet town, and paused in P. Flynn's Corner

House to make some notes in my journal. Back at Hollywell, I'm sure I was asleep before my head touched the pillow.

TOM MAHER SERVED a breakfast that would have nourished a lumberjack, in a grand sunlit room with glowing furniture and old prints, then suggested that he guide me around the environs of Carrick. I was keen to visit the grave of the celebrated harper and bard Turlough O'Carolan, and Tom took me there by a circuitous drive. We passed by Drumsna, a tiny village on the Shannon. Its two intersecting streets of old and pretty houses would make a fine set for the film of a Trollope novel, and I recalled that when Anthony Trollope was a postal surveyor at Banagher, downriver, he conceived his first novel, *The Macdermots of Ballycloran*, after seeing ruined Ballycloran House here.

A little farther we came to Mohill, which seems to claim Carolan—as he is familiarly known—as a native son, although authorities place his birthplace near Nobber in County Meath. At the foot of the main street is a larger-than-life-size bronze sculpture of the bard. Carolan is shown seated with his Irish harp, fingers plucking at invisible strings, his blind eyes closed.

Tom led me up and down the main street, inquiring in various shops for a postcard showing the storied harper, but without success. Yet Carolan's place in Ireland's cultural history looms large. Born in 1670, he was stricken with smallpox in his teens and blinded. Oliver Goldsmith called Carolan "the last and greatest" of Ireland's bards, poets who from time immemorial occupied positions of honor in the halls of chieftains or kings, to sing their praises. In ancient Ireland a poet enjoyed a rank (there were several degrees) and dignity only second to a king's. His role required not only the ability to compose works celebrating the prowess and renown of his hosts but also to recall their valorous deeds and achievements from generation to generation.

Carolan passed from one to another house of the surviving Irish gentry, his music and poetic talents making him welcome and rewarded. Some two hundred of his compositions survive; the air to that difficult anthem "The Star-Spangled Banner" is attributed to him. Some years ago I commissioned The Chieftains to provide the music for *Ireland Moving*, a documentary film I made, and Paddy Moloney, the group's leader, proposed

"Carolan's Concerto" to open and close the film. Their exuberant performance implanted Carolan's music in my heart.

Not far from Carrick, in County Roscommon, we passed through the village of Keadew, neat as a bonbon box—a winner of the Irish Tourist Board's Tidy Town Award—and just beyond came to a lonely graveyard on the lower slope of Kilronan Mountain, beside the scant remains of the fourteenth-century church of Saint Lasair. It overlooks desolate Lough Meelagh; by its shore is the holy well associated with Saint Lasair, daughter of Saint Ronan, a woman of the sixth or seventh century, still venerated here.

Tom picked our way through deep, wet grass to the enclosure marking the ancestral burial place of the MacDermott Roes, great chieftains and patrons of Turlough O'Carolan. In 1738, the bard died at Alderford, The MacDermott Roes' house, and was interred among the MacDermotts. The sun shone softly on Carolan's resting place, illuminating the words in Irish and in English on the stone which marks it:

> IN GRATEFUL MEMORY OF
> TURLOUGH O'CAROLAN
> HARPER, COMPOSER, POET, SINGER.
> "OUR GREAT SOLACE IN OUR GREAT NEED."
> BORN AT NOBBER 1670
> DIED AT ALDERFORD 1738
> R.I.P.

Beneath, on a plinth placed there in 1978, is a sculpted portrait of Carolan in low relief. Before it lay a handful of fading flowers. I stood for a moment remembering what I knew of Carolan. Not enough, surely, but I knew that his thirst was as redoubtable as his talent. Carolan's verses were in Irish, and one of his poems, "Why Liquor of Life?" (translated by John D'Alton) is a paean to whiskey—*usquebaugh:*

> Why, liquor of life! do I love you so;
> When in all our encounters you lay me low?
>
> You're my soul and my treasure, without and within.
> My sister and cousin and all my kin;

I've the sprightliest kin of all the Gael—
Brandy and Usquebaugh, and Ale!

Oliver Goldsmith, who as a lad is said to have heard Carolan pluck his
harp, wrote that

> his death was not more remarkable than his life. . . . When just at
> the point of death, he called for a cup of his beloved liquor. Those
> who were standing round him, surprised at the demand, endeav-
> oured to persuade him to the contrary; but he persisted, and,
> when the bowl was brought to him, attempted to drink but could
> not; whereupon, giving away the bowl, he observed, with a smile,
> that it would be hard if two such friends as he and the cup should
> part at least without kissing, and then expired.

On the outskirts of Carrick, Tom Maher pointed out a sprawling factory,
a plume of white smoke drifting from its tall stack. "That's the Masonite
factory," he said. "It employs about five hundred people. A big factor in
the local economy."

Leitrim has attracted little industry during Ireland's boom, while
other counties have. Nor has Leitrim been favored in the Irish government's program of devolution, the relocation of government offices from
Dublin to other cities and towns. So the coming of Masonite, the big U.S.
producer of hardboard, to Carrick-on-Shannon was a boon. But while
Masonite's payroll sweetened the lives of its employees and filtered into
the pockets of local shopkeepers, it was a bane to others, who complained
about a foul odor that sometimes emanated from the plant. In the so-called
developed world, we learn that progress has its price.

AFTER ROSALEEN MAHER produced a little lunch in the drawing room
of Hollywell, Tom kindly put me onto a byway I'd have missed on my
own and pointed me toward Strokestown. It had been difficult to decide
which bank of the Shannon to follow on my tramp south from Carrick-on-
Shannon. The left bank, south of Drumsna, led to Newtown Forbes in
County Longford.

There was the seat of the Earl of Granard, a descendant of the Scottish Sir Arthur Forbes, a recipient of a land grant from James I, who had relieved some Irishman of its ownership. The demesne of Castle Forbes boasts a splendid forest I had admired when cruising on Lough Forbes, through which the Shannon flows. The castle's history intrigued me: in the war that followed the regicide of Charles I, Sir Arthur's widow successfully defended the castle for the Crown against the parliamentarians. At the Restoration of Charles II, the Earldom of Granard was conferred upon another Arthur Forbes, forebear of the present earl.

The romance of Castle Forbes drew me that way, but the pull toward Strokestown, across the Shannon, was greater. For there I could learn many things about the Great Famine of 1845–1847, which changed Ireland forever and dispersed tens of thousands of the Irish to other continents.

My route took me through little-settled country, skirting the ethereally beautiful and remote Lough Grange and Lough Kilglass, both linked to the Shannon. I had been told that somewhere near Lough Kilglass there was a mass rock. Such places, still hallowed, are scattered about the countryside, vestiges of the long years after the Penal Laws were enforced, which severely repressed the practice of Catholicism. A Catholic could not vote, could not join the army or navy nor practice law; no Catholic could carry a sword or possess arms, nor own a horse worth more than five pounds. There were many more statutes designed to extirpate Catholicism among the Irish. Catholic priests had to be registered, which required their swearing allegiance to the Protestant succession to the British Crown. As few priests would do so—and no Catholic prelate could remain in Ireland under pain of death—masses were offered clandestinely in out-of-the-way places by priests who lived an often hidden and fugitive existence at peril to their lives. It would not be until 1829—when Daniel O'Connell, the indefatigible lawyer who became a Member of Parliament and effected Catholic emancipation—that Catholics achieved the right to vote. Though I prospected along my way, encountering no one to guide me, I did not find the mass rock.

At dusk, as rain began to fall, I presented myself at Church View House, the handsome old dwelling of Harriet Cox near Strokestown. Downstairs, in the parlor, I noticed photographs of various Coxes astride or leading fine animals that had brought home trophies. The bedroom I was given overlooked a pasture where horses grazed, one a fine chestnut Thoroughbred.

In Strokestown, I dined indifferently in the barroom of the Percy French Hotel, named for the prolific nineteenth-century composer and lyricist, who was born nearby. Back at Mrs. Cox's, I drifted off to sleep recalling the melody of French's lovely ballad "The Mountains of Mourne."

The Shadow of the Great Famine

.⚜.

WHEN TRAVELING TO DUBLIN ON THE WAY FROM FISHING HOLIDAYS in the West, I had often passed through Strokestown, in County Roscommon. I would wonder at the extraordinarily wide streets intersecting in the square at the center of the small town and the imposing gate at its south side, behind which lay the demesne of an unseen great house. It was a house with a remarkable history.

Now, on a gray morning, I walked through the gate erected by Maurice Mahon, 1st Baron Hartland, in the eighteenth century. The drive winds through a spacious park, where sheep grazed beneath gnarled oaks and paused to stare at the lone pedestrian. Through the misty light, I saw the house named Strokestown Park, its central block of three stories balanced by wings of two stories. Extending from the mansion's right wing are former stables and outbuildings; beyond them a long wall encloses the garden. A discreet sign led me to a small restaurant and the admissions booth for the Famine Museum, which had brought me here.

It is appropriate, if ironic, that Strokestown Park should be the site of Ireland's Famine Museum. For Major Denis Mahon, nephew of the 1st Baron Hartland, inherited the estate of nine thousand acres in 1845—the year the great potato blight struck Ireland—and Roscommon, indeed Strokestown, was virtually at the epicenter of the ensuing plague, which

devastated much of the country. For his treatment of the tenants on the estate, Denis Mahon was to pay with his life.

In eleven rooms, letters, diaries, government reports, photographs,
prints, artifacts, and models—and a fifteen-minute video presentation—
illuminate the appalling story of the Great Famine, in which not less than
a million Irish people perished and another million emigrated, a diaspora
that settled largely in North America.

By the 1840s, the potato had become the principal sustenance of the
Irish peasantry; more than two million acres were cultivated for the crop.
According to the historian James S. Donnelly, Jr., in his authoritative book
The Great Irish Potato Famine, "The average adult male of the labourer,
cottier, or small holder class consumed 12 to 14 lb of potatoes every day."
When the blight appeared—later attributed to the fungus *Phytophtora in-
festans*—it spread quickly. Ireland was a largely agricultural country,
dominated by Anglo-Irish peers and gentry, often the absentee landlords
of great estates. Their tenants, who tilled plots as small as a quarter acre,
paid rents to the landlord's agent or to a middleman who leased a substantial acreage from the landlord and, in return, rented small allotments to
farmers who frequently dwelt in a little community—a clachan—of low,
thatch-roofed cottages and farmed collectively in the system termed run-
dale. In the first room, I walked around a large model of a clachan and
tried to imagine life in one of the low, one- or two-room cabins not far
away from the sprawling mansion of Strokestown Park.

When Major Denis Mahon inherited the estate, it had been managed, and
badly, by the Court of Chancery for ten years after the third and last Lord
Hartland was declared mentally deranged. Denis Mahon found that his property was encumbered by debts of as much as fifteen thousand pounds and that
a number of his several thousand tenants were in arrears with their rent. The
bad situation soon deteriorated for landlord and tenants. When the potato
blight worsened and the crop was destroyed in 1845, the Irish peasantry, de-
pendent on their habitual food source, artful in their cultivation of the tuber
(the Irish yields per acre were the largest in Europe), and doubtless trusting
in God, planted potatoes again in 1846 and 1847, only to see them blighted.

In 1846, attempting to avert disaster, Prime Minister Sir Robert Peel
ordered the importation of grain to Ireland from North America, after effecting the repeal of the Corn Laws, which had been conceived to protect
British agricultural interests. The grain—such grains as wheat, oats, and

barley are called corn in Britain and Ireland—was to be sold at low cost from government depots.

A system of so-called Unions was established throughout Ireland; they were administrative districts based on groups of parishes, which required that landowners and lessees of a certain scale pay a "poor rate" to provide relief to the destitute among their tenants. Men able-bodied enough for such work as road building received meager payment, while other family members were confined to workhouses associated with the Unions. These minimal steps hardly stemmed the march of famine in Ireland.

Charles Trevelyan, Britain's assistant secretary of the Treasury (1840–1859), reflected the view of the ruling classes toward the Irish when he wrote, "The great evil with which we have to contend is not the physical evil of famine but the moral evil of the selfish, perverse, and turbulent character of the people." Trevelyan would receive a knighthood for his role in administering Irish famine relief. The Whigs, led by Lord John Russell, succeeded Peel's Conservative government in 1846, in part because of Peel's abrogation of the Corn Laws. Russell enacted the Irish Poor Law Extension, which put a stop to the government's role in providing welfare to the indigent in Ireland. Thereafter, Irish taxpayers were solely responsible for maintenance of the indigent in their districts. In attempting to comply with the act, many were ruined.

By 1847, famine stalked the land. The workhouses, packed beyond their limits, became pestholes. The desperate inmates wallowed in filth; fever, dysentery, and typhus killed thousands. In the countryside, travelers witnessed whole families strewn dead about the roadside, their mouths stuffed with grass or even nettles. Doctors reported entering cabins where they found children reduced to near skeletons. John Mitchel, the Irish revolutionary journalist, wrote, "A calm, still horror was all over the land. Go where you would, in the heart of the town or in the church, on the mountainside or on the level plain, there was the stillness and heavy pall—like the feeling of the chamber of death. You stood in the middle of a dread, silent, vast dissolution."

Urged on by his agent, John Ross Mahon, who pressed for the eviction of tenants who would not or could not pay what they owed, Denis Mahon ordered the eviction of more than three thousand persons in 1847. Usually the dwellings of dispossessed families were burned or pulled down to prevent their return. Like other major landholders, Denis Mahon hoped that after the clearances he effected, his land could be redivided into larger hold-ings suitable for the grazing of cattle or sheep on Ireland's abundant grass.

John Ross Mahon pointed out to the landlord that it would be cheaper to pay for the emigration of the evicted than to contribute to their long-term support in the workhouse. Though Denis Mahon was reluctant, he put up £4,000 in March 1847 for the passage and feeding of one thousand of his tenants, who embarked for Canada, as the cost was less than for their transport to the United States.

Emigrés sailed on ships built for the purpose, which became known as coffin ships because of the terrible loss of life among those stacked be-lowdecks in unsanitary conditions, where great numbers succumbed to dysentery, typhus, and relapsing fever. James S. Donnelly, Jr., writes that "unfortunately for his [Mahon's] reputation, as many as a quarter of his emigrants perished during the Atlantic crossing."

Not long after spending a few months in England, Denis Mahon at-tended a meeting of the Board of Guardians at the Roscommon Union workhouse on November 2, 1847. As he was en route home that evening, two shots rang out when his carriage came to Doorty bridge. He was killed instantly.

Already stirred by the evidence of the national calamity presented in the museum, I had an eerie sensation when I came upon the alleged confes-sion to the murder of Major Mahon, by Patrick Hasty, proprietor of a she-been (where illegally distilled liquor, poteen, was dispensed). Close by this document was the pistol said to be that with which the landlord was slain.

Patrick Hasty was convicted of the murder of Major Denis Mahon, and the government was determined that his execution would not be the occasion for an insurrection nor for an attempted rescue. On August 8, 1848, a mounted squadron of the Scots Greys, three companies of the 31st Foot, and more than one hundred of the Royal Irish Constabulary assem-bled in the town of Roscommon to control the crowd. Patrick Hasty—who protested his innocence, saying he had nothing to gain from the murder, was not a tenant of Major Mahon, and believed him to be a decent landlord—was hanged.

IT WOULD BE HARD to exaggerate the fateful consequences of the Great Famine of 1845–1847. The population of Ireland before the famine was about eight million; afterward it was near six million. Continued emigration, by people in search of a livelihood and perhaps the dream of liberty in a new world, reduced the population of Ireland to what it is today—some 3.75 million in the Republic and a little over 1.5 million in Northern Ireland.

The bankruptcy of great estates—some of whose landlords pledged their all to succor their tenants—and the subsequent dismemberment of their properties led to surviving farmers' acquiring land in their own right. On their deaths their holdings passed to their eldest sons. Other sons and daughters, often with little tangible to offer in marriage, married later, if at all. Ireland's birthrate declined.

The decimation of the peasantry during the famine resulted in the ratio of the Catholic clergy to the rest of the population being greater. As this followed not long after the Catholic emancipation of 1829, the influence of the Catholic church in Ireland's affairs grew increasingly pronounced.

Perhaps the most significant consequence of the famine for the United States, Ireland, and Britain was that the vast host of Irish driven onto the shores of North America, scarred with the memory of centuries of oppression, arrived with the added grievance of dispossession and exile. Irish memories burn brightly, fueled by song and story. For many of the descendants of the famine exiles, a vision of the ancient homeland would be forever green; so, too, for some, would be resentment of the British government and colonialism. The Irish Republican Army has drawn on that capital to finance its struggle to sever Northern Ireland from British rule and reunite it with the rest of Ireland.

As Irish-Americans made themselves a force in U.S. politics, Boston, New York, Chicago, and other big cities have danced to the pipers' tunes. The British government has shown its awareness of the influence that the Irish in America could wield. (There are more than forty million Americans who claim at least partial Irish ancestry and ten million who claim entirely Irish descent.) Eamon De Valera, born in New York of an Irish mother and a Spanish father, was the only major commander of the 1916 Rising to be spared execution by the British. Ironically, as a revolutionary, Irish parliamentarian, prime minister, and president, De Valera was to dominate Irish affairs for fifty years. In various ways he proved a thorn in Britain's side, not least by maintaining Ireland's neutrality in the Second

World War, although tens of thousands of Irishmen served in the British Army in that war, as, paradoxically, they had for centuries.

IT WAS MY LUCK that autumnal day at Strokestown to be the sole visitor guided about the mansion of the Pakenham Mahon family by a charming schoolgirl, Averill Hanly, with eyes as blue as Gary Cooper's and a deadpan delivery quite as good. I peered into the evanescent world of privilege enjoyed by the Anglo-Irish gentry in its heyday; the vestiges were rather like a few rich colors and heady scents lingering in a potpourri when the flowers have faded and crumbled.

We started in the immense kitchen, where recent preservation work had demolished a modern wall, exposing the huge stoves and culinary gear of the eighteenth-century cooks. Then, leading me through a passage into the dining room, Averill paused to take out a very large porcelain bowl from a cupboard and explained, "After dinner, when the ladies withdrew and the gentlemen sat enjoying their wine and cigars, the butler crept about under the table with the bowl, so the gentlemen could relieve themselves without having to leave the room."

In the library, bookcases are filled with the volumes collected over generations, and tables hold family photographs. Averill pointed out one of Olive Hales Pakenham Mahon, great-granddaughter of Major Denis Mahon and, until 1980, the ultimate chatelaine of Strokestown Park and last of the Mahon family to occupy the house. Indicating a murky painting on the wall—a barely passable version of a Caravaggio, *Young Men Playing Cards*—Averill said that as the family fortunes declined, "Olive would sell a valuable painting and replace it with a copy. As you'll see from the empty frames in the dining room, eventually even copies were not affordable." As we were leaving the library, Averill put her hand on one of a pair of huge and splendid antique globes and said, "Nicholas Hales Pakenham Mahon"—Olive's son—"took these to England, but Jim Callery paid sixty-four thousand pounds to bring them back for the library."

That was the first time I heard the name of James Callery. As I would learn, his is a kind of Irish Horatio Alger story: a young man growing up near Strokestown, making his hard way in the world, catch-as-catch-can, kept at arm's length by the lady of the great house even after he had become a wealthy entrepreneur. But eventually Jim Callery would buy

Strokestown Park, found the Famine Museum, and preserve the house as the visitor finds it today.

In every room one glimpses the life lived here. In the master's bedroom, hunting boots await the hunter; dinner clothes hang ready for the evening. I asked about a long brass horn I noticed, and Averill said, "It was blown by an outrider when Lord Hartland was driven out of his gate and along the broad street of his town, to alert his tenants, as Lord Hartland preferred that they not look at him."

The children's playroom, on the top floor, is filled with their toys, rickety, well used, and likely well loved. There is the usual teddy bear, dolls, a tiny tea service, and a remarkable wooden motor car that Averill said was Olive's precious own. I stood in that room for a moment or two, absorbed; as I looked at the faded patina of time on the playthings of children who had lived here and were gone, a poem of my own childhood, Eugene Fields's elegiac "Little Boy Blue," plucked at my memory.

UNLIKE CASTLE COOLE and Florence Court, the great mansions I had visited in County Fermanagh, Strokestown Park was still furnished with all the appurtenances of daily life, for Jim Callery had kept it just as Olive Hales Pakenham Mahon had left it. I wanted to speak with him, and after leaving there, I telephoned him at his home nearby, and he invited me to join him for tea at Strokestown Park.

I arrived before Jim Callery and was met by John O'Driscoll, the head gardener and marketing manager. Having heard that the demesne included one of the largest and finest formal walled gardens in Ireland or Britain, I asked if I might view it before the light faded. An enthusiastic professional horticulturalist, O'Driscoll led me through a gate into a mini-Eden. We strolled along graveled walks whose herbaceous borders are cited in the *Guinness Book of World Records* as the longest in Ireland or Britain. Alongside are hedges of plaited beech and hornbeam. The garden was in the process of being restored to glory, but what one could already imagine, walking by the sere plantings in the mid-November light, was how the Mahons and the Pakenhams and their friends must have pleasured themselves along the flowering walks and in the pretty gazebos by the reflecting pool. John O'Driscoll pointed out that the towering Irish yews by the pool sprang from the ancestor at Florence Court.

In the adjacent walled kitchen garden all was still in ruin. Gazing about, I could only liken it to a horticultural equivalent of Miss Havisham's home in *Great Expectations*. All was overgrown. There was a wild sea of grass; vast glasshouses were fallen in, their underground heating ducts, once fired by charcoal, now fractured and laid bare. In one wrecked glasshouse an immense and venerable fig tree rose from a midden of shattered glass.

John O'Driscoll led me to the derelict tea pavilion, a tower in one corner of the kitchen garden, and assured me that it and the kitchen garden, too, would be restored, as the formal garden had been, through the contributions of various horticultural organizations, other benefactors, and the European Union. (Some months after completing my walking trip, I returned to Strokestown Park and found the formal garden and kitchen garden luxuriating, and the teahouse restored as well. The ancient fig tree, which had been drastically cut back, was laden with fruit in its pristine glasshouse.)

JAMES CALLERY—or Jim, as he seems known to all—is a tall, slim, broad-shouldered man with a merry laugh and a self-deprecating way about him. John O'Driscoll introduced me to him in the drawing room of Strokestown Park, arranged for tea, and left us to chat.

I found Callery open and engaging, and he responded readily to my questions about what had brought us together in the drawing room of Strokestown Park: "My grandfather was a tenant farmer near here," he began. "My father educated himself in England and became a solicitor, but he also farmed. I did, too. In the 1950s, I tried everything to keep body and soul together. I had a filling station . . ." He laughed. "My partner and I sold hay, old horse machinery, anything to make a go. After a time, I got into cars and obtained the agency for Chrysler and Dodge trucks. I was learning the business, just before Ireland joined the European Community, the Common Market, in 1973."

Then Jim Callery had a brainstorm. He realized that "trucks built for long-distance haulage would be wanted." Off he went to Sweden, to see the people at Scania, who build superior trucks. He got two Swedes to come to Ireland to see the operations of what had become the Westward Group at Strokestown, and he took two of Westward's directors to Sweden. The way Jim Callery tells it, he's just lucky: "One day at the Ulster

Bank in Dublin, I ran into the chairman on the staircase and made my pitch." He got the financing Scania required, the Westward Group put Scania trucks all over the roads of Ireland—as I could testify—and Jim Callery made his fortune.

TALKING AMIABLY in the comfortable, slightly tatty drawing room among indifferent antique furniture, pictures of familial interest and marginal quality, and charming bibelots, with old books and magazines—*The Tatler, Country Life,* and *Vogue*—scattered about, just as the Pakenham Mahons had left them, one felt almost one of the family. I half expected that others of the Pakenham Mahon family might return any moment from a hunt or a fair. I asked Jim Callery to tell me about Olive Hales Pakenham Mahon and how he came to acquire Strokestown Park from her.

"Grace, Denis Mahon's daughter, married Henry Sanford Pakenham, who added twenty thousand acres to the property and the Mahon name to his own. Her granddaughter, Olive, was an only child. She married Edward Stafford King Harman on July 4, 1914, and moved to the great estate of Rockingham. He disappeared, was declared 'missing in action' in the First World War, and after seven years, a widow and mother of a daughter, Olive married a Captain Hales. She became Olive Hales Pakenham Mahon, and she and her husband lived in this house, where she had grown up."

Jim Callery's relationship with Olive was long but not always harmonious. "When my partner and I were in farm machinery, Olive complained that we were tearing up *her* road," he recalled with a chuckle. "As time went on and our business grew, we needed room to expand our facilities. Our new garage was adjacent to her property, so I got someone Olive and we knew to intervene and ask her to sell us a piece of land, but she wouldn't. Olive was very forceful.

"After this, however, she sent for me and said that her son now owned the property and that it was going to be sold by public auction. Our relationship improved, and we had many discussions often about history. After some time, Olive said the property would be sold by silent auction in London, and she encouraged me to bid."

Acting for the Westward Group, Jim Callery bought Strokestown Park and what remained—some three hundred acres—of the once great estate (for £1,000,000, Averill Hanly had told me). "My partners agreed with me that the Hales Pakenham Mahons could remain in the house," he said. "After Captain Hales died, in 1980, Olive moved to London and died there the next year. We made a separate deal for the contents of the house and the family papers were donated to us."

Jim Callery credited Luke Dodd, a historian and the son of Callery's first cousin, as the moving force behind the Famine Museum. Callery himself is absorbed by history and is well read. Since the acquisition of Strokestown Park, with its trove of family papers preserved here for over three hundred years, Callery is determined that it should become a research center for Irish history, with those archives as a nucleus. The intermarriages evidenced by the Pakenham-Mahon-King-Harmon-Hales unions perfectly illustrate the nexus woven by the small minority of Anglo-Irish aristocracy and gentry to protect and perpetuate themselves.

AS JIM CALLERY led me to the entrance hall, he added a footnote to the clouded history of Strokestown Park, saying, "During the Troubles of the early 1920s a detachment of British soldiers, Lancers, were stationed here. Their commanding officer, a Captain Peake, and six others were ambushed and slain by Irish irregulars." As Callery was speaking, I noticed behind him the portrait, in full-dress uniform, of General Edward Pakenham. He was with Cornwallis at the fateful surrender of the Irish and French at Ballinamuck in 1798. General Pakenham was less fortunate at the Battle of New Orleans, on January 8, 1815. He was killed while commanding the British force defeated by Major General Andrew Jackson two weeks after the treaty ending the War of 1812 had been signed at Ghent, on December 24, 1814.

The Pakenham family, however, is extant. Its present head is Thomas Pakenham, the 8th Earl, son of the late Frank Pakenham (7th Earl, author of some twenty books, and the Labour minister dubbed Lord Porn for his censorious role in British government) and his late countess, the distinguished biographer Elizabeth Longford. The literary family includes Thomas's sisters, the writers Antonia Fraser and Rachel Billington. An admired historian himself (*The Year of Liberty: The Great Irish Rebellion of 1798*), Thomas Pakenham resides at Tullynally Castle, seat of the Earls of Longford.

After crossing the Shannon again, to County Longford and the county town, I slept that night in the Longford Arms.

Through Goldsmith Country

. ✤ .

ON A SUNDAY MORNING IN NOVEMBER, I AROSE IN THE OLD,
nicely modernized Longford Arms and attended mass in Templemichael,
the nineteenth-century neoclassical cathedral of the Catholic diocese of
Ardagh and Clonmacnoise. A single priest, the celebrant, dispensed
enough incense for three, and a fine choir was accompanied by an organ
whose bass reverberations tickled my toes. An echo of the great Irish
famine reached me here; in my pew was a newsletter with an announcement of a service soon to be conducted at "the Famine Graveyard."

Along Longford's lengthy main street, among the pubs, several smart
apparel shops, and pharmacies, I'd noticed several fast-food establishments, interchangeable with those in Buffalo or Manchester or Paris. Having been the lone diner in the Carvery, at the Longford Arms, the previous
night, whose very good curry dinner was spoiled by a maid determined to
vacuum around me although it was not yet 8:30 P.M., I did not care to lunch
there. Eager to take to the road, I opted for the Deli Pizza. The place was
all shiny plastic, with a big, illuminated bill of fare. The most appealing
feature of the Deli Pizza was a tall serving girl, who might have been
snapped up by the Ford or Wilhelmina modeling agency in New York.
What I really wanted was coffee and a scone with butter and jam, but I settled for coffee and a minimum-size pizza. Shortly the nymph called out,

"Your pizza's ready. Tomato, cheese, and peppers. Nine inches. Three-eighty." The coffee was not bad; neither was the pizza. But in food, everything counts: the Irish make excellent cheeses. Not for pizza.

THE DAY WAS MILD and lightly overcast as I headed due south, toward Ballymahon, into Goldsmith Country, on a straight road with little traffic, passing a ruined church but nothing else I remarked until Keenagh. There my attention was caught by an impressive stone clock tower with a scaffold about it. It dominated an otherwise bleak little village. On the tower was the bust in high relief of a bearded gentleman and beneath it this inscription:

ERECTED BY THE TENANTS AND FRIENDS OF
THE HON^BLE LAURENCE HARMAN KING HARMAN
WHO DIED OCTOBER 10TH 1875
IN GRATEFUL MEMORY OF A
GOOD LANDLORD AND UPRIGHT MAN.
"JUSTUM ET TENACEM PROPOSITI VIRUM."

Some great landlords did strive to assist their tenants in the terrible years of famine. The monument at Keenagh appears to testify to the esteem earned by a kinsman of the first husband of Olive Pakenham Mahon.

I asked the driver of a taxi stopped there if he could tell me of a little-traveled byroad to Ballymahon. Edward Carey, for such was his name, proved jovial and a fund of local lore. First he recommended "a pub a little off the way I'll point you to, where you'd find great *craic*"—merriment—"and good stories from the old ones there." Then he regaled me with one of his own: "There was this fellow who was proud of his greyhounds, do you see? They could catch anything that ran, he said, and he bet my mate and me a hundred pounds there wasn't a hare alive they couldn't run down. Well, we took the bet. We'd been after a great hare ourselves, a twisty great runner he was, and we trapped him. Then we loosed him for your man to set his dogs after him. Oh, they gave those hounds a grand romp and got clean away. So we won the hundred quid. Then we caught the hare again, and we took him way out on the bog and released him. He deserved his freedom; we were in porter [a dark ale] for a week."

Edward Carey was fond of shooting and field sports. He'd just been out, and he offered me a pheasant and asked if I'd care to go duck shooting. Perhaps another time, I told him. Then he directed me to a bohereen that took me through a gently rolling landscape, past several fine old farmhouses in need of restoration, though their livestock looked well cared for. At one such place a number of fine steeds were blanketed against last night's frost.

My bucolic stroll ended all too soon as I emerged on the road to Ballymahon, which was soon joined by a busier regional road. By then it was growing dark, and a drizzle had begun. I leaned against the garden wall of a tidy cottage and did my fandango, getting into the rain pants I pulled from my pack. I put on my reflector belt before slogging onward as the rain became heavier, hugging the irregular verge while cars and trucks bore down on me, their headlights blinding. I had judged my timing badly, and this caper had become scary. But finally, in the distance, the sodium lights on the main street of Ballymahon beckoned.

Usually, if I were certain where the day's tramp would end, I would try to telephone ahead to a B&B, inn, or hotel, to be sure of a bed. But being prone to divagations that made arrival time uncertain, I was not always certain where I would lay my head until it was nearly time to do so. I'd hoped to reach Ballymahon in good time to inquire for lodging, but hadn't.

Coming to a petrol station and convenience store, I went in. It had a trade in video rentals, mostly the same stuff with which much of the world numbs itself. The friendly women behind the counter let me use the telephone to call a Mrs. Doherty, whose B&B was the only one nearby listed in my guides. She said a room was available and that her husband would pick me up.

Mr. Doherty had been in the building trade, working for some years in Britain and the United States as a master mason. He had retired with Mrs. Doherty to Taghinny, a hamlet close by Ballymahon, where they acquired an old rectory and operate it as a B&B, the Glebe. The house was filled with Victorian bric-a-brac and family pictures. This slightly chilled traveler was welcomed with the universal Irish benison, a pot of tea and biscuits.

Already in the parlor, reading a newspaper, was a Japanese gentleman, and we exhanged introductions. Yakinori Ono was an economist, courteous, sophisticated, and friendly. He made regular business trips to Europe and had stopped in Ireland a number of times, rented a car, and traveled widely. After we had chatted awhile over tea, he remarked that he had booked a table for dinner at Wineport, a restaurant at Glassan, about ten miles away, and wondered if I would care to join him. Having been resigned to eating the salami and cheese carried for lunch rations—and not wanting to walk into Ballymahon that rainy night in hope of finding simple pub food—I said it would be my pleasure to do so.

A little later, having got my gray flannels, still well pressed, out of my rucksack and donned the tweed jacket I carried wrapped in a plastic rubbish bag atop the pack, I met the nattily attired Mr. Ono, and off we drove. The Wineport restaurant, sited on Killenure Lough, which opens into Lough Ree, the second largest lake in the Shannon system, was reputed to be very good, and I had long wanted to dine there.

In the inviting little lounge, where we were invited to peruse the menu over an aperitif, I decided to risk a martini, a drink I do not advise ordering in the Irish countryside, except in very grand establishments. The Wineport came through. Full marks, superior. Dinner in the glass-fronted dining room measured up, too. The clientele was sparse this late-November evening, and we lingered at our corner table in amiable conversation. Nori, as Mr. Ono asked me to call him, was a film buff and had a scholar's recall of American films—casts, directors, and memorable scenes. But our talk ranged. We spoke of Zen Buddhism, of which he knew much, and he was interested to hear that I had made a film for NBC with the Zen sage Daisetz Suzuki, whom I had come to revere. Altogether, a most serendipitous evening.

AFTER BREAKFAST next morning, I set off in great spirits. There had been a frost last night, and the weather made for invigorating walking: cool, a bit breezy, and overcast. Facing me as I emerged onto the main street of Ballymahon was a bronze statue of the region's most famous son, to which he has given his name, Oliver Goldsmith. The figure is seated, an open book in one hand, a broad-brimmed hat in the other, gazing reflectively upward. At his feet is a satchel with a tin whistle on it. Beneath is a plaque with Goldsmith's dates, 1732–1774 (his birth year is disputed), and this inscription:

HE LIVED IN BALLYMAHON FOR THREE YEARS
BEFORE EMIGRATING TO EDINBURGH IN 1752.
IN 1755 HE WENT ON A WALKING TOUR OF FRANCE,
SWITZERLAND, AND ITALY. HE SETTLED IN LONDON
IN 1756 AND EMBARKED ON HIS WRITING CAREER.
HE DIED THERE IN 1774.

The sculptor of the appealing work is Eamon O'Doherty. It was unveiled by the U.S. ambassador to Ireland, Michael J. Sullivan, on July 21, 1999.

As I walked toward Athlone on a road with long, straight stretches, unpleasantly busy for the foot traveler, I was traversing a countryside that Goldsmith knew and memorialized. Though Goldsmith springs to life in James Boswell's magisterial *Life of Samuel Johnson* and we know much about his London years, much is unknown or uncertain about the years before. Some writers give his birthplace as Kilkenny West in County Westmeath, roughly five miles southwest of Ballymahon; others say it was near Pallas, some six miles northeast of Ballymahon. All agree that his father was a Church of Ireland rector, as a grandfather had been. After schooling in Auburn (then known as Lissoy) and Elphin in Roscommon, unprepossessing in appearance, scarred from smallpox, Oliver matriculated at Trinity College, Dublin, where, after unhappy years, he received the bachelor of arts in 1750. After a few more years in Ireland, he studied medicine in Edinburgh but left without taking a degree. Then began the itinerant years, which Goldsmith would transmute long afterward into his first major poem, *The Traveller*. In 1756, poor and unknown, he located in London. By 1764, after penurious years toiling at odd jobs and hack writing—including potted histories of Greece and Rome—his work, particularly his clever, witty essays—had earned the approbation of some of London's most accomplished men. That year, Goldsmith became one of the founders of the celebrated Club, which included the already renowned lexicographer, author, and wit Samuel Johnson, soon to be honored as Dr. Johnson; Joshua Reynolds, soon to be Sir Joshua, first president of the Royal Academy; and Goldsmith's fellow Irishman Edmund Burke, shortly to become a famous parliamentarian and polemicist. (Statues of Goldsmith and Burke stand before the main entrance to their alma mater, Trinity College, Dublin.)

Triumphs followed for Goldsmith: the novel *The Vicar of Wakefield*, his poem *The Deserted Village,* and *She Stoops to Conquer,* his play of high jinks in a country inn, which rejoices audiences to this day. All draw on his affectionate and sharp recall of the rural people he had grown up with. And despite his being of the Anglo-Irish class, and his social ascent, he did not forget the circumstances of an oppressed Irish peasantry. In *The Deserted Village* he begins celebrating an idealized rural life and ends scorning the great landlords who evicted tenants and sent desperate peasants into exile:

> Sweet Auburn! loveliest village of the plain.
> Where health and plenty cheered the laboring swain,
> Where smiling spring its earliest visit paid,
> And parting summer's lingering blooms delayed:
> Dear lovely bowers of innocence and ease,
> Seats of my youth, when every sport could please,
> Where humble happiness endeared each scene;
> How often have I paused on every charm,
> The sheltered cot, the cultivated farm.
> The never-failing brook, the busy mill,
> The decent church that topped the neighboring hill, . . .
>
> Sweet smiling village, loveliest of the lawn,
> Thy sports are fled, and all thy charms withdrawn;
> Amidst thy bowers the tyrant's hand is seen.
> And desolation saddens all thy green:
> Only one master grasps the whole domain, . . .
>
> Far, far away, thy children leave the land.
> Ill fares the land, to hastening ills a prey,
> Where wealth accumulates, and men decay;
> Princes and lords may flourish, or may fade;
> A breath can make them, as a breath has made:
> But a bold peasantry, their country's pride,
> When once destroyed, can never be supplied.

Athough he kept sophisticated company in London, Goldsmith never lost his Irish brogue nor the awkward behavior for which he'd been mocked since childhood. Despite earning considerable sums from his writing, Goldsmith was improvident, a reckless gambler, generous to a fault, and continuously in debt. After a brief illness, he died at age forty-six. Admired for the felicity of his writing—marked by irony, wit, pointed and vivid characterizations, and humanity—he was ridiculed for his personal gaucheries of manner and utterance. Nevertheless, the works endure. Samuel Johnson said of his "dear Noll" that he was an author "Who left scarcely any kind of writing untouched, / And touched nothing that he did not adorn."

SOUTH OF BALLYMAHON I came upon the Three Jolly Pigeons, the pub named after the inn where much mischief is started in *She Stoops to Conquer*. Then I passed through Auburn and thought of the schoolboy here who had grown up to be a literary lion of London. Beyond was Glassan and the Wineport restaurant off to my right, where the Shannon wends its way to the sea. I found a grassy place behind a hedge and tucked into the salami and cheese I carried. A split of red wine slaked my thirst. Less than five miles on, I was in Athlone, where I checked into the Prince of Wales hotel in the town's center. (The persistence of the British royal title, in a town that had endured great violence from the English, long amused me as an example of a certain Irish equanimity, or perhaps quixotism. In fact, the Republic is replete with "Royal" academies, yacht clubs, and other institutions, accepted survivors of British rule.) After a long shower to shed the dust of the road and forty winks to recover from the stress of playing dodgem, I dined modestly in the hotel's comfortable restaurant.

AFTER DINNER, I crossed the wide bridge beneath the massive castle to Sean Fitzsimmons's pub, near the lock on the Roscommon side of the river. Here is a pub with character; the walls are hung with bits of marine gear, fishing tackle, and a hodgepodge of memorabilia. At the front of the long, narrow room, packed with patrons, a group of musicians with fiddle, tin whistle, and *bodhrán* were fiddling, whistling, and drumming up a storm of jigs, reels, and planxties. Feet were tapping, and customers were gabbing; it was not a quiet night at Sean's. (Regrettably, Sean was not presiding that evening, for he's famous as dispenser of Shannon lore and master of a barge named *The Iron Lung*.) Cigarette smoke tinted the air; the Irish are demonic smokers. I added to the fug by lighting my pipe before giving myself a large whiskey; the single measure in Irish and English pubs is no proper nightcap. Content, I ambled back to the Prince of Wales, "The March of the King of Laois" or some other martial air ringing in my head.

By the Bloody Ford
a Company Bloomed

. ❧ .

SITUATED APPROXIMATELY AT THE CENTER OF IRELAND AND ON the great river which nearly bisects the country, Athlone had a strategic importance that made it the scene of many battles in Ireland's long and sanguinary history. From early times, there was a ford across the river Shannon here. As *ath* in Irish means "ford," the name of the town may have its source in the seminal Irish epic *Táin Bó Cúailgne*, or *The Cattle Raid of Cooley*, which celebrates the deeds of Cuchulain, the legendary hero of Ulster. In it we learn of the mischief wrought by Queen Maeve of Connacht, wife of King Ailill, who disputed with her husband who had the greater wealth. When they compared their riches—jewels, gold, finery of all sorts, horses, and cattle—they found they were about equal, save that Ailill had a great white bull, which Maeve could not match. Learning that Dáire mac Fiachna possessed a magnificent brown bull at Cooley, in Ulster, that had no equal, Maeve dispatched her warriors to seize it. Indeed, they stole the bull and made for Connacht to present it to their queen. When the two bulls met, a furious combat ensued, which made the earth tremble. In the end the brown bull gored and rent the white bull, whose loin fell into the Shannon here. The Irish for "loin" is *luan*, and so, as legend has it, Ath Luan, "ford of the loin," became Athlone.

Today, with about ten thousand inhabitants, Athlone is the principal town of the middle and upper Shannon. The main highway across the waist of Ireland, from Dublin to Galway, passes through it, as does the railroad, and it is the hub of many bus routes. The town now straddles the river, with the commercial center on the east, or Leinster, side, but it grew from a settlement on the other side and first became notable in Irish history in 1129, when Turloch Mór O Conor, King of Connacht and High King of Ireland, built a fortress on the west, or Connacht, side of the river to guard the bridge he had erected near the ancient ford. Doubtless the fortress was made of timber and earth, in the Irish fashion; in its shelter a town began to grow. Fortress and bridge were contested by rival Irish factions, but by 1199, the Anglo-Normans had taken both and erected a more formidable castle. That year another O Conor torched and looted the castle. In 1210, John de Gray, justiciar of England's King John, constructed, in the Norman way, the massive castle of stone, which, much rebuilt, still looms above the river.

Possession of the mighty fortress and the bridge from Leinster to Connacht alternated between Irish and English forces through battles and sieges in 1381, 1455, 1490, and 1537. The English held castle and town for five months in 1641 against attacking Irish but had to yield to the Irish Viscount Dillon and his troops the next year. In 1650, during the Cromwellian campaigns, General Sir Charles Coote II captured castle and town for the parliamentarians, but by the fateful year of 1690, they had reverted again to Irish and Catholic hands.

Following the Battle of the Boyne, on July 1 that year, when the English and Dutch forces of the Protestant William of Orange, recently proclaimed King of England, vanquished the Irish and French troops of the deposed Catholic King James II, the bulk of James's loyal army, under the overall command of the French general the Marquis de Saint Ruth, withdrew westward behind the formidable barrier of the Shannon. At Athlone a garrison of fifteen hundred Jacobites under Colonel Richard Grace was left to hold off the pursuing Williamite army, twenty-one thousand strong, under the able Dutch general Godard van Reede Ginkel. The garrison of Athlone Castle gallantly resisted while Ginkel's troops, manning fifty cannon and eight mortars, hurled twelve thousand cannonballs, six hundred bombs, and tons of stones, expending fifty tons of gunpowder to reduce castle and town in the most terrible bombardment in Irish history. Under merciless fire a Sergeant Custume led a sortie from the castle to wreck the bridge and prevent the enemy from crossing by it. But ten days after besieging Athlone, Ginkel's troops made a daring passage of the river by the ford and stormed the castle. Colonel Grace fell in the final assault.

If the Irish and Catholic forces could have thwarted Ginkel's advance, the course of Irish history might have been different. The French general Saint Ruth chose not to commit the large force he held nearby as the garrison at Athlone was overwhelmed but held it positioned along a favorable ridge at Aughrim in Galway. However, when the Williamite and Jacobite armies met in battle there, William's army under Ginkel prevailed: Saint Ruth was decapitated by a cannonball, and seven thousand of the Jacobite army fell in the single bloodiest battle in Irish history, on July 12, 1691. Major General Patrick Sarsfield, Earl of Lucan, rallied the Irish and, with a remaining French force under Brigadier Boisseleau, retreated to Limerick, where he successfully defended the city against Ginkel's far greater army until he could secure terms of honorable surrender. In the treaty negotiated with the assent of England's victorious King William, Catholics were to be accorded "rights of worship," and some restrictions on them eased. Sarsfield and his army of about eleven thousand were allowed to embark for France with personal weapons and banners. Theirs would be the greatest flight of the Wild Geese, those Irish who would distinguish themselves in the armies and navies of the Catholic monarchs of Europe; among them were virtually the last of the old Irish chivalry. Although King William intended to honor the treaty's terms, the Protestant Parliaments of England and Ireland, regarding Irish "papists" as dangerous rabble, had no intention of conferring religious freedom on Irish Catholics or otherwise liberating them. The treaty's terms were soon violated.

OTHER THAN grim King John's Castle, now a museum, hardly a vestige of ancient Athlone survives; in 1697, three hundred barrels of powder in the castle's magazine exploded, causing a fire that destroyed much of the town. Yet in Ireland one constantly comes across reminders of epochal events. Out for a coffee on a brilliant morning, strolling along the quays close by the castle, I paused by the lock in the river—a weir extends across the river from the lock, so navigation must be through it—and looked at the words incised in the massive granite blocks: VICTORIA LOCK, 1845. It was constructed in the year the Great Famine began. Common laborers were paid sixpence a day for a six-day week; a skilled mason earned no more than ten shillings a week.

Matters have improved for workers everywhere in Ireland, but many in Athlone got a particular boost from the establishment here of the Elan Corporation, a pharmaceutical company, in 1978. Its phenomenal growth was frequently heralded in the Irish newspapers since I'd commenced my journey. At one point the corporation's market capitalization nearly equaled the value of all other Irish stocks combined, and Elan's were the first Irish shares listed in the United States, first on the NASDAQ, then on the American Stock Exchange, and then on the New York Stock Exchange. Elan's board of directors glittered with a former attorney general of the United States, a managing director of Goldman Sachs International, a chairman emeritus of Merrill Lynch, and two professors at Harvard Medical School, among others. Elan seemed to be a dazzling exemplar of the Celtic Tiger at its growliest; I was keen to learn its story. In time, that would prove to be a cautionary tale.

ELAN—AS IN ÉLAN VITAL, the life force in organisms—is located just outside Athlone, and the company's facilities resemble the campus of a small American college, with open lawns and walks leading to buildings of tawny brick. At the administration building, I was greeted by David Lundie, vice president and general manager at the Athlone site, in what had been the boardroom until the company moved its headquarters to Dublin not long before. Over coffee and pastries, Lundie, neat in white shirt and tie, friendly and informative, who had been with the company for ten years, told me something about its origins.

Although Elan is an Irish corporation, it was founded by Donald Panoz, an American. "He had been a scientist working in pharmaceuticals," said Lundie, "and after serving with the U.S. armed forces in Japan, he packed up his kit, and he and his wife, Nancy, moved with their five kids to Dublin in 1969. A true entrepreneur, he started dealing in U.S. Army surplus.

"However, Donald Panoz had an ingenious idea," explained Lundie. "He was interested in ways of delivering an essential medication to a patient more effectively. More effective delivery means reformulating a drug so that, say, instead of a patient having to take a dosage of one hundred milligrams three times a day, the same therapeutic effect could be achieved by a dosage once a day." Lundie added, "The reformulated drug might also reduce side effects of the original.

"Panoz was a remarkable advocate in selling his idea of delivery efficacy," continued Lundie. "Elan would go to the original manufacturer of a very effective drug and say, 'Let us improve your formulation.' "

"For example?"

"Cardizem was a so-called beta-blocker for treatment of heart disease, manufactured by the Marion Corporation, a U.S. company which had obtained manufacturing rights from the Japanese originator," said Lundie. "Well, Cardizem SR—for 'sustained release'—is the drug which many Elan people retired on.

"Another aspect of Elan's success is that income from an intellectual property is tax free in Ireland," said Lundie. "A patent for a reformulation by Elan is an intellectual property."

I asked why Donald Panoz had selected Athlone to set up production.

"He had the idea of picking a sleepy little town and making a beautiful front door to it. He wanted to involve local people, and we do," said Lundie, who was the president of the Athlone Chamber of Commerce.

Just then, Joey Moodley arrived to guide me around Elan's facility. A tall ethnic Indian with a graceful bearing, dressed in navy-blue blazer and tan slacks, he was introduced as head of Resource Planning and Technical Support for Pharmaceutical Development. He told me that when he was obliged to drop out of college—the family could only afford the professional education of his older brother—he had been hired by Donald Panoz in 1974 in Dublin.

"At that time, Donald Panoz had a chain of drugstores around Dublin, which he was beginning to dispose of," said Joey, as he invited me to call him. (Everyone at Elan, as everywhere in Ireland, uses the casual form of address.) "In 1978, he set up Elan in Athlone, starting in one prefab building, which is presently being demolished. We have twelve buildings here now and are trying to acquire an adjacent property."

As we walked around Elan's campus, inspecting several buildings, Joey told me that Panoz directed that the company's plant in Gainesville, Georgia, be a virtual copy of his Athlone creation. "However," said Joey, "Donald has added a vineyard." (Panoz retired from Elan's board of directors in 1998.)

In Building 11, where basic raw materials are analyzed, I remarked the youth of many employees. "The average age of our work force is twenty-five," said Joey. "Most young people are restless and must be kept engaged. Athlone doesn't offer a lot for young people." When he noticed me observing several persons with impairments washing laboratory glassware, he said that the company liked to hire handicapped persons for jobs they could perform successfully.

One was constantly hearing about expatriate Irish returning for the opportunities the booming economy offered, and I asked Joey whether Elan had employed any of them. "It's not easy to attract well-trained and educated expats," he said. "Taxes are high in Ireland, and housing is very costly." However, he introduced me to Graham Jones, a financial officer at Athlone, who had spent two and a half years in the United States.

We met in Jones's small office, of clinical austerity. Thirty-five years old, tall and lean with dark hair and wearing mod granny glasses, Graham Jones told me that after graduating from University College, Dublin, he had been employed by Elan on a six-month contract. "I availed myself of the opportunity offered for a study course in accountancy," he said, "and I qualified. When there was an opening at Elan's facility at Gainesville, Georgia, I went for it." In January 1996, he and his wife, Louise, and their two-year-old son, Robert, moved to the United States and stayed until July 1998. Their daughter, Emily, was born there and is thus a dual U.S.-Irish citizen.

I was curious to know what, if any, differences Graham Jones had experienced in working and living in the United States, and I asked him.

"In Ireland we treat people differently," he replied. "We—referring to managers—are very demanding. The Americans seem to feel pressure in the workplace more, and they are more likely to feel stressed out. However, a not very well educated worker on the floor will stand up for himself and express his point clearly."

"And your lifestyle there?"

"Well, there's an American lifestyle, which is very seductive," said Jones. "Louise and I are sports buffs. We saw a good deal of the Olympics at Atlanta—beautifully organized—rowing and field sports; we were there when Sonia O'Sullivan just missed winning the gold for Ireland in the five thousand meters. Louise had coached basketball, and we watched the best teams in action, the Hawks and the Bulls with the legendary Michael Jordan."

"What brought you home?"

"Family, primarily. We'd kept up with Irish affairs on the Internet and kept up with the Irish teams—Gaelic football, hurling, and soccer. We went to Atlanta to a couple of Irish pubs to watch the big matches on the telly. So, I wasn't like Rip van Winkle, waking up and finding it all changed when we came home.

"I did notice, comparably, a lack of service here. In a big shop three clerks might be standing about talking while a customer needed help. We mock the have-a-nice-day bit, but while American sales and service might be aggressive, it's friendly and helpful.

"Fortunately, we had kept our house and let it while we were away; it had cost about eighty thousand pounds, and if we'd had to buy it back when we came back, we couldn't have afforded it."

"But you're seeing opportunity in Ireland now?"

Graham Jones laughed and said, "Oh, yes. We're turning out millionaires. I remember when a professor proposed a course in entrepreneurship and that was considered a novel idea!"

DONAL GEANEY, who succeeded Donald Panoz as CEO of Elan in 1995 and as chairman in 1997, invited me to join him for lunch in Dublin, and I bused there and back for the day. Elan's HQ is in a new building adjacent to Trinity College's back gate. Donal Geaney met me in the boardroom, where a very good lunch was served to the two of us. Fairly short, with a ruddy complexion and dark, clipped mustache, he struck me as lucid and enthusiastic, as one would expect of a CEO, low-key and likable.

Since taking the helm at Elan, Geaney had pursued an aggressive course of expansion, acquiring or entering joint undertakings with fifteen companies in six years. Elan's total revenues had grown from nearly $700 million in 1998 to $1.86 billion in 2001. Geaney said that Elan then had about three thousand employees worldwide, including those in firms of which Elan had a 50 percent interest. Besides the operation in Gainesville, Georgia, which mirrors Athlone, there was a marketing division in England and manufacturing and analytical operations in California, Florida, Switzerland, and Israel.

Geaney told me that Elan was undergoing a deliberate shift from reformulating drugs developed by other companies, while intending to remain preeminent in that field: "As pharmaceutical companies have changed and merged, we have had less influence; we had to change the value of our own contribution. We have had to move into the R and D of new products and their marketing." He spoke with pride about Elan's research laboratory just across the way, in Trinity College, of which he is a graduate. "It's our core research group, about fifty people," he said. "Trinity has the minds and the facilities essential for deep research."

I remarked that I'd heard about Elan's development of a medication for the treatment of Alzheimer's disease, and I asked about its status.

"The initial research was by a company called Athena, now a division of Elan, at Oyster Point, near San Francisco," said Geaney. "They were specialists in the field of neurology, dealing with disorders like epilepsy and Parkinson's disease and with drugs for the treatment of pain. We think the potential for the Alzheimer's medication is enormous. Twenty-five percent of people over eighty will get Alzheimer's disease, and the growing longevity of the population increases the number of potential victims." (Elan was then awaiting FDA approval of the medication, but there have been setbacks.)

"Was your acquisition of Athena a shift toward the area of neurology?" I asked.

"Yes. Cardiovascular drugs are more expensive to develop, and existing effective drugs had somewhat limited the opportunities," said Geaney. "We're awaiting FDA approval for Ziconitide, a nonsedating drug for the relief of acute pain."

Donal Geaney urged me to visit Elan's research group at Trinity College, but I felt I'd better return to Athlone and resume my march south. Bidding him good-bye, I said that I'd sensed an almost palpable esprit among his troops. Small wonder; they had been participants in what had been a meteoric success story.

(In July 2002, like countless others, I was stunned to read in *The New York Times* that Donal Geaney had abruptly resigned as chairman and CEO of Elan, as had the vice chairman. After inquiries into Elan's accounting methods—and perhaps because several drugs in development had so far failed to win FDA approval, as well as the licensing of generic alternatives to certain brand-name drugs produced by Elan—the value of the company's stock crashed 96 percent during the year, from a high of $65 per share to $1.80. It posted a loss of $2.4 billion for 2002; its shares closed in New York at $4.03. A dazzling entrepreneurial company that had looked golden saw its image tarnished. It still has valuable products and a talented staff. But like Icarus, Elan may have flown too high or too fast.)

Where Saints and Scholars Toiled

. ❧ .

THE AIR WAS CRYSTALLINE, THE SKY LIKE LAPIS, AS I STARTED
south from Athlone by a road paralleling the left bank of the river. I had
chosen to lie up for the dark, wet months from December through February, fleshing out my journals and researching sites of interest ahead. Now,
light of heart as I resumed my tramp this fine March day, I found myself
humming "Where the River Shannon Flows," a song made famous by
Count John McCormack (as he is always known in Ireland, after his papal
title), the great Irish tenor, who was born in Athlone. With no one to object, I sang:

> Where dear old Shannon's flowing,
> Where the three-leaved shamrock grows,
> Where my heart is I am going
> To my little Irish rose,
> And the moment that I meet her
> With a hug and kiss I'll greet her
> For there's not a colleen sweeter
> Where the River Shannon flows.

I paused at the grocery and post office in Ballynahown to pick up some
picnic fare and mail a few cards home, then, somewhat parched, dropped

into Flynn's pub across the road for a glass of beer. Two clients were speaking with the woman behind the bar about the "unwanted influx of so-called refugees," as one of them put it.

"Disgusting people," the other added, "begging outside or even inside the churches, they are."

Although looks in my direction invited comment, I stayed mum. Disputation pervades Irish pubs as ozone does the Paris metro, but it seemed a little early and too nice a morning for it, so I forbore from stroking my oar in the murky waters swirling about the controversial issue of refugees or asylum seekers pouring into the country (some seven thousand in 2000). The proprietress, with a face like Mother Machree's, gently demurred to the stance of her regulars: "God help us, think of all the Irish from the famine years landing in Canada or the States or the convicts shipped to Australia. Weren't they all refugees?"

"Sure, but we worked wherever we went," said the more scornful customer, who was chasing a whiskey with a glass of Guinness. I might have commented that illegal immigrants to Ireland—most of the refugees from Africa and Eastern Europe seeking resident status—were not permitted to obtain employment until the Irish authorities had determined the legitimacy of those claiming asylum, a tedious process. (Ironically, Irish companies and businesses were recruiting abroad because of the scarcity of workers.) However, I kept my counsel and drank my beer.

When I hoisted my pack, the discourse changed to whence I came and where I was bound. Farewells were cordial.

TURNING OFF the busy Athlone-Birr road, I turned west onto a byway that would take me to the Shannon's shore again. To the south a vast bog spread over this part of County Offaly. Much of the turf had been peeled away by a giant machine, to be compressed into peat briquettes for fuel by the government's Bord na Móna, the enterprise charged with extracting wealth from the miles and miles of bog in Ireland. Mae West's line to her maid, "Beulah, peel me a grape," popped into my head as I observed the skin of Offaly neatly skinned off. With each step I took, the parallel lines of the drainage ditches, their water glistening in the sunlight, led away to successive distant vanishing points.

On my right hand, to the north, fields of brilliant green surrounded the occasional house. Little details to be noted along the march delighted this rambler. As the late Irish poet and screenwriter H.A.L. (Harry) Craig first pointed out to me, "Beside each clump of stinging nettles grows the antidote—the dock leaf." Unmarked on the Ordnance Survey map, a low hill appeared, as perfect as a breast, and I supposed it was a tumulus, a dome of earth covering one of the prehistoric tombs with which Ireland is littered, many of them unexcavated. Farther on, I passed a lush hillside on which a large flock of swans were grazing, some four miles from the river. On a bush just beyond, a pair of lacy knickers fluttered like a captured flag. Still farther, near Clonfinlough Catholic church, was the Clonfinlough Stone, a massive boulder with strange symbols inscribed. Some resemble the Greek theta, θ, others simple crosses. Apropos these markings, I had read in Killanin and Duignan that "affinities are to be sought in the Iberian peninsula. According to Macalister they depict a battle." Archaeological evidence accords with ancient tradition, holding that one of the successive waves of immigration during the Bronze Age (before the arrival of the Celts, about 500–400 B.C.) appears to have come from northern Spain and Portugal.

As I was coming down a gentle incline, Clonmacnoise came into view. There, on a slight rise above a sweeping S turn in the broad Shannon, appeared two round towers, the shell of the cathedral, the remains of seven other churches, and a field of crosses marking many graves. Close by, there rose the shattered remains of a castle, testimony to the Shannon's tumultuous past.

Whenever I first glimpse Clonmacnoise—"meadow of the sons of Nós"—my heart catches, so powerfully do these mute stones evoke this place's extraordinary history. Here, to a desolate stretch of the Shannon, came Saint Ciarán (anglicized Kieran) with eight followers on January 25, 545, to found a monastery. After Armagh, where Saint Patrick established his seat (and where the two primates of Ireland, Catholic and Anglican, maintain the archepiscopal succession), Clonmacnoise became the most important ecclesiastical foundation in Ireland. As a center for art, literature, and learning, it would become preeminent. For in time it grew into an ecclesiastical city where thousands of students came from all over Ireland and Europe and from as far away as Egypt to study with the learned abbots and monks who succeeded Saint Ciarán and his disciples. What was taught and what was learned were not merely theology and the doctrines of the Church. Here classics of Greek and Latin literature were studied and preserved, and students were schooled in the accumulated knowledge of the West and Middle East in such fields as mathematics and geography. The French scholar Roger Chauviré has written of such great monastic foundations as Clonmacnoise that they were centers

> not only of spiritual but also of intellectual life; they were in a sense the universities of their day. Being surrounded in their own country with religious respect, and being protected by distance from the great barbarian invasions and the relapse into savagery which they caused, they were the only lights still burning in the night which had come over the West; for two centuries Ireland, being thus privileged, was truly to be the teacher of Europe.

From Clonmacnoise and other Irish monastic centers such scholars as Alcuin—said to have been a pupil of the learned Colcu at Clonmacnoise and later tutor at Charlemagne's court—carried the torch of knowledge to illuminate the darkest corners of Europe. Their achievements have been delightfully told by Thomas Cahill in *How the Irish Saved Civilization*.

These Irish scholar-monks were neither prudish nor humorless. Thanks to them the lusty sagas of the pre-Christian Irish were preserved, by painstaking and beautiful calligraphy, in the scriptoria of Clonmacnoise in such works as the *Book of the Dun Cow* (named for a cherished cow of Saint Ciarán, on whose hide the earliest version was written; for losing the beast, a servant was buried outside the consecrated ground, and his supposed grave is still to be seen). It contains *Táin Bó Cúailgne, The Cattle Raid of Cooley,* which celebrates the feats of the heroes Cuchulain and Fergus, the wiles of Queen Maeve, and much else from the mythic, pagan past of Ireland. In the *Annals of Clonmacnois,* now one of the riches of Oxford's Bodleian Library, scholars of the monastery recorded one of the earliest Irish histories.

When first I came here, long ago, one could wander freely about the ruins. More than four hundred early gravestones—many decorated with incised crosses, Celtic knots, and weathered invocations in Irish to pray for the soul of the named departed—were stacked against a wall. Today there is a low, unobtrusive visitors' center with a theater offering a video presentation of Clonmacnoise's history, several dioramas, and exhibits, maintained by Dúchas, the Heritage Service. There is a modest admission charge.

I entered, then stepped out onto the green grass with the widely spaced crosses and grave slabs scattered about the church ruins and thought of "The Dead at Clonmacnois" by T. W. Rolleston, based on the Irish of Angus O'Gillan (Irish names and words have varying translations in English):

> In a quiet water'd land, a land of roses,
> Stands St. Kieran's city fair;
> And the warriors of Erin in their famous generations
> Slumber there.
>
> There beneath the dewy hillside sleep the noblest
> Of the clan of Conn,
> Each below his stone with name in branching Ogham
> And the sacred knot thereon.
>
> There they laid to rest the seven Kings of Tara,
> There the sons of Cairbrè sleep—
> Battle-banners of the Gael that in Kieran's plain of crosses
> Now their final hosting keep.
>
> And in Clonmacnois they laid the men of Teffia,
> And right many a lord of Breagh;
> Deep the sod above Clan Creidè and Clan Conaill,
> Kind in hall and fierce in fray.
>
> Many and many a son of Conn the Hundred-Fighter
> In the red earth lies at rest;
> May a blue eye of Clan Colman the turf covers,
> Many a swan-white breast.

Within the bare walls of the the little cathedral, open to the sky, I stood where the high altar had been. Turloch Mór O Conor, High King of Ireland, who died in 1156, is buried to one side of it; on the other side his son Rúairí O Conor (Rory O'Connor), the last High King of Ireland, who died in 1198, was laid to rest; Turloch Mór's grandson Dermot and Rúairí's son Conor were interred close by. Their graves are all unmarked.

Stepping through the doorway on the river side, I turned and looked above it at the carved figures of Saint Dominic, Saint Patrick, and Saint Francis (now headless). Over them a damaged inscription in Latin is carved: DOM[IN]US ODO DECANUS . . . ME FIERI FECIT ("Lord Odo, Dean [of Clonmacnois] had me made"). It commemorates the 1460 reconstruction work of Dean Aodh (Odo) on the edifice erected 1080–1100, after the original stone church, built by Abbot Colmán and High King Flann Sinna in 900, had been burnt in 985, 1020, and 1077.

UNTIL THIS VISIT, I used to stand in wonder before the so-called Cross of the Scriptures, or King Flann's Cross, which stood for more than a thousand years where Abbot Colmán had erected it, perhaps at the grave of his friend the High King Flann Sinna, who died in 914. Through the centuries it had endured fierce winds and rain, its splendid sculptures in high relief visibly worn by the elements but remarkably discernible. To prevent further erosion, the Heritage Service has installed King Flann's Cross in the visitors' center. Its illumination by spotlights in an otherwise darkened room is not ideal, but an impression of viewing the cross in natural light in its original setting may be had by observing the full-scale copy placed there. Carved from a single block of stone, twelve feet ten inches high, King Flann's Cross is a superb example of the high crosses that are a signal achievement of Irish Romanesque sculpture. On its west face the Passion of Christ is represented. Within the characteristic circle between the arms of the cross, the Crucifixion of Christ is depicted. Below, in three panels, are representations of Christ bound and held by soldiers, Christ supported between two men (before Pilate?), and the entombed Christ guarded by soldiers. On the east face may be discerned Christ at the Last Judgment, two panels of unidentified personages (one of armed Irish warriors), and one thought to be Saint Ciarán and King Diarmait I of Tara setting the cornerpost of the first church here, as described in the *Annals of*

Clonmacnois. Less imposing than King Flann's Cross is the so-called South Cross, which stands before the little church called Temple Dowling. On it one can make out the Crucifixion.

Clonmacnoise has the distinction of having two round towers. The precise purpose of these distinctive structures, so often found at Irish monastic sites, is seemingly not documented in the numerous early manuscripts that have survived from the long monastic period. It is generally supposed that the towers, conical in cross section, with immensely thick stone walls, served primarily as places of refuge in the attacks the monasteries so frequently suffered. For the entranceway is almost always located high above ground level; it could be reached by a ladder, which the retreating monks would pull up after them. The tower could also function as observation tower and belfry. The taller of the two here, called O'Rourke's Tower, is sixty-two feet high and fifty-eight feet in circumference. It is believed to have been built, or at least begun, by Fergal O'Rourke, King of Bréifne (essentially the present Counties Cavan and Leitrim), who was killed in battle in 964. The upper section was added by High King Turloch Mór O Conor and Abbot Gilchrist Malone in 1120, as recorded in several Irish annals. The top was demolished by lightning in 1135, leaving the tower without its conical cap. Close by is the so-called MacCarthy's Tower. Only fifty-six feet high, it retains its conical cap and is well preserved. The round tower is attached to the tiny church called Temple Finghin, or MacCarthy's Church. Since the tower's entryway is at ground level, it may have served as a belfry.

I SAT for a while on the low wall between the river and MacCarthy's Church—in my office there's a lovely photograph of tower and church, taken by my son, which keeps me in mind of Clonmacnoise—and tried to conjure up the throng of monks and acolytes who toiled here in Ireland's Golden Age, their rude dwellings (some 109 were burned in 1179), their singing and their prayers when a bell tolled the seven canonical hours from matins to compline, the sounds of metals being hammered and jewels being cut, and the hiss of forges in the workshops. And what treasures came from them! Here these devout artisans made chalices, patens, abbatial and episcopal croziers, and reliquaries. Through the centuries innumerable precious objects of exquisite workmanship were fashioned of gold, silver, jewels, and enamels—invariably incorporating characteristic patterns of geometric forms interwoven with sinuous designs of dazzling complexity—but few are known to have survived, among them Saint Ciarán's crozier, the crozier of the Abbots of Clonmacnoise, Saint Manchán's shrine, and the Cross of Cong (from the abbey in Galway where Rúairí O'Conor died, after abdicating as High King in 1175). In Ireland's National Museum, in Dublin, one may marvel at some of them.

The treasures wrought at Clonmacnoise invited plunder. The Vikings, those piratical Norsemen for whom the Shannon was a convenient highway for their splendid longboats, devastated Clonmacnoise eight times. The most fearsome of these raiders was Turgesius, whose consort, Ota, a sibyl, pronounced oracles while seated on the high altar of Clonmacnoise in 841. Turgesius burned Clonmacnoise in 844. From the seat he established on Rindoon Point, in Lough Ree, the Norse chief subjugated the area for thirteen years, until lust brought an end to his rapacious ways.

Turgesius coveted the comely daughter of King Máel Sechnaill II (afterward High King) and demanded that she be brought to him. Máel Sechnaill acquiesced, with the proviso that the princess be accompanied by fourteen handmaidens. The Norse chief agreed, thinking he would bestow the maidens on his lieutenants. At the appointed time, Turgesius and his warriors gathered in his hall, their weapons stacked, to await the Irish princess and her handmaidens. Upon their entry the maidens threw back their cloaks, and fourteen well-chosen warriors, swords in hand, sprang upon the Norsemen. Mayhem ensued. Turgesius was taken, and Máel Sechnaill had him drowned in a lake, said to be Lough Owel, near Mullingar.

THE VIKINGS WERE not the only despoilers of Clonmacnoise. The warlike Irish, intensely tribal and territorial, fought incessantly among themselves. Clonmacnoise was attacked by Irish princes and chieftains some twenty-seven times. It is recorded that one such pillager was King Phelim of Cashel, bishop and scribe, and I was startled to read in the visitors' center that in 834, one "Cathal, Lord of Ui Maine, drowned Prior Flann in the Shannon." Anglo-Norman soldiery ravaged Saint Ciarán's monastic city six times between 1178 and 1204. Finally, in 1552, Elizabethan troops sacked Clonmacnoise, and it was reported that "not a bell, large or small, or an image, or an altar, or a book, or a gem, or even glass in a window, was left which was not carried away." Yet the wonder is that King Flann's Cross has survived intact. Miracle enough for me.

ABOUT A QUARTER MILE from the eight churches of Clonmacnoise, one comes on the ruin of the Nuns' Church, a tranquil place to picnic. Little remains of this small edifice, save for two richly carved Romanesque doorways. Its builder played a significant role in what is perhaps the most epochal event in Ireland's troubled history. For she was Dervorgilla, the beautiful wife of Tiernan O'Rourke, King of Bréifne. Dermot MacMurrough (Diarmait MacMurchada), King of Leinster—a contradictory man given to great violence but to poetry, too—lusted for Dervorgilla and abducted her, setting great mischief afoot. O'Rourke retaliated against MacMurrough by raising a revolt among the chiefs of Leinster. High King Rúairí O Conor threw his weight against the troublous MacMurrough and banished him in 1166.

The resourceful MacMurrough appealed to England's Henry II— whom he found in Aquitaine, one of Henry's French dominions—to become his ally in recovering Leinster. As it happened, King Henry had his own designs on Ireland and, conveniently, had already obtained a papal bull, *Laudabiliter*—whose authenticity is disputed—from Adrian IV (otherwise Nicholas Breakspear, to this day the only English pope), authorizing Henry to invade Ireland for the purpose of reforming what Rome regarded as egregious practices of the Irish clergy and the moral laxity of the Irish. King Henry permitted Dermot MacMurrough to recruit leaders among his barons, who would raise soldiery for the enterprise. Dermot sought his allies among the Norman barons settled in Wales and found men hungry for new conquests.

In 1167, MacMurrough landed in Ireland with a small advance party of Anglo-Norman warriors. Though initially repulsed, after some ninety reinforcements joined them, Dermot and his allies held fast. In 1170, Richard de Clare, 2nd Earl of Pembroke, dubbed Strongbow, arrived at Waterford with two hundred knights in armor and a thousand men at arms. The defenders were no match for Normans in chain mail and the English longbow. Strongbow secured the place; wed Eva (Aoife), MacMurrough's daughter, who had been promised to him; advanced and took Dublin; and on Dermot's death, in 1171, became ruler of Leinster. (Dervorgilla ended her days in Mellifont Abbey.) Besieged in Dublin by High King Rúairí O Conor, Strongbow prevailed in a daring sortie of six hundred horsemen, dispersing the Irish.

Determined that Strongbow and the other Anglo-Norman conquerors should not acquire too much land and power for themselves and to impose his own suzerainty, King Henry II came to Ireland in October 1171 with a great force. He received the fealty of Strongbow and the submission of many Irish chiefs and, after a few years, enjoyed the submission and eventual abdication of High King Rúairí O Conor. The die was cast. For more than seven centuries—though there would be periodic uprisings to throw it off—some or all of the Irish would live under the English yoke.

I LINGERED AT Clonmacnoise until the westering sun began to gild its ancient stones. A faint mist began to rise beyond the noble sweep of the Shannon, over the water meadows and the far fields of Connacht. Then, as the fiery orb began to sink below the horizon, the towers, walls, and crosses of Clonmacnoise became a blaze of glory once again. It is not hard to be magicked here.

Saint Brendan's Landfall

FROM CLONMACNOISE IT WAS JUST OVER A MILE TO KATE HARTE'S Kajon House, where I found a soft bed and a good dinner, as the only guest. The menu was in five languages, so travelers from many lands were anticipated.

I had asked that the rhubarb pie be saved for my breakfast, and fortified with it and a bit more, I had a pleasant march to Shannonbridge. The road overlooks the river, with its wide water meadows, called callows, which flood when the river rises with winter rains, harboring waterfowl and making for rich haymaking after they drain in late spring.

In Shannonbridge, I found a room at The Bungalow, Celine Grennan's B&B. My bedroom looked past laundry drying in the sunlight and a meadow with grazing sheep to the Shannon. After nipping along to Killeen's Village Tavern, just down the street, for a spot of lunch, I and the few patrons enjoyed a lagniappe when a musician who introduced himself as Norm Allen dropped in with his wife for refreshments.

After some pleasant chat with proprietor Mick Killeen—to whom he gave a CD, *Lovin' the South*—Norm Allen fetched a guitar from his car and favored us with some of his songs. It transpired that although the couple made their home in Los Angeles, Norm Allen was a Texan. He and his wife were on their first trip to Ireland and had been touring in a rental car for ten days. "We love the country and the towns," Norm said, "but don't care for the cities. After all, we know cities. We just move along until we see a place that looks all right and stay. It's worked out."

Before leaving, the troubador informed us that he was a lieutenant governor of the Kiwanis and that the profits from his *Lovin' the South* album were going to the organization's efforts to eradicate thyroid-disease-related disorders throughout the world by promoting the use of iodized salt. Occasionally one acquires incidental intelligence in an Irish pub.

IN THE AFTERNOON, I inspected the substantial fortifications on the west, or Connacht, side of the river. They were built early in the nineteenth century, when the British, fearing that the French might invade again, erected Martello towers around the coast and fortified strategic Shannon River crossings. Most of the visible gunports face west, and vines and weeds were now the attacking forces. At the bridge abutment, the handsome barracks building, itself a strong redoubt, was under repair, and later I was to hear rumors that it would become a riverside hostelry.

As I was walking across the sixteen-arched stone bridge in the amber light of late afternoon, I paused near the Leinster shore to watch a fisherman. He stood on the deck of a cruiser moored to the quay just above the bridge, spin casting, and he cast well. (The Shannon holds salmon and used to hold many pike of impressive size, until platoons of Continental anglers, mostly Germans, horsed them out in great numbers. The government has since imposed stringent regulations to protect the species. Brown trout and various coarse fish may be found in the river, too.) A vicarious fisherman, I observed the man casting again and again into the fast-flowing, clear stream. Then my eye was riveted by something troubling: just behind the angler's position, from an orifice in the quay just below the surface, a dark stream was gushing, staining the water just downstream from the fisherman an ugly brown. The raw sewage of the good citizens of Shannonbridge was joining the Shannon on its course to the sea, and I remembered swimming with my children from a cruiser not far downriver. As the man slowly rewound his line after each cast, I could see the flash of his metallic lure just missing the odious discharge of which he seemed unconscious. Richening Ireland has some environmental problems to address.

When I was having a simple supper in the Village Tavern, publican Mike Killeen asked me my next destination. I said Banagher, which is on this bank of the Shannon, although I longed to revisit Clonfert Cathedral, one of the supreme achievements of Irish Romanesque architecture. But as it was across the Shannon, that would require a considerable detour from my planned route.

"Why not bike over there and back here?" said Mike Killeen. "I'll lend you a bike and show you a short way there."

NEXT MORNING off I pedaled. The bicycle proved to be Mrs. Killeen's, a vehicle that had seen much service, with a plastic carrier for a child mounted behind the seat. I wheeled merrily on until I came to a long chain-link fence, which enclosed a yard appearing to contain scrap metal; its guardian was a large Alsatian dog, who was offended by me or my transport, perhaps both. He tore along the fence, snout to the ground, snarling and barking furiously and making a persuasive show of getting under the fence or gate, to go for me. I bore down on the pedals, but my bike was not made for the Tour de France, and I was relieved to leave the bellowing beast behind.

When I came to the turnoff Mike Killeen had indicated, it was to an unpaved track along the perimeter of a huge electric-power-generating station beside the river. It was one of two I knew of on the Shannon in which peat from the bogs is the fuel for firing the steam turbines. They are blemishes on a pastoral landscape, but growing Ireland needs power, and its vast bogs provide a ready resource until scraped bare, when they remain a dismal sight until new growth occurs. The track took me beside a high embankment, on which a very narrow gauge rail line leads from the power plant across a bridge over the river and into an extensive bog on the far shore. With difficulty I humped the bicycle up the high, steep embankment and onto the rail line. When I reached the river, I noticed a solitary angler, hooded against the wind, watching me. He was fishing just by the outlet from which heated water from the steam turbines is discharged into the river; cool water is drawn in upstream of the plant. Certain coarse fish, such as tench, flourish in the warm outflow, whereas such game fish as salmon and trout require colder, more oxygenated water.

Mounting the bike, I started to cycle along the narrow concrete walkway beside the raised track bed but could not get up enough momentum to prevent the bicycle from wobbling. I scraped one knee and then the other on the concrete railbed on my left and the low parapet on the right, which just kept me from plummeting into the river. The fierce wind that had sprung up did not help, and I soon dismounted and barely managed to squeeze myself along beside the bike. Midriver I stopped to enjoy the prospect. The Shannon was whipped white with waves, the azure sky laced with high cirrus clouds, promising good weather. Suddenly, as if magically, a fox appeared in the middle of a field on the far side. Perhaps it had darted from its den or been hidden in a low place before I spied it jinking at high speed, maybe after some creature I couldn't see. The fox was a thing of beauty, its red coat brilliant against the field of intense green, bounding over one fence into the next field and over another before it vanished from sight. One almost expected a pack of hounds to appear in full cry, the hunt behind in hot pursuit. Instead, I liked to think that the fox was just stretching its legs in a good run on a fine morning, and its apparent high spirits stirred mine.

Across the bridge, before the little railroad reached the bog, a bohereen led off to the south, and I took it. I was in Galway now, cycling along for about three miles through flat farmland without habitation or livestock, until I came to the few buildings clustered around a small stone church—Clonfert. There was not a soul in sight, and the bucolic place had the dreamy, slightly unreal feeling of a stage set.

About 558, Saint Brendan, called the Navigator, founded a monastery on this site. In the tenth century an early-Irish epic was translated into Latin as *Navigatio Brendani* (*Brendan's Voyages*), which tells of Brendan's legendary journeys. His first voyage to Scotland and the Hebrides is commemorated by place-names incorporating his own, and the priestly sailor is said to have reached Iceland. Legend has it that on his second great journey, Brendan and a group of monks reached America, almost a thousand years before the voyage of Christopher Columbus, their vessel made of skins stretched over a wooden frame (like the currachs still used by fishermen of the Aran Islands and the west coast of Ireland). The holy adventurer is reputed to have sailed to the Mediterranean and the Grecian Isles before he died, at age ninety-three, at Annaghdown, in Galway, where his sister, the saintly Brigid, is said to have been abbess of a nunnery.

St. Brendan's foundation at Clonfert suffered the devastations so common to Irish ecclesiastical establishments: it was laid waste by Vikings in 844 and 845, likely by the dreaded Turgesius, and destroyed by fire four times between 749 and 1179. Nonetheless, it arose like the phoenix and flourished as a center of learning, harboring as many as three thousand students. In the twelfth century, Conor Maenmoy O Kelly, King of Uí Maine, built the church, which served as the cathedral of a new diocese. (Today the Catholic diocese of Clonfert has its cathedral at Loughrea; the Church of Ireland diocese of Clonfert is under the administration of the Bishop of Killaloe and Limerick.) Though modified over time, the small edifice has survived, surprisingly intact, and serves as a parish church for the Church of Ireland. It stands within a walled green haven that must once have been the cathedral close and remains a peaceful country churchyard. I was interested to note that although St. Brendan's has been a Protestant church since at least the seventeenth century, the names on the gravestones—among them Killeen, McEvoy, Egan, Ryan, Nolan, and McCormack, English phonetic equivalents of old Irish names—are usually those of Catholic families.

I stood before the west portal of the church and marveled at what designer and stone carvers had accomplished here more than eight hundred years ago. A single wooden door is set within decoratively carved door jambs joined by an arch; high on each jamb is the single figure of a prelate, whom I guessed to be an abbot, from the flat cap and doffed cowl. The door and arched jambs are recessed within seven receding arches, which spring from pilasters on the church facade, and six pairs of engaged columns, each pair worked in varying patterns, geometric and foliate. The arches are composed of individually carved blocks of stone, with each arch revealing a different motif, such as foliate designs, grotesque animal heads, and geometric patterns. Above the arches are six short, engaged columns, carved with different designs, that support four arches, each of which encloses a carved human head with differing features. Above them, within a triangular pediment pointing heavenward, are ten more carved human heads of marked individuality, in four rows of decreasing number, each head in an inverted triangular recess separated by triangular blocks. Despite the ravages left by centuries of wind and storm, the conception and execution of the west portal are a triumph of imagination and workmanship. With the lichen-covered stones glowing warmly in the sunlight, the effect was memorable.

The door to St. Brendan's Cathedral was locked, but despite some crude restoration to the interior, there is a small feature of the church which has long intrigued me and I wished to see again. I set off to scout for the key, and upon inquiring at a sprucely kept house by the churchyard, I was provided with the large iron key by a kindly woman. Within St. Brendan's, I made for the transept. On a pillar of the chancel arch, almost at eye level, there is the little figure of a mermaid, carved in high relief on the limestone pillar, her large eyes regarding the beholder, unabashed at finding herself out of water and revealing her pretty bosom in this holy place. The figure is charmingly executed, its date unknown. It pleases me to think an abbot-bishop decreed the mermaid be placed so near the high altar, perhaps to celebrate a wonder observed amidst the fastness of the sea by the saintly navigator. Or perhaps some whimsical artisan, maybe a monk, fashioned this lovely mermaid, cutting her figure from the pillar supporting the cathedral's chancel arch, thinking it not likely to be replaced.

After returning the key, I took a turn around the remote hamlet. Adjacent to St. Brendan's Cathedral is a derelict manor house. Unlike most such houses, it is neither the relict of some eighteenth-century grandee who had gambled himself into penury nor the home of Anglo-Irish gentry burnt out by rabid nationalists during the Troubles of the 1920s. No, it had been built about 1650 as the Church of Ireland's Bishop's Palace. Three centuries later it became the home of Sir Oswald Mosley, British fascist imprisoned by his government during the Second World War and husband of Diana Guinness, one of the celebrated Mitford sisters. He settled here in 1952, possibly thinking that since Ireland had had its Blueshirts and German sympathizers, he'd be welcome. Unfortunately for Sir Oswald, who writes sadly of his Clonfert home in his autobiography, occupancy was to be brief. The Bishop's Palace was gutted by fire shortly before Christmas 1954. Between the ruined palace and the cathedral is a renowned avenue of yew trees, said to be a thousand years old. Close by, a small hostel and religious retreat center have been established.

After cycling back the way I had come, at the railroad embankment I picked up a few good stones and put them in the child's carrier seat on the bike, in case the Alsatian at the scrap-metal yard got loose. No need. By now I was a familiar, harmless figure; the dog merely gave an obligatory demonstration of his guardianship, to show he was on the job. At Shannonbridge's Village Tavern, I returned the bicycle to Mike Killeen and pronounced my outing tip-top.

Mad About Castles

·❊·

SHANNON HARBOUR WAS NOT MUCH TO LOOK AT, UNLESS ONE were a fancier of cabin cruisers or a variety of craft, from old barges and "narrow boats" (for English canals) to the occasional sleek motor sailer. Given the escalating cost of real estate, some people found it cheaper to own a dwelling afloat than to own one built on a solid half acre of Ireland. But most of the vessels here belonged to weekend and holiday sailors, who cruise the river Shannon or the Grand Canal, of which Shannon Harbour is its westernmost point. In times past a further section had been open, extending westward from the river Shannon to the sizable town of Ballinasloe, in Galway (site of Ireland's great livestock fair, in October). The Grand Canal, which leads to Dublin and its harbor, is more or less paralleled, farther north, by the Royal Canal, which connects to the Shannon and has its western terminus at Cloondara, near Longford. It is in the process of restoration, and the last section, from Mullingar to Dublin, is being completed as I write. While the canals—part of a remarkable system of waterways that crisscrossed Ireland in the nineteenth century—no longer carry freight, their routes through a lovely landscape, picturesque locks, and graceful stone-arched bridges are a powerful attraction for Irish and foreign holidaymakers.

———

IN BANAGHER, I lodged at the small Brosna Lodge Hotel in the center of this riparian town. After dinner in the lively bar, I took a walk up and down the long main street. Anthony Trollope came here as a functionary of the postal service and began to write novels. He would write no fewer than forty-eight, a number of them with Irish characters or situations, becoming hugely popular, then eventually somewhat neglected until comparatively recently, when critics have applauded his considerable achievements in depicting Victorian society.

It was essential that I pause in J. J. Hough's pub. Small, dim, revealing many years of patronage, Hough's is what Peter O'Toole, an erstwhile connoisseur of such matters and much else, used to call a "proper pub." The credentials may be hard to name, for they must be experienced. Hough's is notable as a venue for traditional music, though this night it was silent except for the conversation of the publican, J. J. Hough, the indispensable fixture of the place. Attired in hoary sweater, with cap atop his flying locks and gap-toothed grin, in a gentler era he would have been called a card as he engaged his regulars in provocative badinage. Drawing on a prodigious memory, Hough exhaled a blizzard of anecdotes about players and great plays in hurling matches decades past. (Hurling is the quintessential Irish game, played by heroes of ancient epics and by athletes today. It pits two teams of fifteen players against each other on a field 150 yards long by 90 wide, who hit a leather ball—on the ground or, more often, in the air while on the dead run—with a lethal wooden stick, called a hurley. It makes World Cup football seem in slow motion. I think of it as mayhem licensed as sport, and it arouses ferocious passions in both hurlers and spectators.) Although the hurling arcana bandied back and forth between ardent patrons and publican were memorable this night, the reputation of Hough's establishment rests on various attractions. Once, in a pub in Birr, a man asked me if I'd been in J. J. Hough's in Banagher. I acknowledged that I had watered there. "Did you see the horse?" my companion asked.

"What horse?" said I.

"The horse hitched to a pillar in the bar."

I confessed that I had not. But I wished I had.

———

AFTER BREAKFAST, I went to have a look at the old fortifications on the Connacht shore, guarding the bridgehead here, then moseyed up the main street to buy *The Irish Times* and enjoy it with a cup of coffee. As I was passing Lyons grocery and petrol station, I noticed the lettering on the fascia: WILLIAM LYONS WOOL BUYER. There was a fair-haired young man filling the tank of a car at the pump, and when it had pulled away, I asked, "Is there a wool buyer here?"

"I'm your man," said William Lyons.

"How is the wool business these days?" I asked.

"It's hardly worth the farmers' while to raise sheep," he said. "It's a poor market. I pay twenty 'p' a pound. To shear a sheep costs one pound ten or one pound twenty, and there are about six pounds of wool from a yoe. So you see . . ."

I'd sometimes thought it would be nice to have a few sheep about, to keep the grass down and for the Easter roast or a nice *navarin du mouton,* but William was discouraging.

"Wool is not subsidized, but the meat is," he said. "But Irish lamb can't compete with the Australian and New Zealand prices. A hundred-acre farm is big here. There, five hundred acres is small. The Australians have developed a chemical that makes the wool fall off, so that they have sheep that need not be sheared."

I wasn't sure if William was trying to pull the wool over my eyes, but I asked, "If there's so little profit in it, why do you keep dealing in wool?"

"Tradition, I suppose," he replied. "My father dealt in wool. Besides, who would look out for the farmers if I gave it up?"

ON MY ORDNANCE SURVEY section map for Galway-Offaly, I noted Cloghan Castle, about three miles southwest of Banagher. Somewhere I'd heard that the castle had been continuously occupied for eight hundred years and that its present occupants opened it to the public. Ignoring several signs that proclaimed it closed, I approached a man driving a small yellow roller around the circular driveway in front of the castle. A burly man in an anorak, with a stocking cap pulled over his ears, he had an air of authority as he stopped his roller and looked the intruder over.

I introduced myself, apologizing for the intrusion, and asked if, perchance, he were the proprietor of Cloghan Castle. He said he was indeed Brian Thompson and that his castle was closed. I apologized again for barging in and said that I was interested in castles, particularly their restoration and preservation, but would have to be far away when his castle would be open to visitors. Much as I hoped to visit the castle, I said, I'd appreciate even more the opportunity of talking with him about the problems of making such an ancient fortress habitable. Mr. Thompson heard me out, then suggested I telephone next morning; perhaps a visit could be arranged.

Next morning, I telephoned, and Brian Thompson invited me to tea.

CLOGHAN CASTLE, with its keep and crenellated battlements, lacked only a moat and drawbridge to seem the perfect setting for the filming of, say, Sir Arthur Conan Doyle's *The White Company*. I was met at the low, stout wooden door by the castellan, Brian Donovan Thompson, and led into the great hall. The lofty space, with its minstrel gallery, was impressive, and despite the stone walls, its handsome antique furnishings made the hall seem less austere than it likely was when the O'Maddens made the castle their stronghold, guarding the Shannon crossing to Meelick on the Connacht side. Instead of the thick mat of rushes with which the O'Madden chieftain would have covered the cold flagstones, now Oriental rugs covered the floor.

Once a boy who liked to construct castles of cardboard or Lincoln Logs, I was beguiled as my host guided me through the castle he had lovingly restored: from great hall to a dining room intimate in feeling, despite a fireplace fit to roast an ox, to the tiny chapel, to various bedrooms furnished comfortably with pieces befitting a medieval building that has been continuously inhabited over many epochs. Throughout there were antiques with family associations and many paintings, prints, letters, and documents about or by forebears or relatives, which contribute to the appeal of Cloghan Castle today.

On the roof of the keep, Thompson pointed out the proximity of the castle to the Shannon's callows—and the wildlife sanctuary he's created—and spoke of sieges and battles long ago. In 1595, Elizabethan troops sacked the castle; in 1651, Cromwell's forces battled the Irish defenders; in 1691, at Cloghan Castle, William of Orange's superior forces vanquished Irish troops loyal to James II. Today, beneath the battlements, piebald Jacob sheep were grazing, and Thompson said his was the largest flock of the rare breed in Ireland and kept primarily for decorative purposes.

In the cozy, pleasingly furnished drawing room, the chatelaine, Brian Thompson's friendly American wife, Elyse, served tea while Thompson talked of his career. Born in New Zealand, growing up in Donegal, descended on his father's side from a Northern Irish merchant family and on his mother's Donovan side from Irish chieftains, he became interested in restoration by what his father and mother had accomplished with an old house overlooking the river Foyle outside Derry. When he was working for an insurance company in England, he bought a hundred-year-old house in Kent and restored it. "I did everything but the plumbing," he recalled. For the next six years he bought, restored, then rented one old house every year. By then a confirmed restoration entrepreneur, he left the insurance company. Restoration of two old English manor houses followed; then, said Thompson, "I was thirty-three and had a business partner, from whom I subsequently parted."

Emmel Castle in Cloughjordan, Tipperary, was Thompson's second castle restoration in Ireland. He and Elyse and their children lived there until he sold the castle, to the actor Patrick Bergin. "I bought Cloghan Castle in 1972," said Thompson, "and I had four men working on it for ten years. The restoration was massive, and I saved all that I could."

Thompson's work had attracted the attention of the mayor of Newburgh, New York, and in 1975, he invited Thompson to undertake a major restoration of old houses in the small city on the Hudson River. "I'm a restorer," said Thompson, "but I like to think of myself as a social engineer."

"How so?" I asked.

"I'm a healer of sick houses; but not only did I restore forty-one houses in Newburgh," said Thompson, "I strove to get deserving and responsible people into housing they would appreciate and care for. I interviewed scores of prospective tenants, often placing blacks among whites."

"But matters became very difficult for Brian," said Elyse.

"When the obstruction from slum landlords made the undertaking unbearable, Elyse persuaded me to return here," Thompson said. "Corruption, the Mafia really, made going on impossible."

Thompson has become a crusader for the restoration of Irish castles. In an essay he gave me, he wrote,

> Our ancestors were not all peasants in perpetual revolt . . . the castles are there standing like beacons all over the land to remind us of the way things were before we lost the right to live in our own way. The Irish tower house . . . was the equivalent of the English manor house for the gentry and the protection of their cattle and retainers. There are thousands of derelict castles all over Ireland . . . and I can personally testify that many could be easily (and not too expensively) made habitable again.

Thompson said that from reactions to his lectures and television and radio talks in the United States, he is sure that the restoration of Irish castles would bring a boost to tourism while revealing a too-little-known aspect of Ireland's history and culture.

Sitting in Cloghan Castle's gracious drawing room in an aura of well-waxed old furniture, interesting pictures, flowers, and perhaps the soundless footfalls of untold generations of O'Maddens, it was easy to find Brian Thompson's ardor for restoring such castles persuasive.

THAT EVENING, I stopped at Birr, a town I'd often passed through but didn't know. This time I wanted to explore some of its renowned features: the recently restored giant telescope and the vast gardens in the demesne of Birr Castle. The castle has been the seat of the Parsons family since 1620, when Sir Laurence Parsons was granted lands held for centuries by the powerful O'Carroll family but declared forfeit to the Crown in the plantation program of King James I. (A displaced O'Carroll founded the Maryland dynasty that produced a signer of the Declaration of Independence and the founder of Georgetown University.) After checking in at Spinners Town House, just below the castle, I went to dine at the Stables, a restaurant of considerable charm, on Oxmantown Mall, a terrace of Georgian houses.

After dinner, I took a stroll around the town, handsomely laid out by Sir William Parsons and his son Sir Lawrence (who succeeded his uncle as 2nd Earl of Rosse in 1807) in the late eighteenth and early nineteenth cen-

turies. It is centered on what is now called Emmet Square (after the unfortunate Robert Emmet, who was hanged and decapitated for leading an
abortive rebellion in 1803). Originally the space was named Duke Square,
for the Hanoverian Duke of Cumberland, known as Billy the Butcher by
the Scots, for the slaughter his veteran cannoneers and infantry inflicted on
the claymore-wielding Highlanders, inexperienced gun handlers, and
some Irish and French soldiery supporting Bonnie Prince Charlie on Cul-
loden Moor in 1745. With the prince's flight after that catastrophe, any real
prospect for the Stuart restoration of the British throne ended. At the center of the square stands a column, which once supported a statue of the
duke, garbed as an imperial Roman. An improbable icon in republican Ireland, the duke has long since vanished.

Pausing in a pub named Dolphin's, I was soon drawn into a conversation by a retired career RAF man named Gordon Henderson, who was
keen on local history. Perceiving my interest, he nipped out, and before I
had my pipe well lit or my drink finished, he popped back and presented
me with copies of newspaper articles about a defunct railway and the 1691
siege of Birr Castle.

A FURIOUS THUMPING on my door made me tumble out of bed in the
middle of the night. On opening the door, I was confronted by a giddy
young woman, as tipsy as a seesaw. Blearily, I gathered she was inviting
me out to play, and I glimpsed other young women dashing in and out of
bedrooms, all of them shrieking with laughter. I failed to rise to the occasion, neither joining the prankster at my door nor inviting her in, but
closed the door and tottered back to bed after glancing at the clock:
3:10 A.M.

When I came downstairs for breakfast, the proprietor—Liam Maloney, a genial chap who only seven weeks before had taken over the stylish guesthouse converted from an old wool store and mews—was still
vibrating from his high dudgeon of a few hours earlier. "I'm truly sorry
about the events of last night," he said, as he cooked me rashers and eggs.
"Outrageous! Would you believe it? I booked in a group of young
women, one of them about to be married, whose peers were going to give
her a send-off. A hen party instead of a stag party. Never again. Shocking

behavior! They were from Dublin, and they picked this provincial town to raise the hell they wouldn't dare at home."

My host went on to tell me that after the town's pubs and a disco had closed last night, his women guests—nineteen, I believe—were followed back to the guesthouse by about a dozen young fellows who were keen to join them inside. "I wasn't having any of that," said Maloney. "When I confronted the ringleader, she threatened me, said, 'I'm a lawyer from Dublin.' She was so drunk two of her friends had to hold her upright."

The innkeeper felt he had no choice but to call the police. Maloney reported that the sergeant said to the still unruly women, "I have a bed in gaol big enough for the lot of you, if you want to come along." Maloney concluded, "The lads vanished, and the celebrants dragged themselves off to bed."

"Not without trying to rout out a few other guests," I said. Rolling his eyes, the harassed boniface withdrew to his desk. After breakfast, I stood by the staircase while the Bacchae of the previous night clomped sullenly by me, somewhat the worse for their revels.

I HAD HEARD that Birr had known memorable revelry in times past and wanted to verify one tale. I called on Frank Egan, former longtime proprietor of the venerable Dooly's Hotel on Emmet Square, at his comfortable, modern house. Retired for some years, a courtly widower, he served us coffee, and after inquiring what had brought me to Birr, he asked how he might be of help.

"I had heard that the famous County Galway hunt called the Blazers got its name by burning down your hotel," I said.

"Oh, that was long before my time," said Frank Egan.

"But it happened?"

"It was after a successful invitation meeting, to hunt the Ormonde country. In the celebrations it appears that people got carried away." All this seemed unremarkable to Frank. He referred me to a book that has an account of the incendiary doings.

Scion of a prosperous County Offaly family, Frank Egan is a fount of local lore. His grandfather Henry, a founder of R&H Egan Ltd. of Tullamore—"they were into every kind of agricultural business and had other interests, of which Dooly's was one"—was a notable conscientious objector, recalled Frank. "He liked to snub the British. When someone close to him was let out of jail, he met him at the gate with his coach and a fine pair."

When I spoke of my intention of visiting the demesne of Birr Castle next day, Frank Egan offered to telephone Lord Rosse and introduce me. Then, speaking of the benefits Birr had enjoyed through the vision and patronage of the Earls of Rosse, he said, "We had street lighting here long before many towns in Europe."

Of a Telescope, Gardens, and an Earldom

ONE ENTERS BIRR CASTLE DEMESNE THROUGH A VISITORS' CENTER constructed in the old block of stone stables and coach houses. In it are a number of well-designed exhibits illustrating Birr Castle's history and the remarkable accomplishments of the Parsons family. The one that most fascinated me depicts the 3rd Earl of Rosse's construction of what was for seventy-two years the world's largest telescope, until the one on California's Mount Wilson was erected in 1917. The exhibit depicts the earl's casting and polishing of the seventy-two-inch metal mirror for the instrument. It was an astonishing feat demanding mastery of metal casting—done over a peat fire in the castle's moat—and requiring the grinding of the mirror to the minute tolerances of concavity essential for astronomical observations, accomplished in the castle's workshop. On an April night in 1845, on first peering into the eyepiece of his huge instrument, the 3rd Earl discovered the Whirlpool Nebula. The precision of his illustrations of spiral nebulae were only superseded by advances in photography decades later.

After lying derelict and dismantled for eighty-five years—its mirror in London's Science Museum, the wooden barrel, fifty-seven feet long and more than seven feet in diameter, left at Birr—the telescope was restored in 1997, at a cost of £1.25 million. I hastened to see it. Sited about 150 yards beyond the nineteenth-century moat and bastions that front the castle, the telescope is supported between roofless, towering stone walls with engaged Gothic arches and, on the side facing the main gate to the demesne, crenellations to match those on the castle. The entire fantastic contraption—with its cat's cradle of chains and winches to move the telescope and the observer's platform, and the flights of stairs—seems as wonderful and improbable as an invention by Rube Goldberg.

The great telescope at Birr Castle.

I was fortunate to arrive at the telescope just as a group of visitors was listening to the head guide, John Joyce, explain the reconstruction of the telescope and demonstrate its operation, elevating and traversing the optical leviathan. We learned that the telescope has a lateral movement of only twelve degrees and that an observer can view 84 percent of the sky visible in the Northern Hemisphere on the fifty days of the year, on average, when weather conditions at Birr permit. I listened and watched, as entranced as I'd been as a boy in a movie palace when the organ rose mysteriously from the depths to accompany the audience in a sing-along to lyrics projected on the screen.

The 3rd Earl of Rosse, another William Parsons, who succeeded his father, was by no means the only scientific achiever in the family. His eldest son, who succeeded as 4th Earl, became renowned as a lunar astronomer. The 4th Earl's youngest son, Sir Charles Algernon Parsons, a brilliant engineer, invented the steam turbine.

In this century the family's scientific proclivities have been manifest in their horticultural pursuits, the results of which are everywhere evident in the one hundred cultivated acres of the demesne. (Sir Laurence Parsons acquired 1,227 acres of arable land, woods, and bog, with Birr Castle in 1600.) On this balmy afternoon, I wandered through them. Starting below the castle, pausing to admire the vast *Magnolia delavayi*—named for a French botanist; another magnolia in the demesne is named the Michael Rosse for the botanizing 6th Earl—then passing the little wire-and-wrought-iron suspension bridge over the pretty Camcor River, constructed in the 1820s (by William Parsons, then Lord Oxmantown, before succeeding as 3rd Earl) and perhaps the earliest remaining wire suspension bridge. At the lake created by the 2nd Earl, I sat for a while on a bench near an immense beech, watching the swans gliding on the silvery surface and wild ducks dabbling among the rushes. Birr's demesne has long been a sanctuary, and there are many species to be observed.

Walking on, gazing at the magnificent trees, oak and weeping beech, chestnut and sequoia, labeled with their common English and scientific names, I came to the formal gardens, approaching by the walk between the three-hundred-year-old box hedges, listed in the *Guinness Book of World Records* as the tallest in the world, part of the garden begun by Sir Laurence Parsons in the seventeenth century. However, it would be in the twentieth century that Birr's gardens would become among the most renowned in Ireland and Britain.

The 5th Earl was interested in horticulture from his youth, and inspired by his friendship with Augustine Henry, the eminent botanist who collected plants from China, he brought many exotic plants and trees from the Far East. An officer in the Irish Guards, he died from wounds received in the First World War and was succeeded, in 1918, by his twelve-year-old son, Michael, who became an ardent plantsman (and served in the Irish Guards during the Second World War). As a young man he sponsored botanical expeditions in the Himalayas and China, collecting specimens himself during an expedition to Tibet, contributing to Birr's richness in exotic species. In 1935, Michael married the ideal partner to realize his dreams for the gardens of Birr: Anne Messel of the notable English family whose garden, Nymans, is a famous National Trust showplace. On their honeymoon, in Peking, the earl obtained seeds from the grounds of a Confucian temple, and together, in 1937, Michael and Anne made another botanical trip to China.

IT WAS THE 6th Earl and Countess of Rosse who created the formal gardens at Birr, which were to become a glory for Ireland and whose major restoration was nearing completion when I visited. Anne's eye and taste complemented Michael's; her watercolor designs for the formal garden, many of which are displayed in the visitors' center, one sees realized as one walks through the alleys of the gardens. The center of the great complex is the box parterre, surrounded on four sides by the alleys of hornbeam she conceived of as "cloisters," with the branches of opposing trees plaited to form arches of greenery, beneath which one walks in shade. In winter, snowdrops flower along the hornbeam cloisters. Anne planned the box to be planted and clipped to display large linked *R*'s, perpetuating the Rosse name. A pair of giant seventeenth-century Bavarian urns provide focal points in the parterre.

While I am modestly knowledgeable about trees, I am ignorant about flowers. Though labels enlightened me, I can't do justice to the delphinium borders of subtle hues outside the hornbeam alleys, nor can I convey the pleasure of peering into extensive glasshouses still crying for restoration but brimming with beauties or coming upon the Pergola Garden, with its stunning Japanese *Wisteria floribunda* and border of Oriental irises and peonies.

The late-afternoon light of springtime burnished shrubs and cast a faint golden gloss on the early-flowering plants, and I was alone in Birr's noble gardens, the castle barely in sight across acres of green meadows. I shared the pleasure of the present earl in his demesne and was eager to talk with him about its perpetuation.

I HAD NOT taken up Frank Egan's kind offer to telephone Lord Rosse on my behalf. Instead, I'd written a note explaining what I was up to and asking if we might talk. The earl responded with an invitation. On a cool, fresh morning, I set out, curious to visit a castle steeped in history and to speak with William Brendan Parsons, 7th Earl of Rosse. Passing through the tall stone gate tower, I glanced up and noted the flag flying from the castle's highest point—three silver leopard's masks on a solid red field,

corresponding to the escutcheon of the Parsonses, the Earls of Rosse—
indicating that the earl was in residence.

Not long after the Anglo-Normans invaded Ireland in the twelfth century, they built a stone fortress at Birr. But from the fourteenth to the seventeenth century, the O'Carrolls maintained the great keep at Birr, called
the Black Castle, which stood about sixty yards to the northwest of the
castle that Sir Laurence Parsons began to construct in the 1620s. Sometime
in the seventeenth century a Parsons built two round towers, called
flankers, outside the central block, and they became incorporated into the
castle I had come to visit.

Birr Castle was twice besieged. A year after Irish Catholics rebelled in
1641 against the repressions and dispossessions inflicted by the English
Protestants, a force of Molloys, Coghlans, and other disaffected Irish descended upon the town of Birr and burnt it. Sir William Parsons, grandson
of Sir Laurence and governor of Ely O'Carroll (the ancient territory of
the O'Carrolls), who held Birr for the Crown, noted in his diary, "And
when they saw the Towne on fire, they blew up their Bagpipes, and beat up
the drums and fell a Dauncinge on the hills." On January 16, 1643, the
Irish laid siege to Birr Castle, for five days. One of the attackers was a
mason who had been employed in the castle, and he supervised the plant-
ing of a mine to blow it up. The threat forced the capitulation of Sir
William and the garrison. He was permitted to withdraw to Dublin, and
the castle was occupied by the rebels. After torching Birr Castle, they
eventually abandoned it. Sir William's son Sir Laurence (created a baronet
in 1677), returned to Birr and rebuilt the castle, including the construction
of a superb staircase of yew, which survives as the oldest staircase in Ireland made of a wood other than oak.

By 1690, the Parsonses of Birr had cast their lot with William of Orange, and their castle was garrisoned by soldiery loyal to King William III.
In August 1690, after some preliminary skirmishing, a Jacobite army of
ten thousand under the nineteen-year-old Duke of Berwick besieged Birr
Castle. About one hundred defenders held out as the Jacobite artillery
blasted away. (The scars of the cannonballs are still discernible on the
north flanker, and cannonballs and shot that flew through a drawing-room
window are trophies in the castle.) The garrison put up a fierce resistance,
though reduced to melting down a giant caldron of Lady Parsons's—said

to hold the carcasses of five or six beeves for salting—for bullets. Then, within two days, the besieging army decamped, for reasons still uncertain but likely because of the approach of a large English force. Birr Castle survived.

MY KNOCK AT the front door of the castle—recessed in the battlemented porch of the gatehouse, built in the 1620s and the central feature of the castle—brought the earl's secretary, and I was ushered into the hall. Four high Gothic windows at the far end lit the elaborate early-nineteenth-century plasterwork ceiling, old tapestries, paintings, and a display of swords. The earl, casually dressed in corduroy trousers and old tweed jacket, quickly appeared to greet me and led me into the study just off the hall. He asked if I would join him in coffee, and his secretary soon returned with it.

We sat before a fire glowing beneath an eighteenth-century chimney-piece of white and colored marble in the book-filled room, and I asked William Brendan Parsons, as he was in 1979, to tell me something of the circumstances when he succeeded as 7th Earl of Rosse, on the death of his father that year.

"I was serving in the UN as a program administrator in Algeria," he said, "doing what I had done for many years in Africa and the Middle East."

"You had always expected to inherit the title?" I said.

"Well, as my father's son, yes." he said. "As a boy here, seated in the dining room under the portraits of my forebears, it was rather intimidating, having those ancestors staring at one. How would one measure up?"

I was curious to know how he had found matters at Birr when he returned as 7th Earl, and I asked him.

He laughed: "I found affairs here disastrous, spinning out of control financially. There were not the resources to run this place as there once had been, but I thought I owed it to past generations, some twelve, to keep the place going and even to build it up, if possible."

"What did you do?" I asked.

"Having been in the UN for many years as an administrator, confronting problems, one thinks of a program," he said. "Do a feasibility study. First, consider your assets. I saw the scientific history that we could draw upon, the great achievements here. You know about the third Earl's great telescope?"

"And the fourth Earl continuing as a lunar astronomer," I said. "I've read that he invented an instrument to measure the temperature of the moon."

"Yes, then his younger brother became a brilliant engineer, inventing the steam turbine, which revolutionized marine propulsion and the generation of electricity," he continued. "There was also the pioneering photographic work of Mary, the third Earl's wife."

Thus the Birr Scientific and Educational Foundation was established. "I'd like to see Birr become Ireland's scientific center," said the earl in what I thought was a visionary flight. The first steps were the reconstruction of the castle's stables and carriage houses for the visitors' center and the conception, design, and installation of the exhibits, focusing on the astronomical, engineering, horticultural, and photographic achievements at Birr Castle.

Meanwhile, the restoration of the great telescope began. A serious handicap was that there were no plans or sketches for the telescope. Daunting as that was, the Office of Public Works, which had undertaken the restoration, and Michael Tubridy, the supervising engineer (perhaps better known as a member of The Chieftains, the renowned Irish musicians), were able to draw on the photographs of the Countess of Rosse, who had recorded the building of the telescope.

The second stage of the earl's plan would be the restoration of the gardens, in the conception of which his countess, Alison, actively joined him. The earl remarked that he was "very pro–European Union" and said that the two stages of restoration in the demesne of Birr Castle were "a five-million-euros undertaking, with about one and a half million euros coming from the EU Structural Fund." The rest of the funding came from the Irish government and private sources. The earl was pleased to note that when he inherited the earldom, Birr Castle attracted twelve thousand visitors a year. In 2000, fifty-five thousand visited the demesne.

As our talk had veered to the gardens, I asked about the 6th Earl's passion for collecting the seeds of exotic foreign plants and trees to add to the gardens and demesne, and William Brendan, his son, told me that since succeeding as 7th Earl, he, too, had been collecting abroad.

"One may legally only bring in washed seed," he said. "That is, seed that has been brushed off. I use a toothbrush and put the seeds in tea bags. In 1993, I brought home seeds from one hundred forty-nine species of plants." Going to the bookshelves, he took down volumes in which all the plant species brought to Birr by the Earls and Countesses of Rosse are recorded. Thousands are listed, giving the species names, locations where collected, and dates.

BIRR CASTLE WAS heavily gothicized in the early nineteenth century, after the fashion of the time. In *Country Life*, Mark Girouard describes the octagonal Gothic saloon as "one of the most sympathetic large rooms in Ireland." It is the castle's principal room, its ceiling a fantasy of bosses, with flamboyant arches springing from engaged columns around the walls. About the Gothic windows, Girouard writes, "The tracery of the three large windows has the delicate absurdity of Georgian Gothic at its best." In the dining room, lit by a vast bay window spanning the room and a huge chandelier heavy with ormolu, the ancestral portraits gaze down from frames hung against dark Victorian flocked wallpaper.

"See here," the earl said, pointing to the portrait of an elegantly attired man. "Notice how the cleaning has revealed the lace at the neck and wrists. That's very much in the French style, appropriate for a follower of James II"—who had been reared at the French court. "Sometime later that finery was painted over, when it became impolitic to be seen as a Jacobite."

With this talk of family history, the earl led me to a landing on the famous yew staircase, where he indicated a small picture. "You didn't expect to see a portrait of Wolfe Tone in Birr Castle, did you?" he asked.

I confessed I did not.

"Sir Laurence Parsons became a member of the Irish House of Commons in 1782," said Lord Rosse, "and he met and became a friend of Wolfe Tone, the Dublin lawyer and nationalist." The earl explained that Sir Laurence (afterward the 2nd Earl of Rosse) was one of the substantial number of Anglo-Irish elite who, while wishing Ireland to remain loyal to the British Crown, worked to maintain an independent Irish parliament, which they hoped to make primarily self-governing. Wolfe Tone wrote: "I was exceedingly assisted by Sir Laurence Parsons, whom I look upon as one of the *very few* honest men in the Irish House of Commons."

Sir Laurence was of an independent cast of mind. When he was an officer in the Irish Volunteers, a militia, he was reluctant to have his soldiers flogged for offenses, when flogging was common practice; he was an amateur of architecture and made sketches for improvements at Birr; he was interested in literature, corresponding with Maria Edgeworth, the renowned writer, and advocating studies of ancient Irish texts; and he refused to send his sons to public schools in England, as was the custom with his class, instead having them tutored at Birr Castle by French-speaking tutors, as his son, the 3rd Earl, did after him with his own children.

Finally, the 7th Earl took me through the archives of Birr Castle to the darkroom of Mary, the 3rd Countess of Rosse, an English heiress who brought a fortune to the earldom (as did the wife of the 4th Earl). Blackened shutters cut off the light, cobwebs draped the dusty bottles filled with the reagents the countess had used to process her negatives and prints. The room seemed perfect for a remake of *The Cabinet of Dr. Caligari*. I was fascinated to think of the photographic work done here by the avant-garde countess more than one hundred fifty years ago.

Remembering that Anthony Armstrong-Jones, afterward Lord Snowdon (the distinguished photographer and ex-husband of the late Princess Margaret), had grown up in Birr Castle, I spoke of him. "Yes," said Lord Rosse. "Indeed he began his photographic adventures here. He's my half brother; we had the same mother." I thought how right that Lord Snowdon should have been inspired by the pioneering countess and her darkroom.

WALKING BACK TO Spinners Town House along Castle Street to collect my rucksack, I noticed the newly renovated row of small Georgian houses. From one a young black man and a little boy emerged, hand in hand, and set off on a walk. The child, perhaps five or six, was dressed in freshly laundered clothes, and his father—or so I assumed—was as neatly dressed. I was struck by their appearance and companionable manner. Moments later, on stopping in a pub, I heard disparaging remarks about the refugees who had been sent to Birr by the government. Since almost every day Irish newspapers carried stories of local resistance to the government's policy of settling refugees or asylum seekers wherever it could find affordable space and building proprietors who would accept them, I should not have been surprised. Still, the mutterings of disapproval about the group placed in renovated housing in Birr were troubling.

However, the asylum seekers, called "lazy parasites come to prey on decent people" by one fellow, were not the only ones I heard bad-mouthed. As I was about to leave the pleasant town of Birr, I listened to one man complain that the Earl of Rosse was letting property he owned in Birr go to ruin, pulling down the value of buildings around his own. "There he is, up there in his bloody great castle, looking contemptuously down on people like us," this chap growled. I wondered whether he realized the money that the Earl of Rosse's fifty-five thousand visitors brought to Birr and if he realized the obligations incurred and the ingenuity required to maintain a Birr Castle and demesne in our time.

The Irish are not practiced in forgiving or forgetting. Years of resentment against great Anglo-Irish landowners continue to fester in the hearts of some die-hard Catholic nationalists. From the 1919–1921 War of Independence (sometimes called the Anglo-Irish War) through the Troubles of the early 1920s, numerous houses of the Anglo-Irish gentry were burnt. A number of their owners left the country; many others, considering themselves Irish after two or three hundred years, stayed. Their great houses, which few can afford to keep, are as much treasures of Ireland as the ruins of her great abbeys, though they often stand on land wrested from their ancient owners and were built with the sweat of Irish peasants. It would be well for grumblers in public houses to remember that Wolfe Tone, Charles Stewart Parnell, W. B. Yeats, and Sean O'Casey, among others, were Protestants and Irish patriots. I was glad that the Earls of Rosse have endured.

Along the Shannon's Grandest Lough

. ❧ .

AFTER LEAVING BIRR, HAVING OGLED THE VICTORIAN OPULENCE of Birr Castle's principal rooms and experienced the smart severity of Spinners Town House accommodations, I arrived at Somerset House, the O'Meara family's big nineteenth-century farmhouse near Lorrha, in Tipperary, which had the pleasing patina of time about it. Vera O'Meara showed me into the library, where we found her husband, Johnny, a smallish man with thinning sandy hair and friendly, twinkly eyes behind clear-rimmed spectacles, relaxing by the fire, book in lap. After he'd given me a whiskey (the first and only time in a B&B I was offered a drink for which I was not expected to pay), we began to talk.

"Like many places, there was much more land with the house when my people settled here," said Johnny O'Meara. "You either had a lot then or virtually nothing. The famine years made it very difficult for all." As Johnny spoke, I was conscious again, as so often in Ireland, how deep the impress of the past remains on land and people.

Johnny studied economics at University College, Dublin, in the early 1960s and had thought about enrolling at Harvard Business School. But after a stint with giant Shell in England, he changed his mind. "Sitting in an office?" He smiled broadly. "No, I came back here."

O'Meara raises cattle, sheep, and hay, and speaking of his farm, he suggested not a whiff of complaint about a farmer's toilsome life. He spoke with pride about a daughter pursuing multimedia studies and talked knowledgeably about virtual reality in filmmaking. After an engaging conversation, I retired to a commodious room, aware that the books on the library shelves here were read and that the life of the mind was nourished in this Tipperary farmhouse.

After breakfast, Johnny O'Meara showed me the old walled garden. "This is Vera's work," he said, gesturing toward beds of tulips and grape hyacinths already luxuriating in the spring sunshine. "Gardens are going to ruin all over Ireland," he said in an elegiac tone, meaning the gardens associated with the big country houses of the Anglo-Irish gentry destroyed in the Troubles of the 1920s or those that simply decayed as the class that had made them drifted toward genteel poverty.

A cheerful, energetic woman, Vera O'Meara could claim other accomplishments besides gardening; a former schoolteacher, she had just accommodated twelve guests who came for an antique car rally at Birr. She also shared my interest in antiquities, and when I spoke of Lackeen Castle, an ancient O'Kennedy stronghold that Brian Thompson had said was ideal for restoration, she said I must see it.

Lackeen Castle was perhaps only a mile away, but it was off my route by a couple of crossroads, so Vera drove me there. A medieval tower house, Lackeen appears surprisingly intact. In front of it is a modest old two-story farmhouse; its roof looked in fair shape, but some windows were broken. House and castle could be made into a handsome dwelling complex, I thought dreamily and said as much.

"They go when the weather gets in," said Vera; then she added, "It belongs to an old bachelor in Birr."

"Just the place a movie star would go for," I said.

Vera laughed and set me on my way, rested and cheerful.

AT THE SMALL crossroads village of Lorrha, the main street was treeless, bare as a bone. There was not a soul in sight near 10:00 A.M. Yet this place had known great days when it pulsed with life. In the middle of the sixth century, Saint Rúadhán founded a monastery here, which grew to be one of the most renowned in Munster, and at the east entrance to the village stand the remains of an eleventh-century church on the site. In the churchyard of the Church of Ireland edifice there, I saw the remains of two very early high crosses that had been shattered by Cromwell's soldiers. Near the northwest end of the main street is the ruin of the thirteenth-century Augustinian abbey, which is distinguished by a beautiful Gothic doorway.

At the southern edge of the village, I stopped to inspect the principal vestige of Lorrha's ecclesiastical apogee, the gaunt ruin of the Dominican friary established in 1269 by the Anglo-Norman Walter de Burgo, Earl of Ulster and Lord of Connacht. I wandered about, aware that within these walls, the silence broken only by the occasional chorus of rooks, were the graves of O'Kennedy chieftains and MacEgans, celebrated brehons, keepers of the ancient Gaelic laws. Beside the ruin stands the modern Catholic church.

Lorrha has an interesting connection with the O'Kennedy castle of Lackeen and with the abbey ruin at Terryglass, the village about five miles on, where I was bound. A celebrated missal, some say the oldest surviving mass book, which was written in the eighth or ninth century at the abbey of Tallaght, near Dublin (then long preserved in the abbey of Terryglass, within a shrine that may have been fashioned at Clonfert), was transferred to Lorrha, probably in the late thirteenth century. Mysteriously, the missal in its shrine was discovered in a wall of Lackeen Castle in 1735, likely hidden at a time when the monastic communities were being persecuted or dissolved. It is called the Stowe missal, after the seat of the Marquis of Buckingham, who acquired it. Today the missal is preserved in the Royal Irish Academy, and the shrine is in the National Museum, in Dublin.

I TRAMPED SOUTHWEST under blue skies intermittently streaked with rapidly moving bands of the hue known as Payne's gray, much favored by watercolorists. When a sudden squall overtook me, I sought shelter by a stone wall and pulled out my rain gear. The ensuing calisthenics, as I struggled into the rain pants, amused the navvies toiling at a drain across the road, who were already togged out in bright-yellow waterproofs.

Coming into the hamlet of Carrigahorig, I paused by the little stone bridge over a stream, watched the dark water pour over a weir, and hoped for a glimpse of trout dimpling the surface. Disappointed, I crossed the bridge and went into a pub beside the post office; it was named O'Meara's, like my hosts of last night. (In Ireland it is common to find people of the same name clustered in a region they have inhabited for ages.) There was no one in the bar, so I opened a door leading to the post office. Through a doorway, I saw a man and woman in a kitchen and called out. "Excuse me," I said. "I saw no one in the bar, but do you serve sandwiches?"

"No," said the woman.

"Is there perhaps someplace else in the village that does?"

"No."

Just then a younger woman emerged in the hallway off the kitchen, perhaps the postmistress, and I said, "I noticed a sign by the house next door that says 'Restaurant.' Would they be open?"

"Closed," the woman answered. "They're in Germany. They come only for holidays."

"Is there anywhere between here and Terryglass I could get a sandwich?"

"In Terryglass" was the response.

Just as I stepped outside, a little green van of the postal service pulled up, and I said to the postman, "I wonder if you would know anywhere between here and Terryglass to have lunch?"

"In Terryglass," the postman said. "There are two pubs."

"Right. Thanks. I know them." Tightening the straps on my rucksack, I strode off.

At the top of a low hill, not 150 yards from O'Meara's and the post office, I stopped, nonplussed. Right at the roadside was a small thatched public house with a sign, THE HALF-DOOR; a board outside announced that pub food was available. The red half door was open, and I went inside, wondering whether I had only dreamt the conversation at O'Meara's and the PO and whether I was having a *Brigadoon* experience.

In a moment, a smiling woman with short gray hair appeared behind the bar, and I said, "Do I read your sign outside correctly? You can manage a bit of lunch?"

"Surely," said the publican. "What would you like?"

I asked for soup and a toasted sandwich, and after a few minutes a savory soup and sandwich were produced. I lingered in the sunlit room, sated but utterly baffled by the misinformation I'd received not a longbow shot away. When a lorry driver came in with a cheery hello, we exchanged pleasantries; then I picked up my pack and moved on.

THE REST OF the way to Terryglass was through an open, gently rolling countryside. To my right was the Shannon, just out of sight, swelling into Lough Derg. I passed patches of bog, small pastures, and occasionally good-size fields, recently tilled, in which the first green harbingers of future harvests were already showing.

At Terryglass, I stopped at Riverrun House, a stylish B&B where I'd stayed once before, then strolled through the pretty hamlet to the small harbor on Lough Derg. Some eight vessels, powerboats and sailing craft, were moored along the breakwater, French and German flags fluttering from several flagstaffs. A fresh breeze off the lough had halyards jangling merrily; a rising wind had chased the bands of gray away, and cumulus clouds sailed like dandelion puffs across a cerulean sky. Out on the lough a sloop, big jib blooming, cut smartly through the sparkling water. An Irish Raoul Dufy could have made a delightful picture of the scene.

I WALKED BACK the few hundred yards to the Protestant church near the shop–cum–post office. In the churchyard, part of two surviving walls give faint evidence of the abbey founded in the fifth century by Saint Colm moccu Cremthannáin, which enjoyed considerable fame during the golden age of Irish monasticism. The saintly anchorite Máel-Díthruib died here in 840; an abbot of Terryglass was slain battling the Vikings at Dunamase in 845. Terryglass was renowned for its literary as well as saintly associations. Here, one Flann, *ollamh* of Ireland, master poet, was buried amidst three kings of Muskerry (one of the several petty kingdoms in Munster). According to Killanin and Duignan, Flann "is the earliest Irish professional poet [eighth–ninth century] of whom any definite tradition survives. He was called 'The Devil's Son' because he was so satirical and burdensome" in a time when a king feared the lash of a poet's tongue and gave him the place of honor at the dining table, where it was hoped that the poet would sing of the prowess and virtues of his lord. Killanin and Duignan comment that "it was believed that [Flann] went to Hell for his avarice."

In the late twelfth or early thirteenth century, Áed Crúamthainn, abbot of the monastery and revered sage, composed the *Book of Leinster,* a celebrated codex, of which it has been said that it "sums up all the learning of the monastic period of Irish writing." Despite the sweeping claim, the *Book of Leinster* is a rich source of information both factual and fanciful. Among other matters its scribe, whose patron was the King of Leinster, Dermot MacMurrough, records and laments that troublous potentate's banishment from Ireland: "O King of Heaven, dreadful is the deed that has been perpetrated in Ireland today, namely Diarmait, son of Donchad MacMurchada, King of Leinster and the Foreigners [the Danes of Dublin], has been banished over sea by the men of Ireland. Alas, alas, O Lord, what shall I do?"

Close by the Protestant church and the scant remains of the abbey are this tiny village's two pubs, Paddy's and the Derg Inn. Once, my wife and I were enchanted by a father and daughter who made memorable music on pennywhistle and fiddle in the bar of the Derg Inn. A few years before that, our cruising party had enjoyed a delightful dinner in an upstairs dining room, where I savored the largest and finest brown trout I have ever been served, but that room has long been closed.

In the bar this evening, I was presented a barely cooked duck breast cut in slices as thick as mutton chops. Next door, in Paddy's, a dimly lit establishment that has at least once been voted the best pub in Ireland, I savored an Irish coffee, serenaded by the click of balls on the pool table near the impressive potbellied stove. Then, returning to the snug lounge of Riverrun House, I sat nodding by the fire over some local history for a while, before repairing to bed and a wanderer's sweet dreams.

AT BREAKFAST, when my hosts, Tom and Lucy Sanders, asked where I was staying next, I replied that I didn't know. They suggested Annagh Lodge, about eight miles on, and telephoned the owners for me. Setting out, I took a little-traveled way through low grassy land that more or less paralleled the ragged shoreline of Lough Derg; across the lough lay Galway. At the little village of Ballinderry, the road rose and began to traverse a ridge some two to three hundred feet above the lough. Beyond it the glacially rounded Slieve Aughty Mountains, which Galway shares with Clare, emerged silvery green on this warm, sunny morn. As the light morning mist dissipated, I looked over fields of luminous green sloping toward the lough, always some half mile or mile distant. Small herds of cattle or flocks of sheep grazed on the rich grass. Occasionally I would glimpse the chimneys of manor houses hidden in the trees along the shore, with names like Waterloo Lodge, Brookfield House, or Bellevue House, each indicated on my Ordnance Survey map.

Lough Derg, covering fifty square miles, like a salamander wriggling from northeast to southwest, is the largest of fifteen lakes in the Shannon system and remains beautifully unspoiled despite the steady increase in cruising traffic. Scattered about the lough, mostly near its shores, are numerous islands, on one of which—Inis Cealtra, or Holy Island—are the remains of perhaps the most important early monastic foundation in Clare, including a round tower, four churches, and two high crosses. Along the shore of Lough Derg are several villages, Mountshannon and Scarriff, in Clare, and Dromineer and Garrykennedy, in Tipperary. Here and there a castle or abbey ruin offers mute testimony to the turbulent history of this waterway.

At a spot quite near the lough, I lunched contentedly beneath a spreading oak while watching a single black lamb amid an all-white flock, grazing like all the others. I wondered about its situation, whether it felt at all estranged from the all-white flock or whether the others—indeed, its mother—thought the black lamb odd. That seemed not so when she suckled it. One of the joys of the footloose is how freely the mind wanders, occasionally stimulated by an observation, sometimes fluttering like a butterfly among memories. Then I settled back against my rucksack and browsed contentedly in *A Book of Ireland*, Frank O'Connor's rewarding anthology of prose and poetry, my unfailing paperback companion on the road.

As I passed the little crossroads place called Coolbaun, to my left, about a half mile off, I sighted a castle, a tower house, dark and mysterious looking, on low, rough ground. (Later I would learn that it was called the Black Castle.) I was tempted to investigate, but my map told me that Annagh Lodge lay just a little bit ahead, and a hot bath beckoned. On I went, reflecting that I'd never had a lovelier day's walk in Ireland.

A long drive ascended past a magnificent evergreen oak and a field of sheep to Annagh Lodge, which I judged to be a very-late-Georgian or early-Victorian building. At my knock, host Andrew Sterling admitted me and in a little while was serving tea. Later, when I came down for dinner, the only guest, I found a drinks tray set out, and over a preprandial martini, while looking at framed wedding photographs of the lanky, charming Andrew and his pretty, blond wife, Rachel, I imagined a sitcom about a well-born young couple turning their country house into an upscale Fawlty Towers. I thought Hugh Grant and Gwyneth Paltrow would be ideal casting.

Just then Andrew came in, introduced me to his wife, and accompanied me to the main reception room for dinner, while Rachel, a trained hotelier and cook, retired to her kitchen to prepare it. Over the tasty repast that Rachel cooked, Andrew and I talked about their life by Lough Derg, where he and his wife have close family connections: Andrew's mother lives in a castle nearby, and Rachel's mother has a house just down the road. Andrew managed a shooting syndicate—raising ducks to add to the migratory waterfowl drawn to the lough—and besides operating a B&B, they had ventured into animal husbandry, obtaining some relatively rare, tobacco-colored Tamworth pigs from the Dublin zoo. Before dinner, I'd seen them usefully rooting through a field of nettles.

IN THE MORNING, Rachel allowed me to meet the appealing Sterling tykes and told me that since the house of her mother, Hilary Henry, was on my route to Dromineer, she would be pleased to have me stop for a cup of coffee. As I was about to leave, Andrew was setting off to fetch a boar of a different breed, which he hoped would add some heft to the progeny of the slighter Tamworths. We all parted cheerily, and I told myself I should return one day for the shooting and to see what had become of the pigs.

Just a little way along the road, I saw an unusual iron gate wrought in floral motifs. It opened onto a short driveway curving up to a white modern house of striking lines, standing in nicely landscaped grounds. Near the house the most chicly garbed gardener I'd ever met arose from the flower bed she'd been manuring; Hilary Henry was no less charming than her daughter Rachel. Pulling off her gloves, she greeted me and led the way into the house and a comfortable living room.

While she went to bring coffee, I admired the antique furnishings and good pictures, which complemented and warmed the white walls; large windows offered views over the countryside. The house and its mistress had flair. It was the only such modern dwelling into which this vagabond was invited on his journey, a friendly gesture, and by a lady alone. It would never have happened in France.

Over coffee, Hilary Henry said that she had conceived the basic plan of the house and determined upon certain distinctive features. Notable among them was the wrought-iron work by a university friend of Rachel and Andrew's. Besides the gate I'd opened, my eye was riveted by the black iron balustrade created for the hall staircase, which zigzagged up to a skylight; like the base of the glass table on which we took our coffee, it intertwined images of fruit and flowers. We talked about the house, the countryside, and my journey, and graciously Hilary Henry saw me on my way. I cannot recall seeing another contemporary house in Ireland of quite such style and appeal.

EN ROUTE TO DROMINEER, I was overtaken by showers and a biting wind. The little harbor there, where I had put in on more clement days, was a welcome sight. I walked along the quay, watching the white horses galloping down the lough and enviously inspecting handsome boats moored snugly within the breakwater.

The Dromineer Bay Hotel had recently been modernized, in the international motel style; it could have been in Cincinnati or Frankfurt. There were hardly any guests at this time, and I asked to be moved from the room I was shown to another, which overlooked the lough and the harbor, beside which stood the massive keep of an O'Kennedy castle. The O'Kennedys had traded it to the Butlers, Earls of Ormond, who with the Fitzgeralds became the most powerful and enduring of Ireland's Anglo-Norman families. The castle ruin was garrisoned by rooks; their raucous sorties persisted until night fell. With the dining room closed, I had a dreary dinner in the bar, beside a family with strident children. In my room, I fell asleep while studying the map for the next leg of my march.

NEXT MORNING, I started for Ballina, at the southern end of Lough Derg, where the Shannon emerges more riverlike again. It is about fourteen miles from Dromineer, and for roughly the first four miles, I had to make a number of left and right turns onto linking roads, all country bohereens. At some point, I found myself on a walking route called the Lough Derg Way, with distinctive trail markers, which should have led to Ballina. But somehow, for the first time on this journey, I went astray. I took a turn that wasn't marked for the Lough Derg Way but nonetheless seemed to take me in the right direction, according to my map. The little road started climbing steeply, and after trudging uphill for a mile or so, menaced once by a dog, I halted. With my magnifying glass, I scrutinized the Ordnance Survey map for this area of Tipperary, then scanned the countryside. I realized that I was getting into the Arra Mountains. Across a valley, I could see the slate quarries indicated on the map. If I had paid closer attention to the contour lines on it, I would have realized that the elevation I was climbing didn't correspond to that of the road I should have taken.

But a wrong turn can prove to be a good turn for the traveler: just ahead was what the Ordnance Survey map labels GRAVES OF THE LEINSTER MEN. I could dimly recall reading somewhere that warriors of King (perhaps not yet High King) Brian Boru (whose seat, Kincora, was at Killaloe) had slain men of the King of Leinster hereabouts. The nondescript stones at this remote place I'd stumbled on were said by Killanin and Duignan to be a "prehistoric chamber tomb." I wondered, for folk memory of heroic deeds is long in Ireland. Just then I had to step aside for the car of a farmer who had driven up here to look at some cattle he had nearby. I told him I'd lost my way, and he took me down the long grade, past the alarming dog, and set me on the right road near Ballina.

BALLINA, IN COUNTY TIPPERARY, is separated from Killaloe, in County Clare, by a bridge over the river Shannon; it once had thirteen stone arches, but the fourth from the Ballina side has been replaced by a higher metal span, to permit the passage of boats. While Ballina is a pleasant riparian town, I was keen to visit somewhat larger Killaloe for its historical associations, so I crossed the Shannon again.

There was a monastic foundation here as early as the sixth century. In 639, Saint Flannán, of a princely family, became the first bishop of Killaloe. The earliest church that survives here, called the Oratory, is believed to have been built in the late eleventh or early twelfth century. The simple structure is unusual for having its stone roof intact. Beneath it is a small croft or living space over the vault of the nave. Beside the Oratory is St. Flannán's Cathedral, erected between 1185 and 1225 and altered over the centuries. Like almost all early Irish churches not in ruins, the formerly Catholic St. Flannán's became a Protestant church, still St. Flannán's but the cathedral for the Church of Ireland's diocese of Killaloe. As with so many other monuments in Ireland, it was being restored through the munificence of the European Union.

The most arresting feature of the cathedral—cruciform and without aisles—is a superb Romanesque doorway, which, oddly, now frames a window at floor level in the south wall by the entrance portal. Also preserved in St. Flannán's is an eleventh-century high cross with a crucifixion, brought from Kilfenora, in Clare, and the shaft of what was probably an earlier cross. It has inscriptions in ogham (the earliest form of Irish writing, composed of a long vertical line with lines of varying length incised at right angles on either side) and in runic (the characters of the Norse alphabet), which have been translated, respectively, as A BLESSING ON TOROQRIM and THURGRIM CARVED THIS CROSS.

No less interesting to me were the memorials on the walls, for one can read in them much history. All appear to commemorate deceased Anglo-Irish gentry. See if a few of those I read do not tell much about the British Empire that is no more:

IN LOVING MEMORY OF RONALD ELPHINSTONE PARKER
LIEUTENANT ROYAL HORSE ARTILLERY
KILLED IN ACTION
IN THE BATTLE OF THE MARNE
ON THE 8TH SEPTEMBER 1914, AGED 28.

IN MEMORY OF MAJOR GENERAL JOHN BOURCHIER RA
. . . .
WHO SERVED UNDER THE DUKE OF YORK
DURING THE CAMPAIGN OF 1793 IN FLANDERS
AND PARTICULARLY DISTINGUISHED HIMSELF
IN THE WEST INDIES UNDER SIR CHARLES GREY
AT THE TAKING OF THE ISLANDS OF
MARTINIQUE, SANTA LUCIA, AND LA SAINTE.
HE DIED ON THE 25TH DAY OF SEPTEMBER 1817

AGED 62 YEARS

AND WAS INTERRED IN THIS CATHEDRAL.

ERECTED

BY THE TENANTS OF THE TINERAMA ESTATE

AS A MARK OF THEIR DEEP REGARD AND RESPECT

FOR THE MEMORY OF

LIEU^{T.} RICHARD PONSONBY PURDON RN

WHO WAS LOST ON BOARD

H.M.S. "CAPTAIN," SEP^{T.} 7TH 1870

AGE 27.

The most famous of all Irish kings, Brian Bóruma, called Boru, had his seat at Killaloe. Alas, unlike Shelley's Ozymandias, not even a stone remains to be seen of Brian's fortress and royal seat, Kincora. The present Catholic church is said to stand on its site. Brian succeeded his brother Mathgamain (Mahon), King of Cashel, who was assassinated in 976. After avenging his murder and making himself King of Munster, the formidable warrior consolidated his power swiftly, by bold military strategy involving many struggles and by shrewd political strokes. At one point, Brian met Mael Sechnaill II (Malachy), then nominally the High King, at Clonfert; they agreed to divide Ireland, but Brian pressed on and forced Mael Sechnaill's submission. By 1002, Brian had won the high kingship for himself. Yet he had still to contend with enemies. On Good Friday 1014, the aged Brian Boru threw his men of Munster and Connacht against his longtime foe Mael Morda, King of Leinster, who had allied himself with Sitric of the Silken Beard, king of the Dublin Norsemen, who had recruited fellow Vikings from the Isle of Man and as far away as the Orkney Isles. What became the great Battle of Clontarf (today a Dublin suburb) was a violent, bloody conflict, in which Mael Morda, Brian, Brian's son Murchadh, and a great many others perished. But Brian's forces were victorious: the power of the Norse in Ireland was crushed, and for some time Leinster was reined in. Mael Sechnaill II became High King of Ireland and ruled until he died, in 1022. For a time, the descendants of Brian Boru, the O'Briens, held the high kingship, until overtaken by the O'Connors. The O'Briens remained Kings of Thomond, a major part of Munster, for several centuries, until co-opted by the English with an earldom.

Brian Boru was buried in great state at Armagh, for he had been a strong supporter of the church. (His brother Marcan was abbot of Killaloe, Holy Island, and Terryglass.) The scribe of the *Book of Armagh* acclaimed Brian Boru as *Imperator Scotorum,* that is, "emperor of the Irish." (In Latin, Scotia, like Hibernia, is a name for Ireland. When settlers went from Ireland to Scotland, they brought the name of their homeland and their language, which there is called Gaelic, the tongue of the Gaels, from Goidelic, the early Irish form of Celtic.)

THAT NIGHT I stayed comfortably in the Lakeside Hotel, pleasantly sited on the Shannon in Ballina. Next day, I took myself back to Killaloe and lunched in a pub called the Dalcassian (from the Irish Dál Cais, the north Munster dynasty from which Brian Boru sprang). The publican was genially mediating a spirited discussion by some patrons about the meaning of destiny. At the table next to the one I took, two ladies of a certain age, who would have been called very "county" in England, wearing impeccable tweeds and good jewelry, one smoking a cigar, were enjoying coffee and a tête-à-tête about local intrigues. I relished my lunch and a report in the *Irish Independent,* supported by a photograph, of the appearance in a Dublin court of model Samantha Blandford Hutton, her alleged associate Karen Leahy, and Ms. Blandford Hutton's brother Stephen, accused by the prosecutor of keeping a bawdy house. The defendants were garbed in hooded red-satin-lined cloaks, and when the hearing was adjourned, they donned black masks and sped off in a van with blackened windows. Joyce would have been amused to think that perhaps Dublin's Nighttown was not quite extinct, if become rather more upscale than his.

I was about to leave the Shannon, which I had more or less followed for about one hundred miles. Below Killaloe, after ten miles, the river begins to veer sharply westward, twisting its way to the city of Limerick, where Sarsfield yielded to King William's general and signed the treaty so abruptly dishonored by the victors. From there the river opens into its great estuary and joins the Atlantic. My way lay more southerly, to Cork, the Republic's second city, and to the port of Kinsale.

I paused on the bridge from Clare to Tipperary and dug a coin from my pocket. It was a ten-penny piece, minted in 1995, showing a leaping salmon on the obverse, the Irish harp on the reverse. I hesitated; it was a very small coin, and I wanted something larger. Dug again. Came up with a one-punt coin, showing a noble stag. Balked. This and a couple more of the same would buy me a pint when I was thirsty. Back into the pocket. This was it: I held another ten-penny piece, but this one, coined in 1980, was almost twice the size of the other ten p. The country was getting richer, but the coins were getting smaller. In a while the euro would replace all of the beautiful Irish coinage. I hefted the big ten-penny coin, and wishing I would return, I flung the salmon into the river Shannon.

PART THREE

A Long Way Through Tipperary

The Rock of Cashel.

Surprised by Priests

⁂

THE ROAD SOUTH FROM BALLINA TO BIRDHILL WAS STRAIGHT, dull, and busy for a mercifully short three miles. Coming to the N7, the main road running northeast from Limerick to Dublin, I paused by The Thresher, a good restaurant and pub and familiar pit stop, and waited until I could safely nip across between speeding cars and trucks. Then I started south on a country road that led to Newport, where I planned to spend the night. The road began to rise along the foothills of the Silvermine Mountains, and I recalled that Corney Magrath, an Irish giant who was a cynosure in London in the mid–eighteenth century, hailed from this area. He had been employed by Bishop Berkeley as a lad, before being exhibited as an oddity. Magrath was only twenty-three when he died, and his body was stolen by anatomy students of Trinity College, Dublin, and brought to their professor for dissection. Corney Magrath's skeleton is preserved in Trinity. His height was seven feet, two and a quarter inches.

I MET ONE curious creature along the way who was not curious at all: some distance ahead a dog lay in the middle of the road, and several cars swerved to avoid it. Perhaps it had already been hit. But no, as I drew nearer, I saw that it was a sheepdog, dozing in the afternoon sun. As I came close, I could see that it was an old dog, head on paws, eyes following me. As I came abreast, the dog lifted its head, regarded me benignly, started to rise, then subsided. As I went by, I spoke: "What a good old dog!" The tribute was acknowledged with a single wag.

Mine was a delightful route. At first, I had lovely views across viridian fields sweeping down to the Shannon, a great silver serpent gliding over a broad plain toward Limerick and the distant Atlantic. Along the road, yellow primroses luxuriated in the ditches, and Queen Anne's lace was just beginning to show. At one point, I saw in a meadow a high limestone massif shaped like a tumulus. Sheep had terraced it, and their horizontal trails that circled it, fertilized by droppings, were green with grass and brilliant with primroses. The whole composed a rock garden fit for a pasha.

Farther on I was transfixed by a single rapturous birdsong, which was coming from a copse across the road. The song went on and on. Crossing over, craning my neck and trying to see the singer, I remembered Keats:

> That thou, light-wingèd Dryad of the trees,
> In some melodious plot
> Of beechen green, and shadows numberless,
> Singest of summer in full-throated ease.

Finally, after it paused and fluttered before resuming, I glimpsed the performer, which appeared to be a blackbird. I guessed from the ardent serenade the singer was a male and wondered if any female could fail to be as spellbound as I was.

At Newport, I lodged at White Walls, the little B&B of Mary Maloney, who suggested that I might like to accompany her and her daughter to a "priests' show" at the parish hall. This had been an annual event for some time, a charitable fund-raiser, and always a sellout. So off we went. The venue was the big hall of the Sisters of Mary Convent, next to the large parish church, which dominates the nondescript town. Admission was I£4.00, and the place was indeed sold out. Doubtless through the pleasant Mrs. Maloney's persuasiveness, I found myself seated with the Maloneys on a bench at the front of the packed hall. Four pounds never bought me more entertainment.

What was formally billed as "The Holy Show" was a surprise. I'm not sure what I expected, but not the assured performers of hard rock, traditional Irish airs, contemporary love songs, and some nearly naughty jokes. They were whisked on- and offstage by a slim, red-haired doppelgänger of Danny Kaye named Father Tony Nolan, the MC, who seemed to have been fine-tuned on the borscht circuit or *Saturday Night Live*.

The musical numbers were of several modes but seemed to favor country-and-western. After Father Dick Brown put over "The Black Hills of Dakota," Father Jamie O'Donoghue (wearing a cowboy outfit and introduced as a "Cork man," to hisses from the Tipperary audience) proposed an homage to John Denver and sang:

> So kiss me and smile for me,
> Tell me that you'll wait for me,
> Hold me like you'll never let me go.
> 'Cause I'm leaving on a jet plane,
> Don't know when I'll be back again.
> Oh babe, I hate to go.

Father Denis Shanahan continued the amatory theme with tender renditions of "Perhaps Love" and "And I Love You So." The mood changed when three padres—Father Dick Brown on concertina and pennywhistle, Father Tom Fanning on accordian, and Father Tony Nolan on *bodhrán* and spoons—cut loose, and we almost had a traditional Irish *céilí*, with the audience stomping and clapping as the boys in black segued through a medley of traditional tunes.

Father Bobby Fletcher, clearly a highly popular curate in the local parish, gyrated as a wild rocker, wearing a shirt of silver sequins, and nearly brought down the house. In a long program that sped by, musical acts were interspersed with comic turns. One featured a pair of portly, bespectacled nuns who cavorted about, revealing a flash of knickers before MC Tony Nolan disclosed that they were two respected matrons doing their bit for charity.

Because we were in Tipperary, where hurling may be a sacrament, a certain Father Peter (whose surname I missed) told one about the chap who turns up at the Pearly Gates and, before admission, asks Saint Peter if there'll be hurling in Heaven.

Most memorable was Father Jimmy O'Donnell's story about the young curate who could not get the attention of the men in the back of the church who went on gabbing about hurling or farming while he was giving his homily, so he appealed to the wise old parish priest.

"Well," said the PP, "start off with something short and snappy to get their attention; then you can get on with your sermon. You could start by saying, 'I spent last night in the arms of a beautiful woman.' That'll get their attention. Then you add, 'It was my mother, Mary.' "

The young curate was all excited at his next mass, and he started his homily, "Last night I was in the arms of a beautiful . . . but, God help me! I can't remember her name. You can ask the parish priest; he knows her better than I do." The audience in the Sisters of Mercy hall howled with laughter.

At the close of the evening, Father Liam Holmes, a Lorne Greene look-alike, brought the crowd along with several rousing airs, then led all in a fervent singing of "The Soldier's Song," the national anthem (by Peadar Kearney, an uncle of Brendan Behan, the playwright and sometime IRA man).

Back at White Walls, Mary Maloney brewed us a pot of tea to top off a jolly evening. After I turned in, I mused on the evening's entertainment. I'd been surprised that many of the priests' songs were about romantic love and that some of their humorous stories played on the erotic. Should I have been surprised, in an Ireland entering the third millennium? In the successful Irish TV series *Ballykissangel,* a young village priest's vow of celibacy is severely tested. Still, all the sermons I had heard on my journey reflected the serious thoughts of serious men. It was amusing to think of parish priests sitting around the rectory of an evening, cracking each other up with ribald jokes. I drifted off, imagining another sitcom, this one with Jackie Gleason—may he rest in peace—and Art Carney as parish priest and curate in a series called *The Rectory.*

Marching Song

CLOSE BY MARY MALONEY'S WHITE WALLS A SECONDARY ROAD
turns almost due south, and I struck off along it. After a couple of miles, I
came to a single-arched old bridge over the Clare River, marking the lower
end of the Clare Glens, which, at least in the region, are renowned for
their beauty. The little river flows from east to west and for some miles
forms the border between Tipperary to the north and Limerick to the
south. Dropping my pack, I lit a pipe and sat on a rustic bench overlooking a pool below the bridge. Trout were dimpling the peaty water, the
smaller ones jumping eagerly to snatch at tiny flies, the larger, more practiced performers rising slowly to engulf their prey almost imperceptibly
before retreating, leaving concentric circles that made an angler's heart
beat faster.

By the bridge, a large map of the river and the Clare Glens had been
erected. On it two river walks and particular beauty spots were marked,
but I could barely make them out because the thick glass covering the map
had been smashed. I took the path upstream, along the right bank. The
glens are a series of steep defiles, their partially rocky slopes covered with
bracken, vines, and brush near the stream; higher up there are stands of tall
conifers and, here and there, great beeches and other deciduous trees. It
had rained heavily in the night, and the river fell with a tumult through a

series of cascades. The ascending path was carpeted with pine needles, and wet stones and slabs made for treacherous footing. After perhaps half a mile, I turned back regretfully. The dim green canopy above the soaring tree trunks, the whisper of water from the leaves, and the music of the tumbling river made the glens seem Edenic. I thought of the ecstatic response to nature in very early Irish poetry; one finds it in *Buile Suibhne,* a long medieval poem in Irish, which has been translated by Seamus Heaney in the memorable *Sweeney Astray.* It is the tale of a king named Sweeney driven mad at the Battle of Moira (A.D. 637). Before the battle, Sweeney had offended Saint Ronan, who put a curse on him, causing Sweeney to be transformed into a bird. Flying from the battlefield and much harried, mad Sweeney seeks respite all over Ireland. In one place above all, Sweeney finds surcease, calling it his Eden, and he sings of another glen, perhaps like the one I climbed through:

> And then Glen Bolcain was my lair,
> . . . .
> I wouldn't swop a lonely hut
> in that dear glen
> for a world of moorland acres
> on a russet mountain.
>
> Its water flashing like wet grass,
> its wind so keen,
> its tall brooklime, its watercress
> the greenest green.
>
> I love the ancient ivy tree,
> the pale-leafed sallow,
> the birch's whispered melody,
> the solemn yew.

But I had to leave the sweet Clare Glens behind. Crossing the bridge over the Clare River, I was in County Limerick. Three miles on, just before the village of Moroe, I passed the gate of Glenstal Abbey, a Benedictine foundation and a distinguished school, founded in 1927. Coming to Moroe, I saw a telephone kiosk at the crossroad and went to it, only to find it trashed. (This was the first and only such serious vandalism I noted on my journey.) However, the Valley Inn across the road was open; refreshment was available, so was a telephone.

Riversdale, in nearby Abington, is the B&B and sizable farm of Mr. and Mrs. Thomas Cooney. Mrs. Cooney was away, and Tom Cooney gave me dinner and installed me in a corner room affording a panorama of a lush countryside. Looking down at a big farmyard with several dilapidated buildings and two large prefabricated metal barns, I watched Tom Cooney, his son, another man, and two Border collies round up a herd of bullocks. Off they went, through a series of fields separated by hedgerows, men and dogs driving the bullocks to a good pasture for the night. As all disappeared in the distance, two frisky billy goats clambered over the farmyard wall and took off after drovers and herd. One collie, left in the farmyard, lay watching as the billy goats scampered over the first hedgerow, then bolted after the vagrants. I watched for quite a while, till all were lost to sight, made a few notes in my journal, then looked out again. The rural parade was returning: two billy goats chivvied by three collies, followed by three cowherds, the evening task done.

In the distance, across the Golden Vale of Tipperary to the southeast, the Galty Mountains appeared like cutouts of tissue, receding from purple to the faintest heliotrope. Close by the lane to the Cooney farm loomed the spire of a lovely, small, isolated chapel, typical of the Church of Ireland. I groped futilely to think of an Irish equivalent to Gray's "Elegy Written in a Country Churchyard."

ON A PALE, gray morning, I walked southeast toward Cappamore, posted some letters, bought a newspaper, and settled into the snug lounge of O'Dwyer's public house. Good timing. As a sudden squall beat against the windows, John O'Dwyer replenished the fire and served a good soup and sandwich. The only other guests in the lounge—as in all pubs, the so-called public bar held more patrons—was a couple from Dublin, Mr. and Mrs. O'Dúill. Eileen was an American, a genealogist whose researches, largely for American clients, took her far afield. She mentioned that she has a sister who lives in Claremont, New Hampshire, and I said that I went there at least once a year, to fish the Sugar River.

Leaving Cappamore, still in Limerick, I continued heading southwest along the edge of the Slieve Felim Mountains, on a road that looked down over lovely, sparsely settled country. Before reaching Cappagh White, the road crossed the county border, and I was back again in Tipperary. By my reckoning, when I reached the border of County Cork, I would have traversed nearly one hundred miles of Tipperary by a diagonal route through Ireland's biggest inland county.

THE RAIN SQUALL had passed, and as I tramped along contentedly, I found myself stepping to the words of a great marching song of the First World War:

> Up to mighty London came
> An Irishman one day,
> As the streets were paved with gold,
> So every one was gay!
> Singing songs of Piccadilly,
> Strand, and Leicester Square.
> Till Paddy got excited, and
> He shouted to them there:
>
> It's a long way to Tipperary,
> It's a long way to go.
> It's a long way to Tipperary
> To the sweetest girl I know!
> Goodbye Piccadilly,
> Farewell Leicester Square!
> It's a long way to Tipperary,
> But my heart's right there.

The song set me thinking of the tens of thousands of Irishmen who wore British uniforms and served under the Union Jack and the banners of British regiments—indeed, a number raised in Ireland—in the First and Second World Wars. This might strike some people as paradoxical, considering the tormented relationship of Britain and Ireland for so long. Consider that while a British Army with many Irish in it (some 250,000) fought and died (25,000) in the mud of Flanders, and on other foreign fields, Irishmen raised a rebellion in Dublin on Easter Monday, 1916, proclaiming an Irish Republic. However, the British had retained garrisons in Ireland, and the "Rising" was ruthlessly put down; the center of Dublin was ruined by artillery and naval gunfire, and fifteen leaders of the insurrection were executed. Only the American-born Eamon De Valera was spared. After escaping from a British prison in 1919, Dev, as he was universally known, proved to be a boil on Britain's neck for many years, not least during the Second World War. Then, although Winston Churchill seemed to offer De Valera the reunification of Ireland in return for full participation as an ally, as *Taoiseach*, or prime minister, of Éire (as the 1937 constitution of Ireland renamed the Irish Free State, established in 1922), Dev insisted on maintaining its neutrality. Nonetheless, thousands of Irish enlisted to serve under Britain's colors in that war. Numbers are disputed: the official British government figure is 42,665 men from Éire; however, according to Major H.M.E. Grogan, administrator of the Royal British Legion in Ireland, General Sir Hubert Gough stated that in 1944 "the official list of next of kin contained 165,000 addresses in Éire, as it was then."

I STOPPED EARLY that evening in Cappagh White at a B&B preciously named Lo-th-Morn and went looking for some supper. At a laundry, I left a tiny bundle, which an obliging woman said would be ready in an hour; then I dropped into Coughlan's pub. The public bar was crowded with horseplayers, two women and some twenty men, almost all smoking, moored to the telly, watching the racing at Doncaster and Sandown Park, in England. A heavy fug hung in the room. If Coughlan's served food, I preferred to skip it. One TV screen showed just the odds on each horse as it changed—and I saw ardent punters in the pub exchanging bets—while on another screen the camera zoomed in on the parade ring as gaily caparisoned riders mounted their splendid steeds, then followed them onto the course to watch them race for wealth and glory.

I picked up some food and wine at a little market and picnicked at a pleasant roadside park, a rarity in Ireland. The evening was balmy, and I had a view over the Golden Vale to the Galty Mountains, their color changing as cloud shadows raced over them. The field in the foreground was verdegris patinated by the lowering sun. In the middle was a single pillar stone, which I imagined was erected in ancient times, perhaps to mark the deed of some chieftain or other notability. This evening it provided the scratching post for a cow.

Next day, I went to mass at the church of Our Lady of Fatima in Cappagh White and learned from the parish newsletter that in three weeks time a special mass and Jubilee celebration would be held in the Fox Covert. This was the site of a simple thatched chapel in nearby woods where mass had been said clandestinely in the time of the Penal Laws. I would have liked to attend but would have to be far along by then.

MY ROAD CONTINUED to skirt the Slieve Felim mountains to the north, with the Golden Vale of Tipperary stretching away to the south. When I reached Dundrum, I stopped at the Rectory House Hotel, a Victorian building set amid broad lawns shaded by venerable trees. This former rectory of the Church of Ireland is a rambling dwelling nicely cluttered with objets d'art, bric-a-brac, period furniture, and assertive wallpaper. I was shown to a huge corner room comfortably furnished with Victorian pieces, which I thought would make a perfect set for an Agatha Christie mystery.

When I went down to the small bar before dinner, I took a stool beside a short, lithe man and his comely blond wife and was soon engaged in conversation about fishing and shooting. "I'm a welder, but I live for the shooting," said Brendan O'Brien. He was full of lore about the sport to be had hereabouts, and seeing that I was interested, he urged me to get in touch with him if I'd "like to enjoy a bit of rough shooting in the neighborhood." I confessed that I'd spent some happy days out after woodcock and snipe in Galway and Mayo.

"Ah, go on with you! Tipperary's the place, and I'm your man," said Brendan O'Brien. "And you needn't bother with a permit to bring in a firearm; I can lend you a gun." I knew I was in Ireland: one wouldn't have this conversation at a first-time meeting in England, France, Germany, or other countries where I'd wandered. I knew, too, that if I turned up next year here, Brendan would be as good as his word.

After a good dinner, I went upstairs to write in my journal until, much later, a nightcap seemed reasonable. Licensing hours do not apply to residents, and the little lounge beside the bar held about six of them. Jennifer Shiel, the daughter of the house, who had taken me in, presided from the bar. All were having a jolly time, and two were professional musicians who had just returned from the United States, where they had been touring, performing traditional Irish songs. They favored us with several, perhaps more, for after a large whiskey, I opted to retire, skirting a chap who was somersaulting across the floor.

AFTER BREAKFASTING ALONE—I supposed that other residents might wish to sleep late this morning—I paid my bill and bid good-bye to Trigger, the big Irish setter reposing on a settee in the front hall. Jennifer's mother, proprietor Una Doyle, tipped me to an archaeological curiosity I might see and put me on a byway to the village of Golden.

The road stretched out straight before me as far as I could see. A gossamer haze hung over the Golden Vale on the warmest day of my walk thus far. Far to the east the Rock of Cashel, with its majestic ruins, was a pale silhouette towering over the great plain. Cashel was my destination this evening, but I was taking a roundabout route to visit several historical sites. It was my sister's birthday, and I thought of her as I tramped along happily. Then my mind, drifting like a trout fly, recalled reports and photographs in this morning's *Irish Times:* neo-Nazi skinheads menacing leftists in Berlin; masked troublemakers in London brandishing wrenches and hedge cutters and promising to strike against capitalism; and thugs on both sides of the unionist and nationalist divide in Northern Ireland determined to wreck the nascent peace process. But on the open road between one Irish village and another in the South, tranquillity suffused the lovely countryside and seeped into me.

I had been told that there was a prime fishing stretch near the junction of the relatively small Multeen River and the grander Suir, one of Ireland's major rivers and one that has known great days for salmon and trout fishing. I had fished the Suir several times in the past but never here and never the Multeen. Although I hadn't packed fishing paraphernalia, I knew I'd come back, so I wanted to have a look. Soon I spotted two landmarks I'd been told about: a ruined church on a rise to my left and a stone bridge over the Multeen.

Just downriver from the bridge, I climbed over a fence along a pasture and walked toward the river. As I reached it, I saw a young couple reclining in the deep grass beneath the shade of the trees at the water's edge. I remembered it was spring Bank Holiday, and a pair of lovers had found a lovely place to spend it. Turning around quietly, I was surprised to find myself looking right at the impressive ruin of a castle with three towers and typically nineteenth-century crenellations, not a third of a mile from me. It had been screened from my view by trees and what I'd call a late-Georgian or Regency villa to one side. I was mystified. I'd studied my Ordnance Survey section map before I set out this morning; I took it out again. No castle shown here. As it happened, I did want to visit Thomas-town Castle today. I hadn't thought it was here, but could this be it? Or was it truly a *Brigadoon* moment? I had to investigate.

The entrance to the house beside the castle was on a little side road just off the one I'd been following. A low gate closed off the driveway, and behind it two dogs heralded my arrival. One was a big red, perhaps cross-bred dog; the other a feisty wee terrier. They barked dutifully. I was keen to see this castle, but there was no bell at the gate. I regarded the dogs and vice versa; I opened the gate and went in. The big red sniffed me carefully, the terrier yapped lustily at my heels, glad for a diversion, and followed me up the drive. I walked around to the front door of the very pretty one-story dwelling beside the facade of the castle, which looked over a broad field to the river, whence I'd viewed it. I knocked, waited. Silence. The dogs were snuffling at my boots. I knocked again, loudly. No one. I walked out in front of the villa and looked at the facade of the castle beside it— how I coveted this place, with its graceful house and romantic ruin, look-ing over the trouty river—then I went up to a high wooden double door in the castle wall and peered through a crack. Within was a well-kept stable yard, with horse boxes and some farm machinery. There was nothing else behind the castle facade except four enclosing walls. It was like something one would see on the back lot of a film studio: a beautiful illusion. As I turned away, not a whit the wiser about what once had been here, I looked over the green acres toward the river. In the foreground two fine horses lay on the grass; on one, two magpies perched. The dogs sent me on my way, barking, wagging amiably.

A few miles on I came to the turnoff for Thomastown and was soon in the hamlet. I had a pub lunch at Sir Rowland's and learned where to find the old drive to Thomastown Castle. Soon I saw the stark, massive ruin, distinguished by numerous unusual chimneys.

The bleak remains give hardly a hint of the grandeur and the gaiety this place had known. For here, in the eighteenth century, dwelt Thomas Mathew, who possessed extensive lands and a considerable fortune. Scion of an old Catholic family connected to the great Duke of Ormond, he was one of those Catholics of rank or wealth who had protected his interests by conversion to the Church of Ireland. Thomas Mathew became perhaps the most generous—not to say stupendous—host in Ireland since the sixth-century King of Connacht, Gúaire Aidhneach. Thomas Mathew's greatest pleasure was to give pleasure, and he went to extraordinary ends to do so. He made of Thomastown Castle a kind of resort hotel: there were some forty apartments for guests, and Mathew liked them fully occupied by persons whose company he enjoyed.

On arrival, guests were told that they were to treat the castle as their own; they were free to do what they pleased, when they pleased. Accordingly, if they did not care to dine in company, they could take meals in a parlor where they would be served whenever they chose. In the castle there was a coffeehouse such as guests might frequent in Dublin or London, furnished with newspapers, chessboards, and other games. Mathew also had constructed a tavern for his guests, complete with billiard room, where one's choice of drink was served by waiters dressed as they would be in a public house.

It seemed there was nothing the host could think of that he did not provide for the entertainment of his guests. For those keen for fishing and shooting, he would furnish rods and guns; for others who liked to hunt, he kept two packs of hounds. Mathew would not permit his servants to accept gratuities from guests, and for them his sole proscription was that gambling would not be countenanced.

Affluent, handsome, well traveled, cultivated, and a member of Parliament, Mathew was neither social climber nor pursuer of the famous. The only celebrity whom he seems to have invited to Thomastown Castle was Jonathan Swift.

The sometimes acerbic dean arrived with a Mathew relative and Dr. Thomas Sheridan, who reported that, stunned by his view of the castle, Swift exclaimed, "What in the name of God can be the use of such a vast building?" Although he proposed to leave immediately, the testy genius was welcomed by Thomas Mathew and agreed to stay, provided he could keep to his apartment rather than mingle with the throng of guests. Swift did so for four days, until, hearing of the good cheer enjoyed by the others, he joined them. Sheridan subsequently wrote that Swift extended his visit to Thomastown Castle for four months.

As I went on my way, I marveled that Thomas Mathew, the prodigious host, was still a rich man when he died. As I walked the short distance to Golden, I wondered, too, what had led to the ruination I'd seen at Thomastown.

THE VILLAGE OF Golden straddles the river Suir, and on a little island in the middle is a shattered round keep, all that survives of a castle that had guarded the ford here. At the base is a bronze bust of Thomas MacDonagh, poet and scholar, one of the leaders of the Easter Rising and a signer of the Proclamation of the Irish Republic in 1916, who was executed for his role. As I read the inscription, I wondered if I would ever see in Northern Ireland such an evenhanded acknowledgment of the multiple heritage that has enriched Ireland:

PROUDLY REMEMBER

THOMAS MACDONAGH

TIPPERARY MAN

COMMANDED JACOB'S GARRISON, EASTER RISING

DIED LIKE A PRINCE 3RD MAY 1916.

AS YOU PASS BY TAKE HEART FROM THE NOBILITY

AND SACRIFICE OF MEN DIFFERING IN RACIAL ORIGINS

WHO GALLANTLY TENDED THE FLAME OF IRISH FREEDOM

DOWN THE AGES IN THIS COUNTRYSIDE

CHERISH NOT LEAST NORMAN FORBEARS WHO

RAISED THIS CASTLE 700 GOLDEN YEARS AGO.

I picnicked at the upstream point of the little island in the middle of the Suir, watching enviously as two anglers were casting close by. Perhaps I was as hopeful as they that a noble salmon would take a fly and a great contest would begin. But despite the haze, the day was bright, very warm, with barely a breeze. Not ideal. I had spent days fruitlessly flogging the waters for the king of fish, so I was not disappointed, but replete, when I hoisted my pack and struck out for Cashel, a place that has drawn me like a magnet time and again.

Cashel of the Kings

IT WAS RATHER A SHAME THAT, COMING FROM GOLDEN, I SHOULD be approaching Cashel from the southwest. For the approaches from the northeast (by the main Dublin-Cork road), north, or northwest afford the most superb views of the Rock of Cashel looming above the great plain of Tipperary, the Golden Vale. The Rock is a limestone outcropping some two hundred feet high, crowned with a round tower, a splendid and intact Romanesque church, the imposing shell of a fifteenth- to sixteenth-century cathedral, an ecclesiastical residential hall, and vestiges of fortifications. As I approached, the westering sun bathed the Rock and its monuments in an amber glow. It appeared as wonderful as an illustration in a medieval book of hours.

Nearing the Rock, I passed Hoare Abbey, rooks wheeling all about the massive ruin. The Benedictines were the first to found a monastery here. However, there is a story that they were expelled in 1272 by Archbishop MacCarvill, who installed the Cistercians in their place because he had dreamt that the Benedictines planned to behead him.

Although I had visited Cashel a number of times, I was eager to ascend the Rock again. The first time, decades ago, one was free to enter and wander about the ruins on the Rock at will. Today, Dúchas administers the site, charges a modest admission, and with funding from the European Union, has effected major preservation work. The entry would be closed well before sunset. I hurried up the busy main street—the principal Dublin-Cork road still goes through the town—and made for the Rock, passing the skeleton of the medieval friary church of St. Dominic.

PERHAPS NO PLACE in Ireland is so redolent of a past at once sanguinary and sacred as the Rock of Cashel. Legend has it that Saint Patrick came here to convert King Aengus. From as early as the fourth or fifth century, the Eóganachta—people claiming descent from the eponymous Eógan Mór—had established a fortress and their seat here. Until the tenth century the kings of Cashel were effectively kings of Munster. Then a rival dynasty, the Dál Cais, laid claim to the kingdom of Cashel. In 976, Brian Boru succeeded his murdered brother, Mathgamain, as King of Cashel, and by 1002 had made himself High King of Ireland. When Muircheartach O'Brien, King of Munster, became High King of Ireland, in 1101, he gave the Rock to the Church and convened a synod here. Cashel was soon made an archepiscopal see, and Cormac MacCarthy, King of Desmond, erected between 1127 and 1134 the little cathedral that remains, astoundingly intact, a masterpiece of the Irish Romanesque.

A synod of greater significance was summoned at Cashel in 1171 by Henry II of England, who had earlier proposed to Pope Adrian IV that he oversee the reform of the Church in Ireland. Having landed and obtained the fealty of the Irish chiefs (save for High King Rúairí O'Conor and the Uí Neill of Ulster), Henry intended that the synod should establish conformity in organization between the Church in Ireland and that in England and confirm his suzerainty in Ireland. Cashel's ecclesiastical importance grew. Successive cathedrals were built on the Rock, and in 1495, Garrett Mór Fitzgerald, Earl of Kildare, incinerated the cathedral, believing—as he told England's King Henry VII—that the archbishop was trapped within. Nor was that the last of the terrible deeds done here. In 1647, Murrough "the Burner" O'Brien, a renegade and opportunist who twice switched allegiance and religion—led a parliamentary force that scaled the massif, fired the cathedral again, and slaughtered some three thousand of the sheltering townspeople and garrison.

———

WITH LITTLE TIME remaining before it closed, I arrived at the entrance to the complex on the Rock of Cashel, in the building called the Hall of the Vicars Choral. Then I wandered about the roofless cathedral, admiring the weeping mourners carved on sarcophagi and the effigies and inscriptions on wall tombs of nobles and prelates. On the south side of the choir I stood bemused by that of Miler McGrath, the infamous turncoat who was consecrated by Pope (afterward Saint) Pius V as Bishop of Down and Connor in 1567. In 1569, he conformed to the Protestant church and was made Bishop of Clogher by Queen Elizabeth. He became the Protestant Archbishop of Cashel in 1571, went on to acquire several other bishoprics, and by the time he was entombed here, about 1622, beside his bishoprics, Miler McGrath had obtained some seventy-seven other benefices, doubtless becoming the most astonishing pluralist in ecclesiastical history.

YEARS BEFORE, I had been able to explore the fortified tower of the archbishop's palace, which remains at the west end of the nave, to prowl through passageways in the cathedral walls, and to climb the great central tower that rises above the cathedral transept, from which one sees an extraordinary panorama of Tipperary. But those areas were now closed off. Still, I could explore Cormac's Chapel, as the little cathedral is usually known. Restorers were working there, preserving the painted decorations of twelfth-century artisans. Their work in the chancel had been completed; from bits scattered like confetti, one could envisage how richly colored the whole interior had been. Subtly lighted, human and animal heads, benign or fearsome, look down from the arches of the vaulted ceiling. I was tickled by the carving in the tympanum of the north portal: a small centaur aiming his arrow at a huge, snarling lion. Pausing by the gaping, fractured sarcophagus in the nave, I marveled at the carved sinuous, complex Celtic design which covers it.

I walked around to look at the well-preserved round tower, so prominent in the best views of the Rock. Authorities surmise that the ninety-two-foot-high structure was erected before Cormac's Chapel and was possibly associated with an earlier church on the site.

Then I went back to the Hall of the Vicars Choral, where I'd entered. What I had first seen as roofless walls had been restored to replicate the structure's supposed state as a medieval hostel. Roofed, it has glazed windows; beams rest on carved corbels with painted human heads; there is a small refectory, with pots swinging on fireplace cranes. The hall struck me as somewhat Disneyesque, unlike the rest of the stark ruins on the Rock, where the despoilation of the centuries reeks of history. There will always be a tension in archaeological restoration, between those who wish not only to preserve but to re-create some semblance of the function and perhaps the ambience of an ancient structure as it may well have been and those who would do no more than prevent further deterioration of the remains on a site, preserving them as they found them.

The main chamber in the hall has become a nicely illuminated museum. At one end is the so-called Cross of St. Patrick, which stood for centuries outside on the Rock, where there is now a copy in its place. On one face of the much-weathered original is a crucifixion; on the reverse, the figure of a bishop. In the hall there is a vitrine which contains a collection of weapons found on the site, including Bronze Age swords and Viking battle-axes. What most held my eye was a *sheila-na-gig* mounted on a wall. This is a grotesque carved stone figure of a woman with pudenda displayed. Such a figure was often a feature of early-Irish buildings. Perhaps a fertility token or guardian against malign spirits, the meaning and purpose of a *sheila-na-gig* is not known but is suggestive of pagan origin. This one was particularly interesting to me, for I was on the Rock of Cashel when it was discovered, or rediscovered, many years before.

Before leaving, I stepped outside for a final look over the town nestled beneath the Rock and the vast landscape about it. A wind had sprung up and whistled through the cavernous cathedral. I imagined I could hear the clanging of swords and the crackling of flames.

SEVERAL TIMES IN the past, when visiting Cashel, I'd stayed at the former archbishop's palace, a beautiful building of rose-red brick, built in the first decades of the eighteenth century, which has long been a notable country hotel. Its large walled garden has a private way leading up to the Rock of Cashel, and a number of its rooms look on fine views of the Rock, which is illuminated at night. However, on this long journey, it was necessary to husband my resources, and as I intended to dine well here for several evenings, I had settled on other accommodations and was fortunate in my choice.

Indaville, the late-Georgian home of the Murphy family, which they operate as a B&B, is tucked away behind a bend at one end of the main street of Cashel, set back in its own little park. As I walked up the drive, I watched sheep butting heads in the thick grass at one side of the house. Jean Murphy, a sunny young woman, and her big friendly dog welcomed me. I was shown to a capacious downstairs bedroom appointed with good antiques.

AFTER A BIT of shut-eye, I walked the little way to the Cashel Palace Hotel, to have dinner in its restaurant, the Bishop's Buttery. It was good but not recordable. Then I stepped across the passageway to the hotel's intimate Guinness Bar. I had hoped to find Dennis Heffernan—who has long presided over the bar and with whom I have enjoyed several long colloquies, ranging from local matters to the films of John Ford—but it was his evening off. A pleasant young man named John was keeping bar, and as we began to speak of Dennis's keen interest in films, John revealed his own strong opinions—never hard to discover in an Irish pub—about recent Irish films. I quickly learned that he was not greatly taken with *The Crying Game,* directed by Neil Jordan, but admired the same director's *Butcher Boy.* As we were deep in cinematic discourse, the large figure of a priest materialized on the seat beside me, and he ordered a Guinness.

It quickly became apparent that the new arrival, like me, had expected to find the redoubtable Dennis pronouncing from his pulpit. Introductions were exchanged, and I learned that Father Richard Fitzgerald was a retired priest from Clonmel, Tipperary's county seat. He was a big, square-jawed man with a gray thatch and a recurrent chuckle. I found him an engaging ironist in attitude. As Laurence Sterne, the seminal author of *Tristram Shandy,* had been born in Clonmel, I ventured to remark upon it. Possibly the overture was ill-advised, since I knew that Dr. Johnson and other savants had regarded Sterne's witty and worldly work as morally dubious. Father Richard, however, had little to say of either novel or Sterne, save that he was the son of an English soldier, as if, perhaps, that accounted for all. He segued to Jane Austen's *Emma,* which he regarded as so much piffle. I observed that in most of her work the spinster author wrote of young women's efforts to acquire husbands. This seemed to evoke some mirth in Father Richard.

The affable priest veered off onto the then current tragedies in Zimbabwe, where black squatters—who were, of course, the indigenous people—were occupying the farms of longtime white settlers. We spoke about the murder of some of the white settlers, who must always have been conscious that they were farming the land from which blacks had been dispossessed. This led to ruminations about colonialism. The matter lies like truffles beneath the roots of so much woe in Ireland.

When John the barman paused by us, Father Richard asked him, "Is it next week that Dennis is to be married?"

I made no note of John's answer, but I asked, "Is it Dennis's first wedding?"

"Oh, no, it's his fifth," I understood Father Richard to say.

"His fifth!" I exclaimed. "How did he ever find time to see all those films of John Ford?"

"If you need a thing done, ask a busy man," said the padre, finishing his glass and sloping off with a cheery good-night.

Noble Steeds, Buried Treasure

THE GREAT PLAIN OF TIPPERARY IS PERFECT FOR THE BREEDING and training of racehorses. Even in a country that has been fattening from high-tech industries, the breeding of bloodstock and the entire racing industry is still a significant factor in the nation's economy. Moreover, it is a vivid thread in the fabric of Irish life. The Republic supports the Irish National Stud, where individual owners may mate their horses with Irish champions, and such internationally famous figures as the Aga Khan maintain their own stud farms. The Irish of every stripe have a love for the superb animals bred to race over the country's green turf and to challenge its stone walls and fences on the hunting field or racecourse. There are some twenty-seven tracks in Ireland, North and South, and racing goes on throughout the year, flat racing controlled by the Turf Club, and racing over hurdles supervised by the Irish National Hunt Steeplechase Committee.

Here the sport of kings is wonderfully egalitarian. The antiquary and author Desmond FitzGerald, Knight of Glin, has written, "It should be noted that the horse was the main bond with the plain people of Ireland [and the landholding, largely Anglo-Irish, aristocracy and gentry] and crossed all social and religious boundaries." Stop by the parade ring of any course where jockeys are receiving last words from trainers and owners before mounting, and you will see tweedy peers exchanging wisdom with weatherbeaten farmers, ardent punters studying both the parading horses and their racing forms, and young ladies in knockout hats making themselves noticeable.

So far on this trek, I'd missed going to the races. Although I'd got a card from the Tourist Board listing all the racing fixtures, their venues and dates, whenever I came near a place with a track, no races were scheduled. There is, however, a whole equine world behind the spectacle we enjoy at the racetrack, just as there is behind the magical productions we see on stage or screen. There are the owners who will pay a king's ransom for a yearling on whose bloodlines they are betting; some will spend immense sums for the privilege of having a mare they own covered by a stallion which has been a great champion. (So enormous is the cost of acquiring such a champion to stand at stud that most such stallions are purchased by a syndicate. There are, too, champion fillies which are acquired to become brood mares.) There are the veterinarians who examine and treat horses and the experts who manage the breeding. There are the trainers whose experience and horse sense are essential to success. He or she is the expert on whom the owner relies not only to ensure the fitness and preparation of the horse but to recommend the track and race in which the horse should run and to select the jockey to ride that race. The trainer supervises a retinue of exercise boys and girls, hot riders, and grooms to care for the valuable and sometimes temperamental animals on which so much depends. Finally, the racing industry includes the many through whose hands passes much money: the bettors and bookies, the tote operators, track managers, and jockeys' agents, as well as the publishers of racing forms and bloodstock books and the purveyors of equipment, feed, and medicine.

At the heart of this industry are the horses, and their breeders and trainers; and some of Ireland's most important stud farms and training stables are situated on the rich turf of Tipperary. For long the most famous has been that of Vincent O'Brien, near Fethard. O'Brien-trained horses have triumphed on many of the world's courses and in many of the most famous races. O'Brien has won the Prix de l'Arc de Triomphe at France's Longchamp multiple times, won the Grand National at England's Aintree, and captured the Irish Sweep on The Curragh of Kildare. I didn't know Vincent O'Brien and had been told that he was largely retired. However, Michael Morris, a respected trainer and second (and twin) son of my friends the late Lord Killanin and Lady Killanin, also had his establishment just outside Fethard, not far from Cashel.

EVERARDSGRANGE, the training establishment of Michael Morris, is just north of Fethard. His pretty stone house, more than two hundred years old, is in a courtyard formed of well-kept stables, in which some fifty horses were in training under his knowing eye. Michael, rusty-haired and wiry, showed me into the house, where he was living a solo life, being separated from his wife. (Their two sons were students at Glenstal Abbey, past which I'd walked.) He made some coffee and settled us at the kitchen table to talk. I was aware that like many trainers, Michael (Mick to his family and Mouse to the racing fraternity) had been a jockey himself. Steeplechase was his passion, and he had ridden and won on many tracks; he had taken the jumps five times at Aintree, the most daunting of steeplechase courses. First as a gentleman rider, then as a professional, Michael Morris had important victories before training and saddling winners for others. At Cheltenham, in England, he had won the National Hunt Chase and twice won the Queen Mother Champion Chase.

I asked him why he had decided to become a trainer.

Michael laughed. "I broke a leg riding at Camden, South Carolina," he said. "That laid me up for nine months. Then, riding again, I broke an arm at Navan. Next I broke a hip. Then another hip." He paused. "It's expected that one of every twelve rides for a jockey will be a fall."

Having had only one sudden departure from a horse in Ireland, with tedious consequences, I could appreciate Michael's reasoning.

Michael said, "Edward O'Grady, for whom I'd ridden, sent me a couple of horses in 1979, and I was a trainer."

One might say that Michael Morris has won his spurs while out of the saddle, for he has trained some notable horses. Buck House won the Waterford Crystal Supreme Novice Hurdle at Cheltenham and three years later was victorious in the Queen Mother Champion Chase, before prematurely and tragically succumbing to colic. At Cheltenham again, with Trapper John, Michael won the Waterford Crystal Supreme Novice Cup for his American owner, Mrs. Jill Fanning.

I was curious to know whether racing—the whole bloodstock industry—had changed since Michael had first saddled a horse, and asked.

"It's much more competitive," said Michael. "There are more people in the game today. There are huge studs, for example. There's more money involved."

"You chose the hurdles over flat racing as rider and trainer," I said, "and you've concentrated on training jumpers. Are there significant differences between the horses themselves and in training them?"

"Some horses are more natural jumpers, but their racing careers start later and end later," said Michael. "Flat racers win major races on the great courses at three years old. We may start training jumpers at three years old; they start racing at four and can go on racing until they are ten or twelve. Let's have a look at the ground we train on."

First we drove along schooling fences on fairly level ground; then we went over Michael's twelve-furlong (a furlong being one-eighth mile) all-weather gallops, which rise uphill gradually. "Going uphill is a great strengthener," he pointed out. Then we visited the stables. Prize animals are cosseted; I savored the sweet smell of hay and noticed the deep straw bedding. Some skittish horses are soothed by the companionship of a pony or a goat in their big box stalls.

Michael asked a couple of the grooms to lead several of the steeds out and walk them in the stable yard for me to see. One impressive horse, with the carriage of royalty, was Foxchapel King, a big bay gelding, seven years old, standing sixteen hands, two inches high, and then the winner of nine races. He was owned by Sir Anthony O'Reilly, emeritus chairman of the Heinz Company and proprietor of the *Irish Independent* newspaper. Foxchapel King had a major race coming up in five days, the Castlemartin Stud at Punchestown, in Kildare. (On that day, I would stop in a pub to watch the race on TV; at the penultimate jump of the two-mile chase, with Foxchapel King leading, I thought I saw a slight misstep, and he came in second by a head. As I write, he has just won the Munster Stakes, at Limerick, for a purse of I£50,000.)

As I was leaving Everardsgrange, Michael offered a tip: "Stop in at McCarthy's in Fethard. A horseman's pub."

McCarthy's proved to be an oasis on the rather dreary main street of a town that once was walled and has the remains of several fortified tower houses and an Augustinian friary. How right Mouse Morris was about McCarthy's pub. Most of the clientele, largely male, appeared to be under five feet, seven inches, browned and toughened, as is often the case with men who spend much of their lives outdoors in the saddle, having dirt and mud kicked in their faces. McCarthy's is a proper old country pub, smoke stained, with a venerable iron stove, much racing memorabilia and the paper money of many nations on the walls. They draw a satisfying pint at McCarthy's. I enjoyed mine as I huddled with the brethren of the turf around the telly while we watched a race at an English course. Spanish Main, the favorite, ran brilliantly, the horse-wise patrons agreed, his jockey bringing him from behind on the outside to win.

BACK IN CASHEL, I went to dine at Chez Hans. When Hans-Peter Matthiä established his restaurant some thirty-five years ago, it was one of the rare restaurants in Ireland to serve Continental cuisine. The chef-propriétaire had taken a former Wesleyan chapel and given it a German baronial ambience. One is given the menu in the intimate wood-paneled bar, which presumably was the vestry. Thereafter, in the high-vaulted nave, eclectically decorated with paintings and porcelains, I dined on quennelles of brill, stuffed quail in puff pastry, and a profusion of potatoes and vegetables. Hans-Peter Matthiä is no subscriber to Ludwig Mies van der Rohe's axiom that "less is more." I could not contemplate the dessert menu but nibbled on a lemon truffle from the bonbons served with coffee.

IT SEEMED UNTHINKABLE to leave Cashel without checking for late intelligence of the town and enjoying a stirrup cup with Dennis Heffernan at the Guinness Bar of the Cashel Palace. We were beginning to resume our exchanges about the films of John Ford, when the evening was enlivened by three stylish and congenial arrivals. Dennis introduced Michael Webb, his brother Timothy, and Timothy's blond ladyfriend. Over a glass, I learned that Michael lived nearby and that Timothy, who lives in Cairo, is president of Abercrombie & Kent, Africa, the renowned travel agents. Dennis added that Michael discovered the Derrynaflan chalice, a treasure of Ireland's National Museum, which I had viewed in Dublin among the museum's superb collection of early-Irish masterpieces wrought of precious metals and jewels. Of course, I wanted to hear the story of how he'd found it, twenty years before.

"It was on February seventeenth, nineteen-eighty," began Michael. "I had given my sixteen-year-old son, Mike, a metal detector for Christmas, and we were out on a walk, over a friend's bog, trying it out. We got a strong signal and started to dig with a trowel. About two feet down, we found the chalice. We took it home and I showed it to an archaeologist friend."

Thus began a long process to establish ownership, value, and the eventual disposition of the chalice. "Soon the National Museum took over at the site," said Michael. "They found some fragments belonging to the chalice and a paten." He recalled that when he visited the National Museum soon after, "the director said, 'We'll see that you are taken care of.' " Michael added that when the door closed behind him, he could hear whoops of exultation. Small wonder the curators were thrilled; the museum had in hand an extraordinarily rare masterpiece of early Irish art.

Years of litigation followed for Michael Webb, to establish compensation for a "priceless object." He told me that, in fact, Sotheby's valued the chalice at somewhere between £6,000,000 and £10,000,000. Charles Haughey, *Taoiseach* at the time, interested himself in the matter, insisting that the chalice belong to the nation. As the litigation drew toward a settlement, Webb's lawyers sued the government for larger fees. In the end, Michael Webb and his son received I£50,000 and the two owners of the property on which the treasure was buried each received I£25,000.

Why such a masterpiece of craftsmanship should have been hidden in a lonely Tipperary bog, and whence it came, we shall almost certainly never know. Perhaps monks hid it from Viking pillagers who attacked nearby Cashel, or later priests intended to preserve it from despoliation by Cromwell's soldiery, who stabled horses in some Catholic churches and torched others. Doubtless, other treasures remain concealed beneath the turf of Ireland. From time to time, such wonders surface.

Great Fortress, Winner's Pub, Wondrous Cavern

·❧·

I WAS SOMEWHAT REGRETFUL, LEAVING CASHEL, FOR QUITE ASIDE from its patina of history, which I find affecting, I've known good times here. The main street always seems busy and inviting. There are a number of good pubs: I favor Pat Fox's, and one can eat well at Hannigan's. When I first came here with my family, what was then called Quirke's Castle and latterly Kearney's Castle, a medieval tower house on the main street, was a ruin; it has now been incorporated into a small hotel. Our children acquired an interesting chess set here: Vikings versus monks. I must have turned up in Cashel on several "daffodil days," for in a little wooden boat on a chest of drawers at home are several silk daffodils pressed on me by young girls selling them in aid of cancer research.

As I was leaving Indaville, Jean Murphy made me feel as if I were a Sunday-afternoon stroller in the park when she told me that she was about to leave home on a solo journey, backpacking about Brazil. A veteran walker in Ireland, she directed me to a little-trafficked route to Cahir.

The first six miles or so were through flat, lightly settled land, with some small farms and homes. Then I was obliged to jink onto a section of the N8. No fun. Big lorries and would-be Formula 1 racers rocked me with their slipstreams as I tried to hug the verge. After a couple of miles, I veered onto a direct road into Cahir, which the national highway bypasses.

The town of Cahir grew around a fortress that had existed from very early times on an island in the River Suir. In 1375, James Butler, 3rd Earl of Ormond, was granted the barony of Cahir. He had a natural son by Katherine, daughter of the Earl of Desmond, a Fitzgerald, uniting two of Ireland's most powerful families. From their union sprang a cadet branch of the Butlers, who remained in possession of Cahir Castle until the death of Lieutenant Colonel Richard Butler Charteris, at age ninety-four, in 1961. Three years later it was acquired by the state and is administered by Dúchas. Largely constructed in the fifteenth and sixteenth centuries, though much restored in the nineteenth century, the castle I eagerly visited remains the largest, best-preserved medieval fortress in Ireland.

Cahir Castle is every child's storybook image: battlements of tawny stone rise from a slight rocky elevation above the river. A massive gatehouse and stout towers guard the four corners of the inner ward, and high crenellated walls with round towers at the angles enclose the outer ward. A barbican shields the entrance. I clambered happily about the castle, peering everywhere, down a murder hole over an entrance to the northwest tower; inspecting the great hall and the very early gatehouse with its domestic apartments; studying the portcullis, one of the very few in Ireland that is operable; and looking out of gun loops.

In a letter (variously attributed to Archbishop Miler McGrath and the secretary to the Earl of Essex) written at the time of the extensive campaigns launched by Elizabeth I, the author refers to Cahir Castle as "the only famous castle in Ireland which is thought to be impregnable and is the bulwark of Munster and a safe retreat for all the agents of Spain and Rome." (The Butlers of Cahir had remained steadfastly Catholic.) Its impregnability was soon tested. Robert Devereux, Earl of Essex and Elizabeth's favorite, was dispatched to Ireland with an army of up to eighteen thousand men, with the mission of chastising and subduing the Great Hugh O'Neill, Earl of Tyrone. However, instead of proceeding north to Ulster to attack that rebellious chieftain, Essex marched south. In late May 1599, with several thousand foot soldiers, two hundred cavalry, and two big guns, he advanced on Cahir Castle and demanded its surrender. James Galda Butler, younger brother of Lord Caher, commanding the garrison, refused. After three days a wall was breached and the castle taken. (A cannonball from the siege remains lodged in the northeast tower.) Eighty of the defenders were slain, but James Galda Butler escaped with some followers by swimming the river. Despite this modest victory, Essex was recalled in disgrace from his ineffective campaign.

Cahir Castle was attacked twice more. In 1647, Murrough "the Burner" O'Brien, Earl of Inchiquin, obtained the surrender of Cahir Castle for the parliamentarians in a matter of a few hours. After it subsequently reverted to Catholic, confederate hands, on February 24, 1650, Oliver Cromwell approached with his army and dispatched a letter to George Mathews, half brother of the Earl of Ormond and warden of the castle (Piers Butler, 4th Baron Caher, being a minor):

> Sir, Having brought the army and my cannon
> near this place, according to my usual manner
> in summoning places, I thought fit to offer you
> terms honourable to soldiers: that you may
> march away with your baggage, arms, and colours,
> free from injuries or violence. But if I be,
> notwithstanding, necessitated to bend my cannon
> upon you, you must expect the extremity usual
> in such cases. To avoid blood, this is offered to
> you by
>
> Your servant, Oliver Cromwell

Prudence prevailed over principle. Knowing that otherwise not one would escape slaughter, Mathews and the garrison capitulated.

I STAYED AT Cahir House Hotel, the nicely modernized eighteenth-century mansion on the town's square, which had been the residence of the Butlers from the late 1770s until the 1850s. Then the 2nd Earl of Glengall, Richard Butler, was declared bankrupt, having depleted his resources on improvement of his estates, including restoration of the castle, and on measures for the relief of the poor during the Great Famine. Cahir House, with much of the estate, had to be sold.

Fortunately, the 2nd, and last, Earl of Glengall had married an English heiress, and at auction in 1853, trustees for the Countess of Glengall bought back much of the estate. Following the marriage, in 1858, of Lord and Lady Glengall's elder daughter, Lady Margaret, to Lieutenant Colonel Richard

Charteris, second son of the Earl of Weymss and March, the couple reacquired the town, including Cahir House, and much of the Butler estates. By that time, Cahir Park House, at the southwest edge of town, had become the family seat.

Before his bankruptcy, Lord Glengall was a notably improving landlord who, before renewing or granting leases, required conformance to his architectural standards. Cahir boasts a number of good buildings and interesting monuments. On the square, which is usually jammed with parked cars, in front of the eighteenth-century Market House, which has been town hall, district courthouse, and town library, is a fine bronze sculpture by Mary Crooms Carroll of Edmund Keating Hyland playing the Uilleann pipes. Hyland (1780–1845) was a famous piper and notable composer, left blind by smallpox in his teens, like Turlough O'Carolan. In the middle of the square is a fountain surmounted by a curious sort of a tabernacle. Erected by Lady Margaret Butler-Charteris as a memorial to her husband, it marks the Cahir estate's then innovative construction of a town water supply, piped several miles from the Galty Mountains.

The monument in Cahir that I found most arresting is the War Memorial, on Castle Street, a rare sight in the Republic of Ireland. For it was dedicated to the eighty-six officers and men of Cahir and the district who fell in the Great War of 1914–1918 while serving in the British Army or the Royal Navy. On it are graven the names of men who died as soldiers or as sailors in such British regiments as the Irish Guards, The Royal Dublin Fusiliers, and the Punjabis of the Indian Army. I looked at the memorial for a long time, seeming to hear the faint strains of "It's a Long Way to Tipperary."

From 1811 to 1922, what came to be called Victoria Barracks sprawled about a mile south of the town, at Kilcommon. It was the principal British cavalry barracks in Tipperary and contributed greatly to the economic and social life of Cahir and the region. A garrison of regular soldiers meant families who traded in the town and the prosperity of shopkeepers who served them. There were parades and reviews, bands playing, and gala balls at which officers in dress uniform waltzed with county ladies. It is reported that in 1893, the square in Cahir would have been destroyed by fire had it not been for the action of the 10th Hussars. Evacuated by the British after the Irish Free State was created, the extensive barracks were burned by antitreaty forces in the Civil War of 1922–1923, to prevent their use by the Free State army. Hardly a trace remains.

HAVING LEARNED THAT an American had won a pub in Cahir in a contest sponsored by Guinness, I was keen to speak with him. Owning a pub in Ireland seemed a dandy idea, though I knew better. Still, for fun, some years earlier I'd fired off an entry in the contest, which requires the contestant to extoll Guinness stout in a limited number of words. I wrote, "Guinness is Ireland in a glass." For my effort, I received a spoon for making Irish coffee—which has nothing to do with Guinness—and a six-pack of Guinness "draught" in cans. Fair enough, but I wanted to know about the pub and the winner.

The pub, called J. Morrissey, a neat, cream-colored building with window frames of robin's-egg blue, is in a prime location, diagonally across the street from the castle. There was an American flag on the facade and the words MUSICIANS WELCOME. The lucky publican, Douglas Knight, was thirty-five years old, tall, fair, and good-looking, with a smile that is money in the bank. He became the proprietor of J. Morrissey's in 1997.

We sat down in the rear room of the pub, which is nicely fitted out with light wood and walls free of ye olde fakery but is no mod cocktail lounge. Drinks were on the house. I had a Guinness, Douglas had a Coke, and I asked him how he came to be a publican in Cahir.

"It was Suzanne's idea, entering the contest," Douglas said, referring to his wife. "It seemed like a once-in-a-lifetime opportunity to live in a foreign country." He told me that Minneapolis had been home and that he was a professional musician, a guitarist.

I was still curious about his winning the contest I'd flunked and wanted to know about the path to Cahir and Morrissey's pub.

"Well, I was selected as one of ten finalists, and Suzanne and I were brought here for a final competition," said Douglas. "We had to do all sorts of things . . ."

"Such as?"

"We had to play darts and, well, we came out the winners."

I asked if he'd found it daunting, taking over a pub, and what life was like.

"The previous owner stayed on for several weeks, to break me in. It's worked out," he said. "We live on the two floors above the pub, and we like Cahir. It's a great town, about three thousand to thirty-five hundred people. In a place like this, you get to know everybody. And it's safe."

"And actually managing this place?" I asked. "How is that going?"

"It's hard work. That goes with the territory. It's like mountain climbing; you can't say it's too steep, it's too windy."

I mentioned the sign out front, welcoming musicians.

"Well, the Irish like music, and it brings people in," said Douglas. "I often play on Sunday afternoons."

Perhaps as musician and pub owner, Douglas is not quite as laid-back as he came across this afternoon. I would have liked to talk with his wife, but Suzanne was away. He's proud of having worked hard to fit in and talked about having sponsored an international *pétanque* tournament. (*Pétanque,* called *bocce* in Italy, is the French version of bowls, played with small metal balls.) "We held it in the park on the island, behind the castle," he said. "And Ireland won!"

As we parted, Douglas said, "It's been very rewarding—not in money terms. We didn't come here to make money. We came for the adventure. And we sure got it." (Some months later, I learned that the Knights had sold the pub.)

I HEADED FOR Mitchelstown, in County Cork, by way of Burncourt and the Mitchelstown Caves. Burncourt is the ruin of a great fortified house built in 1641 by Sir Richard Everard, of an old Anglo-Norman family. David Sweetman, chief archaeologist of Dúchas, has called it "one of the most impressive fortified houses in Ireland with its 26 gables and numerous chimney stacks." The architecture of Burncourt represents a transitional period in Irish life, when chiefs and nobles felt less need to live in a fortress but still required that a more gracious domestic dwelling have defensive features, in case of attack. On this mild, gray day the ghostly pile evoked horrific times. David Sweetman writes that Sir Richard Everard (a Catholic and member of the Confederate Council of Kilkenny, loyal to the King of England and opposed to the parliamentarians) burned his fortified mansion "to prevent Cromwell from seizing it." Sweetman's predecessor as the great scholar of Irish castles, Harold G. Leask, says that Lady

Everard, Burncourt's chatelaine, "set it on fire at the approach of the Cromwellian army." Lord Killanin and Michael Duignan write that "Sir Richard . . . was one of those hanged by Ireton when Limerick capitulated in 1651 [during the Cromwellian campaign]; his great house had been captured and burned by Cromwell the year before." Irish history *is* confusing. With its shattered gables, missing chimneys, and dark, gaping windows, Burncourt was the eeriest ruin I had seen on this journey.

Two miles on, I came to the Mitchelstown Caves, at a place called Coolagarranroe, which was once a part of the immense estate of the Kings, Earls of Kingston, whose seat was at Mitchelstown. (They were a rare lot, even among a rash of eccentric eighteenth-century Anglo-Irish peers. The 2nd Earl was supposed to have conceived the practice of pitch-capping rebels during the revolution of 1798, a practice in which the unfortunate wretch's head was covered with tar, then set afire. This Lord Kingston was perhaps more notorious for having murdered his half brother, who had abducted the earl's teenage daughter, then being acquitted by his peers in Parliament. The 3rd Earl of Kingston built an enormous mansion, called Mitchelstown Castle, greatly improved his town, and went mad. His son, Viscount Kingsborough, spent his life writing a nine-volume work, unfinished at his death, titled *The Antiquities of Mexico,* without ever visiting the country; Lord Kingsborough was persuaded that the Jews had colonized America before the arrival of Columbus and intended that his great work would provide the evidence for his thesis.)

The Mitchelstown Caves include two systems. One is the so-called Desmond's Cave, where Gerald Fitzgerald, 14th Earl of Desmond, fleeing Elizabethan pursuers, sought refuge, only to be betrayed by another Fitzgerald, the White Knight, and ultimately hunted down and slain, in 1583. Desmond's Cave is accessible only to spelunkers with ropes and ladders. The other is the New Cave, discovered in 1833. After the bankruptcy of the extravagant Earls of Kingston, in 1860, the property was acquired, in 1875, by Timothy Mulcahy. His descendants included ardent republicans in the War of Independence, during which the cave was a hiding place for insurgents. The Mulcahys' original house here was blown up in the conflict. Subsequently, through intermarriage, a family named English became the proprietors.

At the entrance to the New Cave, a little way up the hillside, I joined a group of eight, including a Japanese couple and their four children. Our guide, Davinia Robinson, a music student at University College, Dublin, who led us downward into the labyrinth, told us that the interior of the cave remains at a constant temperature of fifty-four degrees Fahrenheit in all seasons. Over eons the action of rainwater, containing dissolved carbon dioxide and filtering through the limestone, reacted with it, eating it away, hollowing out the rock to shape the strange caverns we began to traverse. Some were named for persons associated with the cave, such as Coleman's Gallery, for J. C. Coleman, an Irish speleologist and explorer of the cave, and Mulcahy's Cavern, for the early proprietor. Others have acquired names suggested by their shape and scale and the fantastic formations to be seen in them. In the Cathedral there was one whose shape suggested the Madonna, and in the same chamber a spectacular formation deserved the name Organ Pipes. We were appropriately awed by a fantastic structure called the Tower of Babel, formed when depending stalactites fused with upthrusting stalagmites. The resulting column of variegated color is considered one of the most splendid in any European cave.

The Cathedral is an immense chamber, some 167 feet long by 107 feet wide and 60 feet high. Our guide pointed out some other marvels here, with such fanciful names as the Eagle's Wing and the Pillars of Hercules, and a single pillar aptly named Lot's Wife. I wasn't sure whether my Japanese companions knew about the pillar of salt, but all gaped silently. Indeed, the exceptionally well behaved children had been notably quiet throughout the excursion. I didn't know whether the skillful Davinia wanted to get a rise out of them or whether it was just a standard part of her act when she announced, "There's a remarkable echo to be heard here, if someone will shout." All the visitors stood mutely. A minute passed without a peep. Then I screamed, as loud as I could: *"Wow!"* The reverberation thundered back. Gasps, squeals from my companions. The kids looked at me as if I were demented. Very satisfying.

Still, I wasn't sorry when Davinia said we'd reached the end of the trail—the subterranean complex goes on; further passages have been navigated by spelunkers—and led us back, pointing out fossils embedded in the limestone walls several hundred million years ago, when the sea covered the Ireland that would emerge. Letting the others pass on a little way, I stood still, listening. There was no silence, only the soft *plink* of dripping water, the tic and toc of time. I thought of Tom Sawyer and Becky Thatcher, lost and desperate in McDougal's Cave (which also has a chamber called the Cathedral), and of the Earl of Desmond hiding for his life, of cavers in our time trapped in Stygian darkness. Glad as I was to have visited the Mitchelstown Caves, I was gladder to see the daylight.

AFTER A COUPLE of miles, the pleasant country road I'd been walking led me back to the N8, where giant lorries and big Mercedes sedans went breezing by. For about two miles, I traversed a tiny southeastern bulge of County Limerick, then, at Kilbeheny, I crossed into County Cork. It had been a long way through Tipperary.

PART FOUR

In the Rebel County

Charles Fort at Kinsale.

To Bowen's Court

MITCHELSTOWN SITS ASTRIDE THE DUBLIN-CORK HIGHWAY, THE N8, making something of a bottleneck. I put up at the Palm Grove B&B and supped adequately at the nearby Fir Grove Hotel. Next morning was warm and bright, and I thought I'd look around the town before making a slight zag in my generally southerly course.

There are two large squares in Mitchelstown, the long main street forming the east side of each. The northernmost, College Square, is named for Kingston College, a row of handsome low stone dwellings for indigent Protestant gentlefolk, built by the 3rd Earl of Kingston. The Lords Kingston are entombed in the chapel of the college. The entrance to their demesne is from the square. In 1823, the 3rd Earl, known as Big George, completed the hasty construction of Mitchelstown Castle on the site of the original castle of the White Knight and a later, eighteenth-century mansion, hoping to receive King George IV, who thought Lord Kingston a jolly fellow. Big George had commanded his architect to build a house bigger than any other in Ireland, and he was gratified: Mitchelstown Castle was a huge confection bristling with towers and battlements. However, like other Irish peers who had gone to great ends to be honored by a royal visit, the earl was to be disappointed. The king never viewed the ostentatious pile. (It was occupied by republican forces during the Civil

War, burned, and subsequently demolished.) The earl's building zeal also adorned Mitchelstown with impressive Protestant and Catholic churches; Big George could well afford to. The Kingston estates sprawled over one hundred thousand acres and produced an income of £40,000 a year, at a time when a laborer's weekly pay was less than a pound a week.

On the New Square, long the site of fairs and markets, a statue of John Mandeville and three crosses in the pavement commemorate the fatal shooting of three men by the police on the occasion of a protest meeting of the Irish National Land League. The league had been founded by Michael Davitt in 1879 to oppose oppressive landlordism and to press for peasant ownership of land; the president of the strongly nationalistic organization was Charles Stewart Parnell. The killings here led to the patriotic cry "Remember Mitchelstown!"

EIGHT MILES SLIGHTLY southwest of Mitchelstown, at Farahy, is the site of Bowen's Court, the home of the distinguished author Elizabeth Bowen, who died in 1973. In her many stories and in her novels—among them *The House in Paris, The Death of the Heart,* and *The Heat of the Day*—she writes of an upper-class world of apparent respectability. Beneath its surface she depicts the corruption of innocence, betrayal, and sexual tensions with psychological insight and literary flair. Another master, Eudora Welty, reviewing *The Collected Stories of Elizabeth Bowen,* observes that a number of Bowen stories treat "the dislocations arising from social and psychological disturbance." Welty adds,

> Her sensuous wisdom was sure and firm; she knew to its last reverberation what she saw, heard, touched, knew what the world wore in its flesh and the clothing it would put on, how near the world came, how close it stood: in every dramatic scene it is beside us at every moment. We see again how pervasive this knowledge was through her stories. . . . The collection richly confirms the extraordinary contribution Elizabeth Bowen has made to English letters.

Years ago, driving from Dublin to Cork, I'd gone a little out of my way to see Bowen's Court, only to learn that the house had been pulled down. This day, I determined to visit the site.

———

AFTER LEAVING MITCHELSTOWN, the road ran more or less straight and level through farmland. The smell of grass hung on the air, and bird-song cheered me. After something more than five miles, the road bridged the river Funshion, and ahead of me I saw the town of Kildorrery. It sits atop a hill, up which I toiled before continuing on through a neat place of shops, pubs, police station, and post office. My road then descended for over a mile to a cluster of houses and a bridge over the little river Farahy, which gave the hamlet its name.

No grand gate marked the old lower drive to what had been the finest house for miles around. The former gate lodge—on a tablet over the door was incised R.C.B. 1873—had been transformed into a neat modern house. I walked up a dirt track with water-filled potholes into what had been the demesne of Bowen's Court. A piece of decaying farm machinery and the rusted carcass of an auto lay beside what was now a farm track. I knew that the upper entrance to the demesne was some way up the road, be-tween Farahy and Mallow, and that the upper drive to the house had led through an avenue of beeches. Here the farm track led through good grassland to the desolate space where the house had stood.

IN HER MEMOIR and history, *Bowen's Court*, Elizabeth Bowen writes that the story of Bowen's Court begins with Lieutenant Colonel Henry Bowen, a Welshman, who came to Ireland as part of Oliver Cromwell's army. Cromwell arrived in Dublin on August 14, 1649. (Elizabeth Bowen notes that Colonel Bowen may have come in an advance force.) Like every officer and soldier in Cromwell's army—and the so-called Adventurers who financed Cromwell's Irish war—Bowen was to be paid by a grant of property seized from Irish nobles and gentry who were displaced to Con-nacht, west of the river Shannon.

Just how Colonel Bowen obtained his Irish property is a tale passed down orally through generations of Bowens in various tellings. In *Bowen's Court*, Elizabeth Bowen gives us the version she prefers: It seems that Henry Bowen was addicted to hawking at home in Wales and brought two hawks with him when he went soldiering in Ireland. One day, called to Cromwell's tent, Colonel Bowen entered with a hawk on his wrist. As the great commander addressed him, Bowen seemed to pay scant attention and toyed with his bird. Furious, Cromwell leapt to his feet,

> fell on Bowen and wrung the hawk's neck. Bowen left the tent in a huff. . . . Bowen's incalculability and fierce temper making him more and more a man to be reckoned with, efforts to square him were set on foot. At all events, Cromwell sent for Bowen, again, said, "You know how these things happen," and said he was sorry about the hawk. He then proposed to give Bowen as much Irish land as the second hawk could fly over before it came down, Bowen to choose the spot from which to let off the bird.

Colonel Bowen loosed his hawk near Farahy, not far from Mitchelstown. In the event he acquired more than eight hundred acres of land expropriated, as Elizabeth Bowen writes, from "Garret Cushin, papist. . . . In 1653 'the above mentioned Lands were sett forth to Lieut. Col. Henry Bowen in Satisfaction of his arrears.' " (Colonel Bowen thereupon took a hawk as the crest on his coat of arms, which displayed a stag.) The marriage of Henry Bowen II to the heiress Jane Cole brought additional property to the Bowen line. Henry Bowen III began building a grand house, into which, after some ten years, he and his large family moved, in 1776; it was named Bowen's Court. In 1930, as an only child, Elizabeth Bowen inherited Bowen's Court. She writes matter-of-factly about her forebears and her inheritance: "Having obtained their position through an injustice, they enjoyed that position through privilege. But while they wasted no breath in deprecating an injustice it would not have been to their interest to set right, they did not abuse their privilege on the whole."

AFTER HER BIRTH and early childhood here, Elizabeth Bowen spent much of her life in England, returning regularly to Bowen's Court for long stays. In 1923, she married Alan Cameron, an academic. Their marriage was childless and seemed not to limit her amorous life, which may have informed some of her worldly stories. Her husband died at Bowen's Court in 1952. Eventually Elizabeth Bowen could no longer maintain the house and property and was forced to sell. An Irish farmer was the buyer, and Bowen felt assured that the house would be preserved. All too soon, to her anguish, she learned otherwise. Today a depression marks the area that surrounded the three-story mansion faced in stone. The considerable woods beyond the house—whose lands rose up toward the Ballyhoura Mountains—have been felled for timber. Still, great trees rim the property, as they do so many Irish demesnes. The crowns of the surviving beeches here were festooned with the nests of myriad rooks. Hundreds of them circled, maneuvered, and demonstrated noisily—a great chorus I heard as a threnody for Bowen's Court.

Just beside the old entrance at Farahy, tucked into a notch of the Bowen demesne, is a small Church of Ireland church, dedicated to Saint Colman and rebuilt in 1721 on the foundation of a very old church. The churchyard is a bosky place, sheltered by trees and bushes, recalling Gray's Stoke Poges. Right beside the church is the long, turf-covered Cole Bowen vault, but Elizabeth Bowen was laid to rest beside her mother and father on a little rise facing the portal of the church. For me she had made her people live. As I stood there thinking about the generations of Bowens, a shower burst from the heavens. Not taking time to slip off my pack and extract my rain gear, I ducked into the doorway and sheltered for perhaps ten minutes, until the sun emerged between strands of cloud. It picked out a stone with the name ANNIE COLE BOWEN and the dates 1841–1913 inscribed. Beside it was another headstone, with the legend

ELLEN FITZGERALD, DIED 18TH JAN. 1877 AGED 68 YEARS.
FOR 46 YEARS THE FAITHFUL FRIEND AND NURSE OF
THE BOWEN'S COURT FAMILY. THIS TABLET IS ERECTED AS A
MEMORIAL OF THEIR GRATEFUL AFFECTION AND ESTEEM.

I murmured, ". . . and noblesse oblige."

It was time to move on. I made my way through the deep, wet grass, weaving among the gravestones of Protestants and Catholics alike, among them Roches, O'Regans, and Fitzgeralds. The old stones, with their beautifully cut lettering and often artful abbreviations, had more eloquence and dignity than the modern gravestones, often of polished black marble with gilt lettering and depictions of Christ or the Virgin Mary. An ecumenical churchyard. Peaceful. The choir, the rooks of Bowen's Court, grew fainter as I walked on.

An Inn to Remember and the Hag's Grave

·❧·

I TOOK A BYWAY THAT RUNS SOUTHEAST FROM FARAHY, FOLLOWING the river Farahy until its junction with the river Funshion, just above the village of Rockmills, where my road joined the busier Fermoy-Limerick road. From there on I was walking through the delightful valley of the Funshion, renowned as a trout stream. Coming round a bend, I startled a heifer nibbling at the grass along the bordering ditch. She bolted, trotting smartly ahead of me until she paused to savor another succulent patch. As I neared her, she took off again. And so it went.

I was alarmed lest some driver—and the Irish do not dawdle—careering around a blind bend collide with the heifer, with awful consequences. I remembered driving home late one night many years ago, in Wicklow, and having to brake desperately as I bore down on a horrendous scene: dead cow, smashed car, and lifeless driver. I had driven on and wakened the *garda* in Enniskerry, to take charge at the scene. When first I'd lived in Ireland, it was not uncommon to encounter horses or cattle loose on country roads. Fortunately, enforced laws and insurance strictures have virtually eliminated such hazards, although sheep are to be found grazing or dozing by the roads through the heather-covered mountains of the West. This afternoon the heifer and I continued our pas de deux while I kept hoping to come on a gate that I might herd her through. At last my companion found a gap in the ditch, with a rich pasture beyond, and nipped through it with a click of her dainty hooves.

Just coming to the village of Glanworth, I stopped to look about the shell of the Dominican friary founded by the powerful Roche family in 1475. Of the conventual buildings only the large church remains; a tall, roofless tower rises at the intersection of nave and chancel. A bit beyond is Glanworth's derelict nineteenth-century Church of Ireland building, which stands in its churchyard on the site of the medieval parish church. When this church was built, the fine east window was taken from the friary and installed here. The opening now visible in the east wall exists because the government's archaeologists have seen fit to transport the Gothic window back to the east wall of the friary, whence it came.

The village center of Glanworth, at first glance, was unprepossessing: the unremarkable buildings (one being renovated to become a youth center) consisted of dwellings, a few shops, and pubs (Eileen Fitzgibbon's was the venue for scenes in Atom Egoyan's film of *Felicia's Journey,* a novel by William Trevor, born in Mitchelstown). However, a ruined castle, a beautiful old bridge, and a handsomely preserved mill attract the eye, and I was to find a stop in Glanworth rewarding.

WHAT REMAINS OF once redoubtable Glanworth Castle stands on a crag above the river, where an ancient ford was supplanted by a stone bridge. The castle began as a fortress of the Condons, one of those Anglo-Norman families become thoroughly Irish. Acquired through marriage by the rival Roches in the thirteenth century, it was successively enlarged and maintained until blasted by the artillery of Henry Ireton, who succeeded Oliver Cromwell, his father-in-law, as commander of England's New Model Army in May 1650, when Cromwell left Ireland.

A street beside the castle eminence leads down to the bridge over the Funshion. Twelve-arched (a thirteenth arch was eliminated by the construction of a millrace), the stone bridge spans the Fushion with a one-lane roadway. A little brochure titled "History of Glanworth Village," supported by local advertisers, claims that it is the narrowest, if not the oldest, public bridge in Europe. However, as the brochure's author misquotes Yeats's famous epitaph, one may be doubtful about the assertion. I stood musing by the graceful structure: today the Irish claim to be Europeans, and indeed their connections to the Continent are long and intimate; yet I would not expect to find such an asseveration about its bridge in the historical brochure of an English village. I reflected that Glanworth Bridge's history—its age is conjectural—was nearly shortened during the Irish Civil War, when an attempt to blow it up failed—only the primer detonated, damaging one arch—if I may credit the village's promotional literature.

Turning around, I looked at Glanworth Mill, nestled beneath the castle massif, the greensward about it shaded by a venerable yew. The fine late-eighteenth-century stone building began as a flour mill, became a woolen mill, producing blankets until 1968, and was now a country inn, my destination this evening.

NO SOONER HAD I stepped over the threshold than I felt as if my arrival here had been ordained. For of the ten bedrooms, all named for authors, unasked I was shown to the Elizabeth Bowen Room. The room was delightful, looking from the front of the mill toward the old bridge and the winding green valley of the Funshion, as picturesque a view as a traveler could wish. There was a capacious bed, coffee table with side chairs, a writing table with glamourous photograph of the author—Kitty to her intimates—in a room with off-white walls and tasteful fabrics. After a long, restorative shower and short sybaritic nap in a bed that seemed to demand a consort, I repaired to the little library below.

After being served an aperitif and given the dinner menu, I looked through the small but choice selection on the bookshelves, mostly works by the authors for whom the inn's rooms were named, including William Trevor, Molly Keane, Anthony Trollope, Edmund Spenser, Dervla Murphy, and Patrick "Canon" Sheehan—all Irish, Anglo-Irish, or with significant Irish associations. I took down Elizabeth Bowen's *The Last September*, her second novel and one of only two she set entirely in Ireland. I had not read it and looked forward to indulging myself in what is perhaps for me the most delicious pleasure in traveling: reading a work which invokes the place while one is there, such as wallowing in Victor Hugo's *The Hunchback of Notre Dame* in Paris, Norman Douglas's *South Wind* in Capri, or John Buchan's *The Thirty-nine Steps* in the Scottish Highlands.

Just then Emelyn Heaps joined me. A husky man with a military mustache, he emanates brio and confidence. Heaps said that he and his wife, Lynne Glasscoe, acquired Glanworth Mill in 1997. In twenty-five "furious weeks," with a crew of five, they transformed the old mill into the stylish hostelry I was enjoying.

MY INNKEEPER'S STORY seemed the stuff of fiction: he told me that, while still a lad, he had been taken up flying by George Peppard, star of *The Blue Max,* which was being filmed in Ireland. Infatuated with airplanes, when he was an engineering student, Emelyn became a pilot. After surviving four crashes, he lost his license for flying under the bridge over the river Blackwater at Fermoy—a very low bridge, indeed.

Though grounded himself, the flying engineer wanted to produce an airplane for Everyman. "Like Henry Ford and his automobile," explained Heaps. He designed and built a prototype, dubbed The By-Max. He recalled, "I got backing, and two production aircraft followed before my backers suffered financial collapse."

When Lynne Glasscoe, a designer, went to St. Lucia, engaged in the marketing of crafts, he accompanied her to the Caribbean island. There he was soon involved in the building of the Windjammer Landing Villa Beach Resort and stayed on, working on the design and engineering of projects for Caribbean governments. Though they were then in the Windward Islands, Emelyn and Lynne cast an anchor farther to windward, as a sailor might say about securing a safe anchorage, by buying an old rectory at Conna, in County Cork, in 1993. "Island life was very seductive," recalled Heaps, "but Lynne and I wanted to have a home in Ireland." Thereafter, the Cork County Council approached them about saving the old mill at Glanworth, stipulating that the restoration project provide employment and attract tourism.

When I told my host how charmed I was to find myself assigned to the Elizabeth Bowen Room, having just visited the site of her ancestral home, Emelyn said, "Go have a look at the giant flagstone inside the front door." I duly did so. Beaming, he said, "I went to the farmer who had acquired Bowen's Court, then pulled the house down, and I bought the flagstone which had stood at its doorway."

———

AFTER DINING PLEASANTLY in the conservatory off the dining room, I tucked up in the Bowen bed with *The Last September* and was transported by her novel depicting the widening perceptions of a girl affected by a worldly and disturbing visitor to a country house like Bowen's Court. I awoke on a sunny Sunday morning and breakfasted in the cozy Mill Tea Rooms, at a table separated from the old mill wheel by a sheet of glass. After mass, it was time to march.

At the edge of the village, at the entrance to a small, pretty Georgian house, was a sign:

BEWARE DOGS

KERRY BLUES

I couldn't recall ever seeing the breed of guard dog proclaimed, and although I knew many breeds of terriers to be feisty, this amused me. Not moments later I had another canine epiphany: perhaps a bit over a hundred yards ahead a couple preceded me along the road. They were well dressed; the man, who wore a long topcoat, had a small dog on a lead. I couldn't make out what kind; I guessed a dachshund. Suddenly the dog lunged into the ditch along the way and emerged with a small rabbit in its jaws. A bend in the road prevented my seeing the conclusion to this episode. When next I glimpsed them, master, mistress, and dog were walking on quietly, the rabbit or its remains nowhere to be seen, and they soon turned off.

FOR A MILE the road hugged the river, which then swung more easterly, eventually to join the Blackwater. My way continued southeasterly, and I tramped happily, reveling in the beauty of the Funshion's valley, which I thought supernal along this stretch. Near a ford that had been the scene of an Irish confederate victory over a parliamentary force in 1643, I stopped by a small white cottage, without farm buildings, nestled in the hillside above the river. It was shuttered though neatly kept. I guessed that it might be the weekend fishing retreat of some fortunate fellow, and I was pierced by envy. Then I started up a long hill, at the top of which a massive heap of stones arrested my eye.

The stones were those of a Bronze Age tomb called Labbacallee, marked on my Ordnance Survey map. The archaeologist Seán P. Ó Ríordáin described it as "the most notable (the most elaborate and greatest)" of all the wedge-shaped megalithic tombs in Ireland. A historical marker states that such "wedge-shaped gallery-graves were erected in many parts of Ireland around 1500 B.C. and are particularly common around the south-west of Ireland." Of some four hundred known, most are in Kerry and Cork.

The great tomb stood right beside the road, but not a car passed, nor was there another visitor while I was there. A stone wall separated the grave site from a meadow where cattle grazed. Beech trees and a few pines grew around the great stones that formed the sepulcher; from the branches, rooks kept up a dirge. Around the lichen-covered stones, primroses gave praise to the sun on this golden day.

I had heard locals refer to Labbacallee as the hag's grave; others called it the witch's grave, and I was soon to read in Mary Leland's fascinating and richly informative book *The Lie of the Land: Journeys through Literary Cork* that the tomb was "reputedly the burial place of the daughter of the druid who had named Fermoy," the town where I would spend this night. When archaeologists excavated Labbacallee, in 1934, they found the bones of a woman in the smaller of the tomb's two chambers; her skull was found in the larger one. In Ireland, folk memory is often borne out as history.

I dropped my rucksack, took out the packet Glanworth Mill's kitchen staff had fixed for me, and settled myself on the grass, my back against a sun-warmed stone. With a small bottle of wine I'd got at a village grocer, I enjoyed a collation featuring last evening's pâté while I studied the famous wedge grave. The term comes from the arrangement of the stones with which it was constructed: they are aligned on an east-west axis, and the grave has two chambers, the wider, longer, and higher to the west; the other, narrower, shorter, and lower, to the east. Each chamber is covered by a great capstone resting on walls of upright slabs. Secondary stone walls support the inner walls. An upright slab separates the two burial chambers. Some ten or twelve feet away, on the east and south sides of the tomb, a border of smaller stones appears to be the remainder of a curb that encircled the cairn of stones which usually would have covered such a tomb. Over the millennia those stones had disappeared, presumably put to other uses.

My picnic finished, I inspected the great tomb closely, noticing that a

Labbacallee, or "the Hag's Grave."

corner of the slab dividing the chambers seemed to have been chiseled off. Later I was to read in Ó Ríordáin that the gap created might have been an Irish version of the "porthole" found in megalithic tombs on the Continent, "a ritual feature interpreted as an opening for the passage of the soul of the dead."

Tarrying in this tranquil place, I lit my pipe and ruminated about the hoary tomb. Respectful though I am of the work of archaeologists, I felt a certain regret that the remains of the woman for whom this noble tomb had been erected, with great effort and probable ceremony, more than a thousand years before Christ was entombed, did not repose here. Instead, no doubt carefully labeled, they lay in a museum drawer that is rarely opened.

A Blackwater Idyll

FROM LABBACALLEE TO FERMOY, MY JAUNT WAS PLEASANT AND uneventful. On the long decline to the valley of the Blackwater, I passed one handsome stud farm or training establishment, then soon came to the long, low bridge erected in 1689, and since improved, under which Emelyn Heaps said he had flown. From Mary Leland, I learned that this part of the country was bestowed on Mogruith, a druid, by Fiach Muillethan, third-century King of Munster. Mogruith caused many altars to be built, which gave the name Magh Feine, "sacred plain," to the region. A man who dwelled there was called Fier Magh Feine or Fier Magh, from which the name Fermoy derives.

In 1791, an entrepreneurial Scot named John Anderson acquired the Fermoy estate, provided tracts to the British Army for barracks and training grounds, and laid out the town, principally on the south, or right, bank of the river Blackwater, much as one sees it today. Until 1922, Fermoy was one of the principal British military centers in Ireland. (In Bowen's *The Last Summer* the garrison's social life plays a role.)

I chose to stay at the Grand Hotel, alas no longer grand; my room was the only shabby accommodation I would have on this journey. (The hotel would soon close and the building be put up for sale.) However, my view was splendid: just below was the broad river, the bridge, the weir just above it, and a fish ladder for salmon, for which the Blackwater is famed. Just below the bridge a lone fisherman was spin casting from a bank of shingle. A stroll around town seemed essential.

On the main street, I stopped at La Bigoudenne, an authentic Breton *crêperie,* and enjoyed a café au lait and crêpe. Afterward I moseyed back across the bridge to a pleasant riverside park, where I sat at a picnic table, enjoying the late-afternoon sunlight and writing in my journal as boys coming home from school dropped their backpacks and began whacking a ball about with their hurleys. Later I had a satisfactory dinner in the hotel dining room, then dropped in at nearby O'Sullivan's pub. It was small and authentic, and I savored a whiskey and my pipe but grumbled to the publican about having to pay ten pence for a box of matches advertising O'Sullivan's.

SETTING OFF FROM Fermoy, I stopped at the bridge, hoping to see a salmon vaulting up the fish ladder. By my side, I noticed a small stone commemorating the heroism of members of the Kent family, who fell in the 1916 Easter Rising, during a skirmish with British forces at Castlelyons, where I was headed. The road out of town was steep, and I looked back at St. Colman's College. There Thomas MacDonagh, whose bust I'd seen at Golden, in Tipperary, had been a teacher. One of the school's earliest pupils was John Stanislaus Joyce, father of James Joyce.

Passing the new waterworks, I made for Castlelyons. It is a plain little village, distinguished by several interesting ruins. One is that of a Carmelite friary founded by John de Barri in 1307. Another is the shell of Barrymore Castle, with its soaring Tudor chimneys, gutted by fire in 1771. Just in front of the gaping ruin, on the main street of the village, is the farm machinery business of Kearny Bros. Ltd. Their yard was packed with big, expensive machines; the contrast of ruined castle and flourishing modern business said much about Ireland.

Until the castle was destroyed, it was the principal seat of the Lords Barrymore (the Norman name de Barri having mutated to Barry), whose vast estates spread over much of east Cork, Ireland's largest county. The line ended with three brothers who chose to squander their patrimony in London. (For much of what I learned about the rapscallionly trio—and some other excessives I've mentioned—I am indebted to Peter

Somerville-Large's *Irish Eccentrics*.) As young bucks in the dissolute society surrounding the louche Prince of Wales, afterward George IV, the Barrymores reached notoriety at the top of the pack. Richard, the eldest, who inherited the earldom of Barrymore, was known as Hellgate for his profligacy; clubfooted brother Henry Barry was dubbed Cripplegate; and Augustus, a wastrel whose gambling losses kept him on the brink of debtor's prison, was named for the most famous, Newgate.

Lord Barrymore and his siblings titillated London with their outrageous escapades: the earl's largesse was staggering; at entertainments in the luxurious private theater he had built, sumptuous refreshments were served by platoons of servants in his spectacular livery. A superb horseman, Lord Barrymore raced steeds from his own stable and went tearing through London with his coach, holding the reins of four or six horses while smashing windows with his whip. Perhaps to amuse the Prince of Wales, Augustus Barry urged his horse up the stairs in the Brighton residence of the prince's clandestine wife, Mrs. Fitzherbert; two blacksmiths were required to extricate the animal. Lord Barrymore's huge income could not match his outlay; owing immense debts, he was arrested by two bailiffs, who approached him in the guise of jockeys. Forced to sell much that he owned, he became an officer in the Berkshire Militia and inadvertently shot himself through the head. He was dead at twenty-three. Henry inherited the title—Augustus had died—but was strapped for resources. He took to wearing the livery of a servant at his dinners, to elude the bailiffs. Henry was not popular; indeed, he felt called upon to fight a duel. His fiscal circumstances obliged him to go to France, where he died impoverished, the last Lord Barrymore.

NOT FAR FROM Castlelyons, beyond Bridebridge, is Ballyvolane House, where I was expected. It is approached by a drive winding through a lovely demesne of rolling fields, noble trees, and pretty ponds. The house, of unremarkable exterior, was built in 1728 and remodeled in the mid–nineteenth century in what the present owners, Jeremy and Merrie Green, call the Italianate style. I was welcomed by Jeremy, and stepping into the pillared hall, where a springer spaniel and a Yorkshire terrier snoozed on a settee, I felt immediately at ease in an Irish country house of character. The windows of my spacious, splendidly furnished room looked out on a bucolic prospect: in the foreground a donkey grazed beneath a lofty beech; beyond, many widening rings in two ponds suggested rising trout. When I went downstairs, I stepped through French doors to make a promenade around the wide lawn behind the house. Gravel paths led me to an aviary with fantail pigeons and to a walled garden with luxuriant flower beds and extensive plantings of vegetables for Ballyvolane's tables.

Coming in, I paused in the hall at a chest laden with bottles and glasses and pleasured myself—a little pad was provided for one to keep tab—regarded coolly by an immense cat. (I learned that this formidable personage, of twenty-one pounds, was named Archimedes and "has no principles," said Jeremy.) Then I joined the other guests in a pretty drawing room. Two were from Rome, Luca Montanari, a film editor and writer on angling, and his wife, Giovanna, an actress who frequently dubs the dialogue for American film stars. There were the Gallups from New York, a lawyer and his bride, who were on their honeymoon. We dined together and very well in the beautifully appointed dining room, Jeremy Green acting as maître d'hôtel, taking orders for wine and serving it with the easy, natural manner of the host. Reports of what each had done that day were exchanged, and plans for the morrow discussed. The American couple were keen to see a hurling match, and the Italians had arranged to fish for salmon on beats along the seven kilometers controlled by Ballyvolane House on the Blackwater, Ireland's most renowned salmon fishery. When Luca and I were chatting after dinner, we found that we had fished some of the same rivers, and the upshot was that I was invited to join the Montanaris next morning.

AFTER BREAKFAST we were met in the hall by Norman Gillett, who was to be the ghillie. Tall, lean, and rugged as a blackthorn stick, properly togged in tweed knickerbockers and hat—in style and speech he was unlike other fishing guides I'd known in Ireland, who were usually homespun countrymen. Norman Gillett was clearly of a different cut. As the Montanaris had their own car, Norman took me in his, and I discovered that he had attended Trinity College, Dublin, then Oxford, and had spent years in North Sea oil operations before returning to Ireland and his great love:

fishing. We crossed the Blackwater at Fermoy and drove westward along its north bank.

The river, some seventy miles long, rises in County Kerry, soon enters Cork, and flows due east through Fermoy into County Waterford, past the great castle at Lismore (Irish seat of the Duke of Devonshire, where Adele Astaire was chatelaine, as the wife of Lord Charles Cavendish of the ducal family) to Cappoquin. There the great river makes a right-angle turn and flows due south to Youghal, where it forms the border between Cork and Waterford before debouching into Youghal Bay. About a mile past the village of Ballyhooly, Norman turned off the road, and the Montanaris followed. We parked behind the ghastly burnt-out ruin of Convamore, a once grand mansion of the Earl and Countess of Listowel, now another grim monument to the madness of the 1920s and the vengeance wreaked by Irish republicans on Anglo-Irish landholders for seven hundred years of often ruthless colonization.

A short walk brought us to a sylvan reach of the river called the Scarrif Run, without another dwelling or soul in sight. The handsome Luca Montanari, who writes articles for the Italian angling magazine *Pescare*, suggested by the assured manner with which he rigged his rod and the dazzling array of flies (that he had tied himself, and beautifully) in the trays of his mahogany fly box that he was a dedicated fisherman. Wearing waders, he stepped into the Blackwater and—with his first few long casts, across the river and downstream—revealed that he knew what he was about. Norman Gillett headed upstream to observe. Because I hadn't previously arranged to fish—booked a beat, engaged a ghillie, obtained a license, and had rod, waders, flies, and all the other paraphernalia employed in pursuit of salmon—I sat with Giovanna on a grassy patch above the fine shingle and enjoyed the murmuring of the river, the whispering of Luca's fly line, and the trilling of birds.

It was what American sportsmen call a bluebird day: the sunlight was brilliant; the surface of the river glittered as if a million silver coins had been flung across it; the air was warm, with just enough of a breeze stirring that a cast fly line was slightly hidden in the ripples. Despite the helpful breeze, it was the kind of day that is heaven for picnicking but purgatory for fishing. Luca fished well and steadily for a couple of hours.

I had expected to go back to Ballyvolane House for lunch, but when

Luca came out of the river as luckless as the great heron I'd been watching at the end of the Scarrif Run, he and Giovanna urged me to stay and share the lunch put up for them. Afterward, Norman led Luca well upriver, with Giovanna and me following through broad, verdant water meadows. While the two fished downstream with great care, covering every inch of water in a long, shallow reach, Giovanna and I found a high, shady spot on the riverbank and stretched out in the deep grass to drowse and watch them.

We gathered at the Scarrif Run late in the day, and by then aware that I was keen, Norman handed me his rod and invited me to have a few casts. I followed Luca down the run, and just at the end, in the big bend below, a salmon leaped in what seemed a derisory display. Luca and I both saw it and just looked at each other. Neither he nor Norman nor I touched a salmon that day, as has been the case on many a day when I have cast my fly over other rivers in Ireland and in Scotland. Still, I would pronounce this day on the Blackwater perfect.

BALLYVOLANE HAS A tranquil magic, but I learned that in its history there was one lurid episode. In the early eighteenth century, Sir Richard Pyne, sometime Lord Chief Justice of Ireland, acquired the estate of Ballyvolane and rented it to Andrew St. Leger. On the night of November 4, 1730, Timothy Croneen, the butler, and Joan Condon, a housemaid, burst into the bedroom of St. Leger and his wife, Jane, intent on stealing a chest containing the St. Legers' valuables, and they murdered husband and wife in their bed. For some reason that same night, Croneen also slew the gardener. The villains buried the chest of treasures somewhere in the shrubbery about the place but remained at Ballyvolane, never expecting to be implicated in the crime. As was customary, Croneen and Condon were in the funeral cortege en route to the graveyard when Condon became unnerved by the whimpering of the spaniel following the coffin of its mistress. Croneen dropped off the carriage, seized the dog, covertly slit its throat, and disposed of it in a ditch. (The place is still called Spaniel's Cross.) It is said that suspicion was aroused among other servants by the faithful dog's disappearance and was heightened when horses pulling the funerary carriage balked at a ford; there was talk that a witch would not cross water. Frightened, Croneen and Condon fled Ballyvolane, leaving the treasures of the St. Legers buried. An alarm went out for the fugitives, and they were spied by an alert customs official as they attempted to board ship at Limerick. As the murder of a master by a servant was then deemed a form of treason, Croneen and Condon were tried in Cork by a special commission of thirteen, rather than by a criminal court; its grandest member was James Barry, Earl of Barrymore. The Attorney General of Ireland prosecuted. On January 15, 1731, Croneen and Condon were found guilty. Croneen was immediately hanged, drawn, and quartered, and his head was stuck on the wall of the Cork city jail. Condon was hanged a few days later; the record does not show if the same horrors were inflicted on her body. Folklore holds that she was burnt alive as a witch. Some say it was at a place called Hag's Cross. Despite many attempts to find the treasure of the St. Legers, it has never been unearthed. I inquired if the murder had been committed in the grand room I occupied and was vaguely disappointed to learn that it had occurred in the room next to mine.

THAT EVENING, I found a festive company assembled in the small drawing room, drinking champagne and chatting. I was given a glass and introduced to an attractive, friendly lady named Honor Cattell, a good friend of the Greens, who was giving a fiftieth birthday party for her son Myles, a big, genial chap who was the only man in the room not wearing a jacket and tie. Mrs. Cattell grew up in a great house near Sneem, in Kerry, and later had a small house on the shore there, which she loved. As I had several times been the guest of friends close by, we spoke of an area of which we both were fond. Now she lived near Kinsale, as did the other eleven members of the party, an amiable group that typified the Anglo-Irish gentry long centered on Kinsale. They had taken over the house, and I was made to feel welcome. Until dinner.

Shortly before, the Greens took me aside to say that Mrs. Cattell was greatly embarrassed to ask, but as I would make the thirteenth at table, would I mind if I were seated at a separate table in the dining room. I thought how awful it would be to sit at a small table, like little Jack Horner, reading a book while the party at the long table toasted the birthday boy, and perhaps some would be obliged to turn around now and again to include me in some sally I didn't hear or didn't get. So I politely demurred at the arrangement. Jeremy and Merrie understood, and doubtless Honor

Cattell was relieved. I dined extremely well and enjoyed a good wine and a good book in baronial splendor at the table set up for me in my room.

When I came downstairs later, the house party was gathered in the larger drawing room, and in full if decorous cry. Champagne was instantly proffered, and I felt embraced like the returned prodigal son, or perhaps a Jonah home from the sea. It was a convivial evening.

In the morning the empty champagne bottles stood in ranks like so many battalions of dead soldiers who had done their duty. No other celebrants were at breakfast, but the Greens—indefatigable Merrie, with close-cropped white hair and ebullient manner, from whose kitchen pleasures fly and who manages the fishing, and Jeremy, trim gentleman farmer and unobtrusively attentive host—were already on duty. I parted from them and Ballyvolane reluctantly.

Corcaigh Abú!

.❈.

CORCAIGH ABÚ!—"UP CORK!" OR "CORK FOREVER!"—WAS A CRY
I had heard at hurling matches. It was like the battle cry *O Domhnaill abú!*
with which clansmen and followers of the dauntless Red Hugh O'Donnell, Earl of Tyrconnel, had followed him into the fray during the Elizabethan wars. The cry *O Loingsigh abú!* used to go up for Jack Lynch, the
renowned Cork hurler who became Ireland's most popular and respected
Taioseach and was buried with a national outpouring of mourning and impressive ceremony in Cork in October 1999. Corkonians are notoriously
individualistic and prideful about their city, and although I had been here
before, I didn't feel I knew Cork but wanted to. With a population of
about 180,000—the suburbs add another 50,000—it is the second largest
city of the Republic and, after Belfast, the third largest in Ireland. Cork
was the only city after Derry on the route I'd chosen from north to south
through the center of Ireland, so I was keen to see how it represented an
Irish *urbs* at the end of one millennium and the beginning of the next. I
wanted to take the pulse of the city and learn how it was responding to the
strains of an exploding economy and benefiting from its fallout.

As a racing pigeon flies, it is about fifteen miles from Ballyvolane
House to Cork, but by the little roads I usually preferred to take, it was
considerably farther. Having sought some meetings with various Corko-

nians, I was anxious to get there and chose to travel again along the main Dublin–Cork route, my section being the busy N8.

In Cork, I stopped at Arbutus Lodge in the hillside district called Montenotte, north of the river Lee, whose two channels embrace the core of the city. Long a hotel, the late-eighteenth-century building, now much altered, had once been the home of a Lord Mayor. Happily, the Carmody family, who were new proprietors of Arbutus Lodge, had retained the long-established individual character and nomenclature of the guest rooms. I was lodged in the Irish Rural Magistrate's Room, named after the protagonist of the enduring tales of Edith Oenone Somerville and Martin Ross (the pen name of Somerville's cousin Violet Martin). Their first collection of these stories is titled *Some Experiences of an Irish R.M.*, the leitmotif being the often hilarious efforts of a rural magistrate, a proper young Englishman posted to County Cork in the nineteenth century, to achieve a modus vivendi with the devious Irish locals. The cheerful room was decorated with prints evoking the hunting milieu depicted in many of the stories by the ardent equestrian authors, and it overlooked terraced gardens and the thriving riverine port.

TRADITION IN CORK has it that the city's origin lies in the sixth- or seventh-century foundation of a monastery on high ground above the south branch of the river Lee by Saint Finbarr, an abbot as well as a bishop, who came from Connacht. (Some scholars believe that the actual founder was a disciple.) However, there is evidence that a petty kingdom existed here as early as the third century, when a king named Diarmuid Mór fought in the Battle of Gabhra. Still, Saint Finbarr is exalted as the patron of Cork, and St. Finbarr's Cathedral, a soaring nineteenth-century Gothic fantasy, marks the site of the medieval cathedral and perhaps the site of the original monastery. Like Dublin's medieval cathedrals, Christ Church and St. Patrick's, which became Protestant at the Reformation, St. Finbarr's is the cathedral of the Church of Ireland's Bishop of Cork, while the Catholic Bishop of Cork has his chair in St. Mary's, procathedral of the diocese, on the north side of the city.

Cork's history, as with so many Irish places, is a record of much tumult, but the city has been much favored, too. At the mouth of the Lee, which divided into channels surrounding two islands, was a great marsh, *corcaigh mór,* and eastward, downriver, was a vast sheltered estuary inviting to ships. Vikings repeatedly pillaged the monastery, but they were followed by other Norse, traders who—as Norsemen did at suitable coastal points—established a settlement on one of the islands in the ninth century. In time these Scandinavian seafarers melded with the surrounding Irish.

Not many years after Strongbow's invasion and Henry II's landing to claim suzerainty over all Ireland, the Anglo-Normans garrisoned the settlement of Cork, leaving King Dermot MacCarthy, who had initially submitted, in nominal control. But in 1185, he was killed resisting the invaders. Cork was made a royal borough, and the first of twenty-six charters was conferred on it by King Henry's youngest son, Prince John, and what became an English style of governance was imposed.

Over the next several centuries, possession of Cork changed hands periodically. MacCarthys or other hostile Irish princes would attack and oust the English, only to have the English overlords assault and expel them in turn. Endowed with a great harbor, Cork grew as a trading center, was walled and fortified, and endured some notable sieges. In 1644, Murrough "the Burner" O'Brien took the town for the parliamentarians, driving out the Irish; in 1649, Oliver Cromwell captured Cork, and again the Irish were expelled; and in 1690, John Churchill, later Duke of Marlborough, after a devastating siege, won the city for William of Orange. A year later Patrick Sarsfield and the Irish army vanquished at Limerick sailed from Cork for France, to become the Wild Geese.

Time and again Cork rebuilt from the wreckage of war and flowered as the seat of the country's largest county. By the twentieth century there was a powerful British military presence in and around Cork. (The Royal Navy gave up its major base at Haulbowline, in Cork Harbour, only in 1938; the Irish Naval Service has since had its headquarters there.) During the Irish War of Independence, 1919–1921, much of the brutal conflict took place in County Cork and the other counties of Munster between the Irish Republican Army, a highly irregular force, and the British government forces. The British forces consisted of units of the army and the Royal Irish Constabulary, an armed force augmented by former British soldiers called Black and Tans, for their uniforms of khaki blouses and dark-green trousers, and by ex-British officers recruited as "auxiliaries" and uniformed in navy blue.

On the Irish republican side, "flying columns" conducted feral guerrilla warfare against the British, and the Black and Tans became infamous for the ferocity of their reprisals. The republican Lord Mayor of Cork, Tomás MacCurtain, was assassinated in his home on March 20, 1920; the inquest jury found that the Royal Irish Constabulary had committed the murder. His successor, Terence MacSwiney, who like MacCurtain had been a rebel commandant, was arrested by the British and died in London's Brixton Prison on October 25, 1920, after a hunger strike of seventy-four days. On the night of December 11, 1920, the British burned the center of Cork, destroying much of wide, curving Patrick Street, the principal shopping thoroughfare, and such public buildings as City Hall and the Carnegie Free Library. The following July 11, 1921, a truce was reached between the British forces and the Irish Republican Army (then effectively the military arm of the recently declared Republic of Ireland), which led to the Anglo-Irish Treaty of December 6, 1921, creating the Irish Free State and excluding the six counties of Northern Ireland.

"ONE NOTABLE DEVELOPMENT in twentieth-century Cork's municipal history has been the great prestige of the office of Lord Mayor," writes John A. Murphy, Emeritus Professor of Irish History at University College, Cork, in the *Cork Corporation Millennium Yearbook*. "This role was raised to a very special relationship in 1920 because of the ultimate sacrifice in office of Tomás MacCurtain and Terence MacSwiney. The title of Lord Mayor, though a royal designation, was cherished, paradoxically, by the two martyred republicans." The title of Lord Mayor, conferred by Queen Victoria in 1900, is still a source of pride for Corkonians, and the holder of the office is accorded great esteem by the people he represents.

I knew that the day-to-day affairs of the city were administered by the city manager—an appointed office long held by Jack Higgins—overseen by the elected city councillors, but as the Lord Mayor is the spokesperson for the city and its chief magistrate, I wanted to hear the views of the present Lord Mayor, Damian Wallace, on the state of the city on his watch, and an introduction was arranged.

AFTER SEVERAL HALCYON days at Arbutus Lodge, I decided that it would be prudent to reduce my expenditures, and I moved a little farther eastward, to Lotamore House, a handsome early-nineteenth-century building significant enough to be noted on the Ordnance Survey map. A long drive curves up to the house, sited high above the river. The rooms are spacious, and mine provided a grand vista: on the near shore of the Lee cranes crept back and forth, lifting containers to and from ships moored at the quays of the container port; on the far shore, Blackrock Castle, a picturesque nineteenth-century landmark, stands on the site of an earlier fortress; on the river, crews from the several rowing clubs trained, oars rising and dipping in cadence, shells leaving pretty wakes.

A ring on the telephone pulled me from the window: Mairead Harty, the proprietor, said the Lord Mayor's office was calling and connected me. I was told that Lord Mayor Damian Wallace could give me a little time before an important scheduled meeting if I could be at his office in twenty minutes. I said, "Thank you. I'll be there." City Hall was about three miles distant; even without a backpack, I wouldn't make it afoot. However, the resourceful Dr. Harty (she is a physician) managed to get a taxi, and twenty minutes later I stepped out in front of Cork City Hall, a neoclassic replica crowned by a Georgian pepper-pot cupola. The Lord Mayor's secretaries, Mary Hegarty and Jenny Ahearn, uniformly attired in dark waistcoats and jackets, received me in an anteroom, discreetly remarked that the Lord Mayor had to receive a delegation of mothers in twenty minutes, and ushered me in to His Honor's presence.

Lord Mayor and City Councillor Damian Wallace greeted me warmly in his grand chamber. Still in his early thirties, smartly tailored, wearing his chain of office, well built, with dark, tousled hair and an infectious smile, he had the brio of the hurler he had been (and was now coach of his old school team, the Glen Hurlers). No sooner had we begun speaking than I supposed that, were he an insurance salesman, a flogger of encyclopedias or vinyl siding, he would have sold me. As it happened, outside his mayoral office, Damian Wallace had his own business, in financial services. Damian and his father were one of only three pairs of fathers and sons who have succeeded each other as Lord Mayors of Cork.

While the Lord Mayor drew up a chair near the one he had offered me, I glanced around at the vitrine of trophies, the portraits of his most famous predecessors, Tomás MacCurtain and Terence MacSwiney, and an imposing model of a side-wheel steamship with sails of silver, the *Sirius,* the first steamship to cross the Atlantic from Cobh, the great harbor town of Cork, to New York, in 1838. It was presented to the Corporation of Cork by the Irish Distillers in 1985 to commemorate the eight hundredth anniversary of the city's first charter, granted by Prince John.

"What do you want to know about Cork?" asked the Lord Mayor.

I said that I'd like to know what he would say to the principals of an international corporation considering an operation in Cork. With that the designated pitcher started pitching.

"The biggest attraction has to be Cork's educational facilities and the educational level of Cork's young people," said Damian Wallace. "That has attracted increased foreign business investment and the employment that comes with it. More than that, we are a gateway to the Continent, with ferry facilities and an airport. For a modern European city we have quite manageable traffic. The recently opened Jack Lynch Tunnel under Cork Harbour"—opened May 21, 1999—"connecting the main east-west highway from Waterford to the coast of West Cork and bypassing the city center, is a huge improvement. It has opened up a land bank."

Cork is managed by a corporation under the day-to-day direction of a City Manager, backed by the City Council, of which Damian Wallace is a member, and I asked what were some recent initiatives of the Cork Corporation.

"We have been developing a strategy to establish where the city of Cork will need to be in twenty years, particularly in terms of housing," said the Lord Mayor.

He told me that a major project, long under way, was Cork's main drainage system, budgeted at I£120 million. "It will carry all Cork's municipal waste into a sewage-treatment plant at Carriggrennan, Little Island, near the mouth of the Lee," said the Lord Mayor. "It will greatly increase the quality of the river Lee's watershed and the harbor.

"But we have much more to offer, in educational facilities and the arts—music, dance, theater, and the visual arts . . ." The Lord Mayor was getting under full sail when there was a discreet tap at the door and Ms. Ahearn reminded him that he was wanted in the Council Chamber.

"Come along," said the Lord Mayor, and I could not resist.

A SIZABLE GROUP of mothers from the suburb of Togher awaited the Lord Mayor in the Council Chamber—parquet floors, pilasters, velvet draperies—gabbing amiably while their tots darted about. I was impressed by how quickly the mothers imposed order, and the Lord Mayor, instantly in form, the civic eminence and hurling coach, performed adroitly. He presented a crystal paperweight and a bouquet to one of the women for her contribution to community affairs, and he spoke briefly and convincingly about the importance of child rearing. (Damian Wallace and his wife, Grace, have two preteen children, Daniel and Rachel.) He emphasized the resources and opportunities Cork offers to its youth: "Each can become an engineer or a window cleaner," he said. "Each one of these children can become whatever he or she wants to be. The opportunities are there."

There were occasional screams, suppressed by pacifiers or potato crisps, during the Lord Mayor's formal turn, then, to my embarrassment, he produced me, like a rabbit out of his hat, introducing me as a visiting— he didn't quite say demented—writer who was walking the length of the country and wished to observe these proceedings. Then the Right Honorable Damian Wallace, Lord Mayor of Cork, missed no opportunity to press even the tiniest hands of future voters.

CORK IS A lovely city to stroll in. Although it has almost none of the great eighteenth-century and earlier buildings and the grand Georgian squares that distinguish Dublin, Cork's intimate scale and narrow streets with interesting shops, restaurants, cafés, pubs, and churches give it an old-world charm. The heart of the city, clasped in the two arms of the river Lee, is reached by sixteen bridges. The nearly semicircular Patrick Street, the wide but not so grand Grand Parade, and the South Mall provide major prospects, and long, narrow Oliver Plunkett Street, crammed with all sorts of shops, is Cork's pulsing aorta. A warren of narrow lanes, some of them pedestrian ways, connect the major arteries. On weekdays, I found Cork throbbing with vitality and was struck by the youth of many of the inhabitants. In part that may be because University College, Cork, had 12,000 students (890 from overseas, representing fifty-four countries in 2000) and Cork Institute of Technology had some 5,500 full-time students (many others held jobs and attend part-time).

After calling on the Lord Mayor, I walked to Paul Street, in the old Huguenot Quarter, a district named for the French Protestants who settled here after their expulsion from France in the late seventeenth century. In a swelling of narrow pedestrian Paul Street called Rory Gallagher Place, I stopped for lunch at the Gingerbread House, a Corkonian version of a Viennese coffeehouse. It's a bright, lofty place where patrons—who had ordered sandwiches from the meats, cheeses, salads, and excellent breads available, perhaps with soup, pastry, and coffee—were lingering at the long pine tables, many of them reading newspapers or books. A tall young woman, sleek as a calla lily, with a crown of long, golden hair, slipped into the chair beside me. Her plainer companion took a chair opposite. Each had coffee and a pastry, and each carried books. Having overheard ardent political discourse here in the past, I wondered what would engage these university types and was soon enlightened on the subject of bodices and décolletage and occasions dictating their choice. The discussion of dress reminded me of my mission to Paul Street.

A few steps away I stopped in shock before the shuttered premises of the House of Donegal. I was wearing a Donegal tweed jacket tailored for me here by Anthony Boeg, to whose Savile Row–trained ministrations I had been recommended by the American art historian Nicholas Fox Weber, who has a house in County Cork. I had wanted to treat myself to a new garment to succeed the cherished jacket I had been packing since I left County Donegal. Upon inquiry next door, I learned that Tony Boeg had died of a stroke. Cork had lost a gifted tailor and an amiable man.

The district, which has a variety of restaurants, also has several good bookstores. One of which, almost beside the Gingerbread House, is Mainly Murder, whose shelves hold the expected sanguinary stock. Next door, Pinocchio's Toy Shop has unexpected wares in wood.

Not far off, one of Cork's treasures, which I had visited but once, beckoned. The Old English Market can be entered by gates opening from Patrick Street, Princes Street, Oliver Plunkett Street, and the Grand Parade. Inaugurated in 1788, it has since been enlarged and reedified. A central skylit arcade has striped arches, which recall the great mosque of Córdoba; a towering, wrought-iron fountain; and tiled floor. Vendors in some fifty stalls—names like Moynihan, Casey, and O'Connell above them—offer a panoply of the finest Irish meat, poultry, fish, cheese, produce, and specialties from the Continent and around the world.

Being as fond of cooking as of dining, I found the English market as exotic as an Arab souk, and my senses tingled at the myriad offerings. In an aisle of fishmongers I gaped: heaped on ice were turbot, cod, plaice, black sole, monkfish, salmon, brill, prawns, and a variety of oysters, among other briny specimens. Should a rack of lamb or a choice leg be your fancy, you could consult one of the O'Flynns, who raise their own lamb on the family farm. In season there is wild game to be had—including pheasant, grouse, woodcock, snipe, venison, and hare. Need a rare condiment—say, cardamom from India or saffron from Spain? Mr. Bell will have it. At one stall, I marveled at the ranks of wooden tubs brimming with green, black, and purple olives from around the Mediterranean. At another, I savored the aromas of coffees from Africa. Finally, I wandered past ramparts of fresh green vegetables and out to the Grand Parade, wishing that I were going to my kitchen carrying some deep-green, firm, thin French *haricots verts*, a few of Mr. O'Flynn's loin lamb chops, some spuds from nearby Ballymaloe, and a wedge of Cashel blue cheese.

I WALKED TOWARD the north channel of the Lee and crossed it by Griffith Bridge. Passing the Dominican Church of St. Mary, with its great colonnaded front on Pope's Quay, I ascended Shandon Street, bent on visiting St. Anne's Church, Shandon, which has come to be a symbol for the city of Cork. (The tweed cap I've been wearing on my march has a label saying SHANDON and an embroidered picture of the church.) Turning right onto Church Street, I came to St. Anne's, with its lofty ziggurat-like campanile towering over me and much of the city. The church was erected between 1722 and 1726, with the tower added in 1750. St. Anne's is distinguished by having two sides of its tower faced with white limestone and two with red sandstone. The weather vane atop the cupola is an eleven-foot salmon, saluting the bounty of the Lee in bygone times. But the fame of St. Anne's, Shandon, is doubtless primarily due to the doggerel of Father Prout, titled "The Bells of Shandon":

> On this I ponder, where'er I wander,
> And thus grow fonder, sweet Cork of thee,
> With thy bells of Shandon,
> That sound so grand on
> The pleasant waters of the River Lee.

Francis Sylvester Mahony, who adopted the pen name Father Prout (and
also wrote as Don Jeremy Savonarola), must be one of the most remarkable characters in Cork's long history, a rara avis, a stormy petrel. Born in
Cork in 1804, he was educated in the Jesuits' Clongowes Wood in Ireland,
and at Amiens, Paris, and Rome, becoming a classical scholar and a lin-
guist. Aspiring to become a Jesuit, he returned to Clongowes Wood to
teach as a master of rhetoric, but he was judged unsuitable for the order:
an episode in which he led some of his pupils on a tipsy outing became notorious. Mahony then went to Italy, where, in 1832, he succeeded in being
ordained a secular priest. Returning to Cork, Mahony served as a pastor
but was soon at odds with his bishop. In 1834, he settled in London and
embarked on a career as a journalist, beginning as a frequent contributor
to *Fraser's Magazine for Town and Country*, then edited by a fellow Corkonian, William Maginn, and later for *Bentley's Miscellany*, edited by Dickens.
Witty and convivial, Mahony became a familiar in a literary circle which
included Coleridge, Southey, Carlyle, and Thackeray. In print he had a
penchant for barbed satire; wielding his pen like a rapier, he crossed
swords with various important persons whose views he opposed. Daniel
O'Connell, Ireland's beloved Great Emancipator, was a particular target.

No longer performing priestly functions but always regular in his de-
votions, Mahony was an odd bird of passage, moving to Rome, where he
was correspondent for *The Daily News*, and then to Paris in the stormy
year of 1848. There, for many years, he was a correspondent for the *Globe*.
He died in Paris in 1866, shriven by the Abbé Rogerson, and was buried in
the family vault at St. Anne's, Shandon. Mahony's friend Robert Brown-
ing wrote his obituary for *The Pall Mall Gazette:*

> He was a Jesuit and a humourist; a priest and Bohemian; a scholar
> and a journalist; a wag and a song writer; a Cork man familiar to
> everybody in Rome; a Roman Catholic ecclesiastic well known in
> the convivial clubs of London.

I had read that one could ascend the tower of St. Anne's, passing the great
works that operate the clocks, with their fourteen-foot dials, on each side
of the tower. The climber is rewarded with superb views over the terraces
of the city on this north bank, the old heart of Cork wrapped in the river's
arms below, and the low green hills beyond, to the south. However, the

church was locked, and I walked back downhill to the river, past the fine, round mid-nineteenth-century Butter Exchange, which has become the Firkin Crane Cultural Centre, transformed into theaters and studio spaces for drama and ballet.

CORK HAS AN active cultural life: it has an opera house; the Crawford Municipal Art Gallery; a ballet company; a long-established film festival (at which, many years ago, a film I produced was presented). Several of its writers—Daniel Corkery, Seán O'Faoláin (christened John Whalen), and Frank O'Connor (pseudonym of Michael Francis O'Donovan)—became pillars of Ireland's literary pantheon. But I knew almost nothing about what was happening in the arts here now. When I'd said this to my friend David Nowlan of *The Irish Times,* he gave me an introduction to Mary Leland, saying, "She can put you in the picture." A contributor on the arts to *The Irish Times* and *The Sunday Independent,* Mary Leland is also the author of several novels, a collection of short stories, and *The Lie of the Land: Journeys Through Literary Cork,* a stylishly written, vastly informative trove of lore on writers great and modest who constitute the county's literary heritage.

Early one evening, Mary picked me up in her car and proposed that we dine at a restaurant called Number 5 Fenn's Quay. The former quay proved to be the now-landfilled Sheares Street, named, like so many of Cork's thoroughfares, for patriots, the brothers Henry and John Sheares, who were executed for their roles in the rebellion of 1798. Number 5 was small, austere in decor, and serious about food, which was northern Italian in kind. My grilled fish was a treat.

Mary Leland, charmingly informal and acute, gave me a sketch of what was what and who was who on Cork's theatrical, literary, and artistic horizons just then. That evening she suggested I might want to see Sophocles' *Antigone,* being presented by Donad Productions, a group devoted to Greek and Irish classical drama. The production was near the end of a limited run, after which it would be mounted in the ancient stadium at Delphi and in the Roman amphitheater at Carnumtum, in Austria.

The Half Moon Theatre is in the short Half Moon Street, just behind the Cork Opera House (then in process of major restoration) and the Crawford Municipal Art Gallery. I recalled that Seán O'Faoláin had grown up in Half Moon Street, in the boardinghouse of his mother, who catered to a theatrical and operatic clientele. His father was a policeman in the Royal Irish Constabulary. Like his contemporary, friend, and literary rival Frank O'Connor, O'Faoláin wrote affectively and mordantly about his natal city. In *An Irish Journey,* he writes, "It is one of those towns you love and hate. Some wag said that in Cork you do not commit sin, you achieve it. You do not, likewise, enjoy life in Cork, you experience it." A remark quintessentially Irish and perhaps preternaturally Corkonian.

This evening there was a sparse audience in the Half Moon Theatre, which has an open-space arrangement. Chronologically *Antigone* is the last play in the trilogy Sophocles devoted to the doom-laden royal family of Thebes, following *Oedipus the King* and *Oedipus at Colonus,* but it was the first to be staged, about 442 B.C. The text of this *Antigone* was a translation by Marianne McDonald, Professor of Theater and Classics at the University of California, San Diego; the play was directed by Donal Courtney, who also performed as the Chorus.

Antigone is a tragedy in which Antigone, daughter of the late King Oedipus; her betrothed, Haemon; and Eurydice, Haemon's mother and the wife of the present king of Thebes, Creon, all perish because of Creon's moral certitude. Watching it, I reflected that Sophocles' play was not irrelevant to the absolutism, the righteousness, of unionists and republicans in Northern Ireland, which has left so many dead in our time. Sophocles' moral tale of the conflict between the conscience of a compassionate woman and the authority of the state vested in its ruler seems pertinent. After twenty-five hundred years, it still has the power to move us.

Peadar Cox as Creon was particularly noteworthy, conveying the gravity of a king resolved to uphold the law yet anguished by that responsibility and its terrible consequences. The staging was at once hieratic and modern, and the chanting of dirges by the Chorus and the spine-tingling beating of the *bodhrán* gave the production an Irish tint. I missed only the sense of regal grandeur and scale that you would expect if you were seeing a production in the great amphitheater at, say, Epidaurus; perhaps this company would evoke that sense performing in the stadium at Delphi, where it was soon to appear.

Meanwhile, I carried away from the production of *Antigone* in Cork a realization of the consonance between the classic Greek tragedies and the ancient Irish sagas about the exploits of the mythic heroes Cúchulainn and

Fionn mac Cumhail (Finn MacCool). In both the Greek dramas and the Irish epics there are instances of fosterage, powerful kings, formidable queens, doomed heroes, and bloody deeds. The composition of the Greek and Irish works might even have been contemporaneous.

WHEN MARY LELAND was cluing me in about theater in Cork, she spoke about the Everyman Palace Theatre (on MacCurtain Street; it was dark just then) and its imaginative productions, mentioning Conal Creedon, then the theater's writer in residence, and Pat Kiernan, who has directed a number of its productions.

"Pat Kiernan directed a play called *Disco Pigs* by Enda Walsh for Corcadorca Productions at the Triskel Arts Centre here," said Mary. "It was subsequently presented in Dublin and London and created a stir. Enda Walsh is a Dubliner living in Cork who writes about Corkonian characters. He's written the screenplay of *Disco Pigs*, which is set in Cork, for producer Ed Guiney's company, and they've been shooting here."

IN THE LAST COUPLE of decades there has been an extraordinary flowering of filmmakers in Ireland. Until the 1970s, while there were several distinguished makers of documentaries, there were almost no Irish producers, directors, and writers of feature films. Now such filmmakers as Neil Jordan (*The Butcher Boy*), Jim Sheridan (*In the Name of the Father*), and Terry George (*Some Mother's Son*), among others, were making films—some on Irish subjects with Irish actors—that were achieving critical acclaim, if the sometimes modest audiences that low-budget independent films usually draw. It turned out that Kirsten Sheridan, Jim Sheridan's daughter, twenty-three years old, had finished shooting *Disco Pigs*, and I arranged to catch her for a drink and a talk one evening between her jaunts to London on postproduction matters.

ENDA WALSH'S screenplay of *Disco Pigs* is the story of a boy and girl who have an obsessional bond from infancy. The boy, Darren, is called Pig by the girl, Sinead, whom he calls Runt. They communicate in a lingo of their own, part baby talk and part Cork slang, spattered with obscenities.

By their teens they are dysfunctional at school and at home, living in a hermetic world, and Pig's pubescent sexuality leads to violent, jealous rages. To separate them and normalize Runt's life, she is sent to a rehabilitation center in rural Donegal. Making his way hundreds of miles, Pig finds her, and the pair flee to a deserted beach and the sea, which has always been a magnet and a wonder for them. This extraordinary love story does not end happily, and, as scripted, it tested my credulity. I thought the screenplay would be immensely challenging to realize as a film.

KIRSTEN SHERIDAN is a pretty blond slip of a woman with an easy, self-effacing manner, beneath which one senses considerable determination. She was wearing jeans and a ribbed pullover; wire-rimmed granny glasses framed sapphire eyes. She dropped into a chair and began talking as if resuming an interrupted conversation, immediately likable.

"What got you into filmmaking?" I asked.

"Growing up, I always knew it would be theater or film for me," Kirsten said. "There were always actors in our house. I spent two years studying psychology and philosophy, some in adult education in UCD, then went to the Institute of Art, Design, and Technology in Dun Laoghaire. Afterward I made two commercials for TV."

I asked what had led to directing her first feature film.

"Ed Guiney, a producer who has a company called Temple Films, saw a short film I'd made, called *Patterns,* and he offered me *Disco Pigs.*"

I wondered what control she'd had over casting and selecting key crew members, and I asked.

"Primarily, I got my choices, with OK's from the producer," said Kirtsen. "We knew we wanted Cillian Murphy for Pig; he'd been brilliant in the play, toured with it, and had been in three feature films. There were many auditions and tests; Elaine Cassidy was cast as Runt."

"When shooting starts, there is pressure on any director," I remarked, "the schedule, budget, artistic temperaments, sometimes gambits by the unions. For a first-time director of a theatrical feature, that could be tough. Did you feel any pressure from the front office?"

Kirsten laughed again. "Not while I was shooting. The financiers left me pretty much alone. Oh, there were tears. Not on the set. At night, at home."

I asked if she had an overall aesthetic concept for the film before shooting.

"I wanted a distinct photographic style to stand for each principal character. Pig's is a tunnel vision. Runt's widens out. Our DP"—director of photography—"Igor Jadue-Lillo, who had photographed three features, loved the script and saw my concept. There were three disco scenes that were difficult and demanding and in which key events occur. Igor was up for them. I was fortunate in other people on the team: Brenda Yeates, the editor, on her second feature; Sophie Janson, the AP"—associate producer—"experienced in development, was sound and supportive."

I asked what the postproduction experience had been like.

"The financiers didn't interfere while we were shooting," Kirsten said. "Afterward, in postproduction, there were a lot of faxes, memos, and e-mails involving the lab, Technicolor, and the editing. There was a shot, a three-and-a-half-minute monologue, holding on Pig, tracking in slowly. They thought it was too long. Argument. That sort of thing. I probably did need a kick up the bum about then."

"I imagine you learned a hell of a lot," I ventured.

Kritsen took a beat: "I've learned I've got to hold firm."

EVEN WITHOUT THE annual Cork Film Festival, which brings dozens of new films to the city, filmgoers can view a large number and variety of films. At the Gate multiplex cinema on North Main Street, one can choose from six giant-budget, would-be blockbusters. Kino, a cinema on Western Road near UCC, is an art house offering well-regarded contemporary English-language and foreign films and classics. Film buffs can also sate themselves at the Triskel Arts Centre. Its literature describes it as the "only Multi-disciplinary Arts Centre in the Cork Region."

Off I went to Tobin Street and was astonished at the breadth of presentations that Triskel listed in its calendar for the month. The center's Cinematek would be showing twelve works: feature films, documentaries, and experimental digital and graphic animations from several countries, including Spain, Denmark, Germany, Russia, the United States, and Ireland.

Today there was an eighty-six-minute documentary by Gough Lewis from the United States, *Sex: The Annabel Chong Story*. In Triskel's brochure, I read: "Porn star Chong brought herself to international fame when she led the largest 'gang-bang' in history, involving 251 men. The event shook the U.S. press, the porn industry, and the university where she studied." Somehow Chong's shaking up of the U.S. press had escaped me. However, if I had any lingering doubt that Ireland was undergoing a radical transformation from the country I had first known—and whose board of film censors I had dealt with when the Catholic Church's influence on government and public mores was heavy—Chong's celebration at Triskel dispelled it. (While the Church's profile is lower, it is no mere silhouette: Ireland still has a constitutional ban on divorce and on abortion, except to save the life of a pregnant woman. Annually some seven thousand Irish women travel to Britain for abortions. And when married but separated *Taoiseach* Bertie Ahern's unmarried consort cohosted a state reception at Dublin Castle, it was tactfully arranged that she not be presented to the Catholic archbishop of Dublin.)

Although occupying a surprisingly small space, Triskel crams into it many multidisciplinary arts. I learned that this month one could hear performances by Cork guitarist Mark O'Leary with bass violist Anders Jormin and drummer Auden Kieve or the eclectic rock, electronic, and spoken work of the recording group called DeConfidence. Besides drama and craft workshops, the poet and playwright Paula Meehan was to give a reading.

Triskel was again hosting Intermedia, a month-long festival of new art forms in places scattered about the city. In a gallery at Triskel, I was introduced to the kinetic sculptures of France's Baschet brothers, whose works, many in stainless steel, balanced wondrously or moving eerily, might have riveted the eye of a NASA engineer or a nuclear physicist as much as they did mine. For those whose thirst for art leaves them parched before, during, or after performances, there is the center's Yumi Yuki Club, a sushi and sake bar and café.

WHILE TRISKEL emphasizes the cutting edge in the arts, Cork is also fortunate in having a museum that is a treasury of painting and sculpture by Irish and British artists of past and present and of graphic work by Irish and international artists. The greater part of the Crawford Municipal Art Gallery, on Emmet Place, is a fine late-nineteenth-century building that includes the early-eighteenth-century Customs House and was erected through the generosity of the brewer William Horatio Crawford. Although Dubliners and many of the world's drinkers of the dark beer called stout favor that brewed by the successors of Arthur Guinness & Sons, Corkonians and others are loyal imbibers of two stouts brewed in Cork—Murphy's and Beamish, the latter a brew of Beamish & Crawford. I would not call the Crawford's holdings extensive, for other than the bequest of fifteen thousand pounds sterling by Joseph Stafford Gibson in 1919, the gallery has had very limited funds for acquisitions. Nonetheless, it has some fine representative works by such Irish painters as James Barry, Walter Osborne, Jack B. Yeats, Sir William Orpen, and Louis Le Brocquy. Among the sculptors represented are Joseph Higgins and Seamus Murphy. (Murphy, the most renowned of Cork's sculptors in the twentieth century, did the fine heads of Lord Mayors Tomás MacCurtain and Terence MacSwiney in the City Hall.)

Wandering through the museum, which I had prowled before, I found its intimate spaces, its grand staircase, and the warmth of polished wood pleasing, particularly as a background for the nineteenth-century works. Among paintings I admired were Daniel Maclise's *Lear and Cordelia,* a remarkable, rather Rubenesque watercolor; the British artist Frank Bramley's charming interior with two young seamstresses, titled *Domino;* a superb window, *St. Brendan and the Unhappy Judas,* depicting the saintly navigator and the apparition of Judas in flames, by the Irish stained-glass artist Harry Clarke; and Jack B. Yeats's tumultuous oil of fishermen in their sea-tossed currach, *Off the Donegal Coast.*

A happy surprise was a painting I had somehow missed before: a life-size oil titled *The Goose Girl* by the multitalented Edith Oenone Somerville (1858–1949). Although best known as an author, Somerville trained as an artist in London, Düsseldorf, and Paris (unusual for a daughter of Anglo-Irish gentry). The oil, painted when she was thirty years old, depicts a dark-haired, large-eyed girl in a green smock, sitting on a flagstone floor against a stone wall, cradling a goose in her lap. Beside her are large cooking utensils and a cabbage; in front of her is a copper basin holding what seems to be cornmeal. The handling of space in the picture leaves something to be desired, but the painting of the goose is splendid, and Chardin would not have despised the caldron, stockpot, and comestibles.

In a small gallery, I was intrigued by a remarkable bequest by Father

John McGrath, who left three prints (a Hockney, a Dalí, and a Braque) and forty-five paintings to the Crawford. Father McGrath was a rural parish priest for many years in Tipperary and Limerick. Somehow he was introduced to opera by a sacristan, John Cody, who did not even have a secondary education. His artistic tastes stimulated by Cody, Father McGrath began collecting such eighteenth-century paintings as William Saddler's *The Revolutionaries,* the early-nineteenth-century landscape *Moonlight Scene* by James Arthur O'Connor, and works by such estimable twentieth-century Irish artists as Louis Le Brocquy, Brian Bourke, and Barrie Cooke.

Shortly after my visit, a strikingly unusual gallery in a new addition was about to open. It was designed by the Dutch architect Erick van Egeraat (designer of the new theater at Stratford-upon-Avon), whose design won an international competition. Construction was funded by a grant of I£1.8 million from the European Union. Intended for temporary exhibitions, primarily of contemporary art, the new gallery is a grand single space, two floors in height, connected by a long sloping floor, with an immense window at one end.

An attractive amenity of the Crawford Gallery is its restaurant. With its soft French-blue decor, modest size, unobtrusive service, and good food, it is one of the nicest places I know to lunch in Cork. Happily, I was shown straightway to a table, lunched well, and lingered over a glass of wine and some postcards from the gallery's shop.

IN MY DAILY READING of the newspaper (as there is no Sunday edition of *The Irish Times,* I read *The Sunday Independent*), I could not help noticing what seemed an increase in crime from what I remembered in earlier years. Perhaps it was only a difference in the kind of crimes deemed worthy of reporting by the *Times*'s editors. Reports of murders, rapes, and brutal robberies, while surely not of the frequency in New York or Boston, were not uncommon. The result of a poll published in *The Sunday Independent* on October 24, 1999, indicated that 94 percent of persons questioned believed that "crimes committed against the person" were becoming "more violent." Much crime, not necessarily violent, was drug related. Discos seemed to figure in the reports of many crimes; "hooliganism" (which *Webster's* attributes to an Irish name) was not uncommon in the disco scene.

As Cork was the largest city on my itinerary, I obtained an introduction to Superintendent Kieran McGann of the Garda Síochána to inquire about crime in Cork. Remembering when many of Ireland's cops rode around on bicycles and blew their whistles to raise the alarm, I hoped to learn how Cork's police force operates today.

Cork's police headquarters, a severely functional building as in many another city, is adjacent to City Hall. But I was happy to see that unlike the police stations I'd seen in Northern Ireland, it did not appear to be fortified against possible assaults by the citizenry. Superintendent Kieran McGann's office was on an upper floor.

He sat behind a large desk, speaking on the telephone, and waved me to a chair. I looked around the sunlit, uncluttered office while the superintendent soothed the person on the telephone with a repeated "Good man . . . so . . . good man, yourself" and other cheery reassurances. He sounded as if he were a ward politician in Chicago or Boston. Then the superintendent, a tall, sturdy man with close-clipped red hair, who appeared in vigorous early middle age, stood up and shook my hand. He reminded me of the kind of big Irish cop of my youth, who stood at the corner of Fifth Avenue and Fiftieth Street in New York, in double-breasted blue tunic and white gloves, whistle in mouth but weapon invisible, moving traffic and keeping an eye on St. Patrick's Cathedral and Saks department store. Massively reassuring. However, when McGann talked to me about policing Cork, it was with the concise assurance of an executive.

"Our strength is six hundred and fifteen officers, headed by the chief superintendent, away on an investigation just now," McGann said, "and four superintendents. I'm assistant divisional commander and chief of the Anglesea district and have thirty years in police work. There's one detective superintendent, thirteen inspectors—of whom two are detective inspectors—then the sergeants, and the *gardaí*. Cork city constitutes a division, which extends into the periphery and is comprised of four districts." He named each of them.

I asked what were the major problems for the police in Cork.

"Ours are predominantly burglary and shoplifting. There's a downward trend."

"What's the situation with drugs?"

"There are drugs. They're available," he said. "But no heroin," he said emphatically. "We rarely have shootings or killings. Cork has an airport, and we're a seaport; there's a long, broken coastline, so we're vulnerable. We work closely with Customs, the Navy, and Public Health people, as well as with Europol in The Hague and with Interpol. There's a growing internationalization of crime." (Soon afterward a supposed major Cork drug lord was shot dead at his front door.)

I asked about a recent gruesome gang-related killing of several men at Scheveningen, in Holland.

"Yes, they were from rural Ireland," said Superintendent McGann. "There are certainly international connections."

"In the best of all possible worlds, what would you wish for, to improve policing in Cork?" I asked.

The superintendent laughed. "The holy trinity of policing," he replied. "More personnel, more money, and more equipment. But short of those gifts what you have to do is develop a strategy.

"The great stride was the establishment of the Criminal Assets Bureau for the investigation of major crime," McGann continued. "It was the concept of persons in the Department of Justice, and the Bureau is headed by Barry Galvin. Commissioner Byrne—chief of the Garda Síochána—has built on his predecessor's innovations, establishing specialized bureaus, such as fraud and road safety."

I asked if there had been other significant developments in addressing crime.

McGann said, "One factor in crime reduction is that in rural areas, everybody tends to know everything about everyone else. You've seen the 'Community Alert' signs"—indeed I had, in villages and little outlying settlements. "Community surveillance, keeping an eye out for suspicious persons, is a helpful deterrent to crime. The 'Community Alert' idea was imported from America."

"What's the drill when a crime is reported?"

"Come along," said the superintendent; "let me take you to Communication Control."

IN A SLIGHTLY darkened room five police officers sat by softly glowing computer monitors. A few of them were speaking quietly into microphones. Superintendent McGann introduced me to Sergeant Alan Cronin and left me with him.

Tall, trim, somewhat balding, and blue eyed, the sergeant explained that Communication Control is manned by five officers on three eight-hour shifts. Today his command came on at 2:00 P.M. and would be relieved by another sergeant and four *gardaí* at 10:00 P.M.

"Every one-one-two call"—the all-Europe emergency number—"made in Ireland is routed to one of two centers in Ireland: Dublin or Mullingar," said Sergeant Cronin. "If it concerns the Cork division, it's passed to us, and we handle it. Cork has fifteen uniformed mobiles and eleven detective cars, three traffic cars, and three traffic bikes on duty. It might be an ambulance or the fire brigade that we dispatch."

While I was conscious of hearing some of the officers on duty responding to emergency calls, none seemed to be about serious crimes, but then I realized that the dispatchers are trained to respond to all communications calmly, as they were doing. "Can the bad guys tap into your system?" I asked.

"It's a very secure system. But we're moving from an analogue system to digital encryption in about two years."

I was looking at a monitor over one man's shoulder, and as the display was largely Greek to me, I asked what kind of information came up on their screens.

"Since November ninety-nine, we've had the PULSE system," said Cronin. "The acronymn stands for 'Police Using Leading Systems Efficiently.' An officer here in Control can feed in data from someone detained or a witness, and we can click and search whether, for example, someone is known to the intelligence service or has a firearms or court conviction. In short, we have access to an enormous database."

Sergeant Cronin's enthusiasm for his work was palpable, and I asked how he had come to Communication Control.

"I attended the central Garda College at Templemore, Tipperary, for two years," he said. "After that I served in Tallaght and Rathfarnham, Dublin suburbs, for several years before going to Millstreet, Cork, for two and a half years, next at Togher in Cork for four years, then to headquarters. I spent a year downstairs here, and now I've had a year in Communication Control."

"And the future?"

"Guards, sergeants, and inspectors must retire at fifty-seven. Superintendents at sixty. Full pension is half salary plus gratuity."

I thought Cork would be well served if McGann and Cronin went the distance.

EVER SINCE I'D set out on my journey, I'd hoped to arrive somewhere when a race meeting was on, but there were few racecourses on or close to my route and no race meetings scheduled when I was near—until I reached Cork. Cork Racecourse is actually at Mallow, about twenty miles to the northwest, but it seemed unthinkable to end my tramp through Ireland without taking in a race meeting. I caught a bus that put me in Mallow in good time for the first race, at 5:30 P.M. on a glorious spring day, the sun still high. I remembered that the town had a famous past:

> Living short but merry lives;
> Going where the devil drives;
> Having sweethearts but no wives,
> Live the Rakes of Mallow!

Today little remains to suggest Mallow's glory days as a spa, an Irish mini-Bath, but the town is sited on the beautiful Blackwater, and there is the considerable ruin of a castle supposed to have been built by Sir Thomas Norris in the late sixteenth century, with a rare herd of white deer in its demesne.

At the Cork Racecourse, I joined the throng passing through the main gate. Just inside, I bought a cheap admission to the stands and a race card to find out which horses were entered in the seven races and something about them. Unfortunately, I'd left behind *The Irish Examiner* (formerly the venerable *Cork Examiner*, until April 12, 2000, when it announced its "ambition to overtake *The Irish Independent* and become the country's biggest newspaper"), whose racing pundits I would have liked to consult, for while I'm not an ardent punter, I like to have a little flutter, *pour le sport*, as the French say.

Before going to the new grandstand, with its bars, restaurants, and the official tote windows for betting, I went to the parade ring, to have a close look at the horses being led around and around by their grooms. The Irish know a lot about horses, and even if you may not, you might overhear

shrewd observations about the horses being shown, perhaps from a grizzled farmer with dung-splattered boots or a ruddy fellow who's trained a
horse or two, or a *racée* lady who's ridden quite a few. Many of my favorite
moments at the races have been at the parade ring, watching these beautiful animals, curried and brushed and combed and polished to a fare-thee-
well, showing their stuff, some stepping as proudly as chorus girls, others
mettlesome and champing at the bit, some skittish and blinkered, some
barely held back, raring to go. A racing veteran likes to believe that by observing a horse closely, he or she can discern something that can't be read
in the race card, the racing form, or the prognostications of pundits, something perhaps ineffable, a horse's style, its heart, and its chances.

At last the jockeys, caparisoned in their owners' colors, appear beside
their horses, always with the trainer, often with the owner or owners; last-
minute instructions may be murmured, a cinch may be tightened. Then
these knights of the saddle vault onto their mounts and move out to the
course.

I was certainly unsure but rather fancied the bay colt Cashel Palace. I
noted my hunch on the race card and made for the tote windows. (The to-
talizator, or pari-mutuel machine, controlled by the racing authorities,
constantly records bets and adjusts the odds so that bettors who hold winning tickets divide the total moneys bet in proportion to the amounts they
have wagered, less the racecourse's share.) I joined a long queue and, like
the others in it, glanced at the TV monitors displaying the constantly fluc-
tuating odds for each horse in the next race. The first race was to be a flat
race of six furlongs (six-eighths of a mile, or 1,320 yards) for two-year-old
"maidens" (horses that have never won a race). Factice Royal was the favorite; the odds were not long. When I got to the window, I plunked down
a punt on Cashel Palace, betting the horse each way—that is, to win or to
place.

The course at Mallow lies in the flat bottomland of the Blackwater, in
a bend of the river. Beyond the track is an immense sugar factory. To the
south, across the Blackwater, rise the modest hills called the Boggeragh
Mountains. As an Irish racecourse it is neither as spectacular as that on the
vast Curragh of Kildare, where such great races as the Irish Derby are
run, nor so picturesque as, say, the rural course as Listowel, where there's
a week of racing on lush turf framed by a ruined Fitzmaurice castle and

Kerry's Stack's Mountains. Still, on this evening, as I looked over Cork Racecourse's emerald turf toward the gauzy purple hills beyond, I was content.

Aside from the beauty of the settings, one reason I find racing in Ireland and Britain more colorful and entertaining than in the United States is the presence of the bookmakers. On the whole a rakish lot, here they were lined up beside the grandstand, perched on boxes or steps, their names on placards above them, quickly making bets with punters who approach them, exchanging cash for flimsy slips of paper with the bets recorded. Up in the stands their confederates, the white-gloved ticktack men, wigwag signals as they perceive the odds changing from their perspective among the horseplayers. A racegoer has the choice of betting with a bookie—whose exchequer reposes in the satchel at his feet—or at the official tote window.

The stands were not crowded on this Monday evening. There were not the number of very stylishly dressed women to be seen at such great races as the Irish Derby or the Guinness Oaks, but nonetheless there were some handsome fillies with gentlemen in well-cut tweeds, as well as farmers in their best and unmistakably horsey men in well-worn trilby hats and stovepipe twill trousers, trainers and dealers, among the rank and file of racing fans.

Suddenly, with an announcement, the horses burst from the starting stalls. I focused on the jockey in dark blue, with the number 4 on his saddlecloth, heard myself shouting "You can do it, Cashel Palace!" and in minutes this gallop for novices was all over. Softly Tread was the winner, taking home I£10,000. Factice Royal, the favorite, came in third, and *voilà!* the French-bred Cashel Palace came in second, to place, so my bet paid off. I collected my winnings (I forgot to note what they were). The odds were short, I didn't need a bodyguard, but I could afford a beer.

I worked my way to the bar, got a lager, and found myself standing beside a tall woman bent over her race card; her face was obscured by a large velour hat with an impressive brim. I couldn't see her eyes, but her scent was spicy, unfamiliar. "Bloody hell!" she said quietly, looking up. "I lost a packet." The eyes were mauve, almost the same as the hat and the pantsuit.

"Betting on a maiden. Never can be sure," I said.

"Hahhhh!" It was a well-bred cackle.

I thought her situation rather called for a drink. She already had a pale, full glass before her. Just then a plummy voice spoke near my ear: "I say, old cock, have you a light?"

A man with a lemon-yellow waistcoat and houndstooth jacket was holding out a cigarette. I took out a box of matches and looked at him. Chap well-tanned, dark thin hair that had been brushed back by two brushes. Soldier. I struck the match. Another hand, long and olive skinned with magenta nails that could have cut throats, also held a cigarette. I lit both.

"Whom do you fancy in the second race?" asked the man.

"Thirty runners?" I said. "Worse than roulette."

The PA system blared. "They're announcing the scratches now," said Lady Mauve. Turning, she barely whispered "sherry" in a voice no barman would ignore and that Scott Fitzgerald had nailed.

"Whisky," Yellow Vest added to the barman. "Canadian?" he said to me.

"Yank," said the lady before I could reply.

"You know how to pick 'em," I said, tapping her race card and finishing my lager. "Good luck, though. You always need that."

THE SECOND RACE, two miles, for four-year-olds or older, over hurdles, was under way when I got back near my former place. Despite what I'd said at the bar, I wished I'd taken a chance on a horse I'd liked the look of, Fnan, which came in second. I hurried down to the parade ring before the third race.

The Dairygold Cork Sprint Stakes would bring the winner a purse of I£25,000. It was for three-year-olds and older. The savants at the parade ring looked closely, studied their forms. Some confabulated. I was tempted by One Won One, an American gelding sired by Naevus out of Harvard's Bay, an Argentine mare. But finally I liked the cut of the bay filly Desert Magic's jib and wagered an Irish punt on her nose, to win.

The experience of race going is powerfully sensory, compounded of the press of bodies, the emanations of excitement, the smell of tobacco, the occasional whiff of perfume, the thunder of hooves, the swelling cheers of the onlookers—"Come on! One Won One." "You're home and dry, Namid!" "Run, you divil, run!" As the horses raced for the finish line, my own exhortations of "Go, Desert Magic! Go, babe, go!" were part of the cacaphony. Then came the exultations, imprecations, and final concerted exhalation when the first, then second horse passed the winning post. Namid first, Desert Magic second, One Won One third. The short man with a wind-cured face and a prodigious mustache who'd been standing just below me turned away with a snort. "Miserable bugger," he muttered and tore up his ticket.

As for me, I'd lost my punt, and my place bet on the first race barely paid for my beer. There were four more races, but I'd already had a grand evening. I bused back to Cork in time for dinner.

WHEN IN CORK it is hard not to be conscious of the river Lee. Two branches enfold the city's center, now seemingly one island, although the arc of Patrick Street covers another branch, which once separated the two islands on which the city grew. I first became aware of the river's charms through two books by Robert Gibbings. Writer, artist, and printer, he was the son of a rector of St. Finbarr's Cathedral, and in *Lovely Is the Lee* and *Sweet Cork of Thee,* he hymned the river and his birthplace and illuminated both with his graceful wood engravings.

Thinking of Gibbings's words and images, I wandered along the quays toward University College, Cork, about a mile to the west of City Hall. Along the way, I passed the National Microelectronics Research Centre on the riverbank in old brewery buildings that had been imaginatively reinvented. This high-powered research-and-development facility was instituted at UCC, where its first director, Gerard Wrixon (a prime supporter of the Triskel Arts Centre), is now president of the university. The National Microelectronics Research Centre, usually referred to as NMRC, which originally concentrated on research for communications and information technology, has expanded into a multidisciplinary research facility, with a staff of 260, that offers support to industries within and beyond Ireland. As of 2000, it was the only such European research facility participating in all the advanced research initiatives of the European Union's Information and Communications Directorate. NMRC is well placed in Cork because the city is a major industrial center and many Irish and multinational companies have facilities there and in the city's environs. Among them are such high-tech manufacturers as Apple, Kodak, and

Motorola. Several major pharmaceutical companies are located in or close to Cork, including Schering-Plough at Inisshannon, Eli Lilly at Kinsale, and Pfizer at Ringaskiddy. Pfizer produces bulk chemicals as well as some finished medicines. Given the Catholic church's views on sexual matters, some people in Cork are amused to think that fellow Corkonians at Pfizer are producing Viagra or ingredients for the celebrated male potency restorative.

UNIVERSITY COLLEGE, CORK, was founded in 1845 as Queen's College (about the time of imperial Britain's apogee, when the port town of Cobh was Queenstown and that of Dun Laoghaire, outside Dublin, was Kingstown). After the Irish Universities Act of 1908, it became one of the colleges of the National University of Ireland. Today UCC is effectively a university itself, with eight faculties headed by their own deans, including arts, science, law, medicine, and engineering. While the growing institution has been spreading over Cork, the heart of the university remains the quadrangle surrounded by distinguished buildings designed by the firm of Sir Thomas Deane. They are in the Gothic style favored as far afield as Yale and evocative of Oxford and Cambridge. I strolled about with interest, having once aspired to teach here, conscious of the heterogeneous ethnicity of the students and admiring such striking modern buildings as the National Food Biotechnology Centre and the library.

Looking at the library, with its wealth of books, I thought of how many writers associated with UCC had contributed to that treasury. One was Daniel Corkery, professor of English here for many years—author of the seminal book *The Hidden Ireland,* an eloquent panegyric to writers in Irish faithful to ancient bardic traditions—and before that an early mentor of Seán O'Faoláin and Frank O'Connor. They turned against Corkery, in a typically Irish, disputatious way, disdaining his advocacy of the Irish language, nationalism, Catholicism, and socialist principles as too constrictive.

UCC has long had a strong English faculty; the department's present chairman is Professor Colbert Kearney, a novelist whose scholarly works include critical studies of Sean O'Casey and Brendan Behan. There are other scholars and creative writers of accomplishment in the department. It has been particularly fortunate in its poets. John Montague, who taught at UCC for sixteen years and has a home at Ballydehob, in West Cork, is a major poet who became the first professor of poetry given a chair shared by Trinity College, Dublin, and Queen's University, Belfast, and supported by the Arts Councils of both Northern Ireland and the Republic. Other poets writing in English who have emerged from UCC and attracted notable attention are Patrick Galvin and Thomas McCarthy. UCC has also been distinguished in its Celtic studies. Seán Ó Riordáin and Seán Ó Tuama have made significant contributions as poets writing in Irish, and Ó Tuama, a student of Corkery's and now emeritus professor of modern Irish literature, has written important critical studies of poetry in the Irish language.

I WAS TO MEET Mary Leland for a farewell lunch, and she suggested Esau's in Carey's Lane, a narrow pedestrian passage between Patrick Street and Paul Street, peppered with ethnically diverse restaurants within a short block. Esau's was the relatively new enterprise of Michael Ryan, proprietor of the convivial, dependable Isaac's in MacCurtain Street. (Michael is the brother of Declan Ryan, former proprietor of Arbutus Lodge, and their contributions to cuisine in Cork have been major. Michael has since sold Esau's to the young, internationally trained chef Chris O'Brien, who has renamed it Table 8.) We lunched at a table in a bright upstairs room of minimalist decor, choosing from a short and tasteful menu, and Mary talked of the National Sculpture Centre, which provides instruction and studio space, the Cork Printmakers (whose workshops in well-restored old buildings she had already shown me), and the West Cork International Music Festival, held in the summer. I asked about Cork's writers today, and she spoke admiringly of the poet Thomas McCarthy, who examined contemporary regional writers in *Accents of the South*, and Antonia Logue, author of *The Shadow Box*, who was currently writer in residence at UCC. As I thanked my cicerone for all I'd learned, she added that Martin Kelleher, a young Corkonian, was to give a reading from his first book at Waterstone's Booksellers that evening.

WHEN I GOT to Waterstone's, a goodly number of people were already listening to Martin Kelleher talking about the path to publication of his novel, *Small City Blues*. A tall young man in black turtleneck and trousers, with dark blond hair pulled back in a ponytail, wearing metal-rimmed glasses on a soft, unchiseled face, he was speaking about another writer, whose name I think was Jerry Twomey (I had difficulty hearing; it was rather like being at mass in Ireland, with crying babes in arms): "I shared a bed-sit with him for nine months. He taught me about the nobility of what I was doing. I owe him a great deal." Kelleher spoke ardently, in spurts, hands gesticulating. But when he read sections from his book, he was calm and measured. The first was a quiet, reflective passage about a character named Quigley, from the point of view of the book's protagonist, Mackey, who grows up in the place the author calls Small City, manifestly Cork.

I enjoyed the reading and bought a copy of the book, which Martin Kelleher inscribed, and I read its 136 pages later that night. *Small City Blues* traces, though not chronologically, the arc of Mackey's life from his coming-of-age with his mates—Tracey Boy, Pedro, Quigley, and the lovely Clodagh Quirke, with whom he first makes love—as he drifts through a series of dreary jobs, gets an education, and eventually marries a beautiful woman, whom he desperately loves but betrays, is betrayed by in turn, and loses. Kelleher's mosaic is a bleak picture of vacant lives. But it is written with hard-won knowledge, pungent social observations, and bursts of sometimes rapturous writing, occasionally straining for effect. Kelleher was once a musician, and the sad notes of the blues in his title reverberate.

I SPENT A NUMBER of evenings in Cork writing in my journal, forgoing the camaraderie of a local pub, which is often more entertaining and sometimes more informative than the offerings on television. Cork, of course, offers a plethora of pubs. In places they are clustered like peas in a pod. On clement days, and Cork has many of them, one sees Corkonians sitting outside on beer kegs or in the ubiquituous white plastic chairs, savoring the local brews. Everyone has his or her favorite watering hole; I'm partial to Jim Cashman's, on Academy Street; Counihans, on Pembroke Street; and (especially for lunch) The Oyster, on Market Lane. But the pub I like best is Henchy's, at St. Luke's Cross, a place named after the Protestant church at the edge of the district called Montenotte. Since I had last been here, Henchy's had been bought by Dubliner Paddy O'Reilly, who has spruced it up (not tarted it up, in the plastic way that has despoiled so many old smoky, wainscoted Irish pubs that are imitated as far afield as Paris and Boston). In ages past, Henchy's had been an upscale grocer's, a purveyor of fine teas. The bar back, which has seen legions of bottles and countless pounds of Darjeeling come and go, is still here, as is the scarred wooden bar, which has supported countless elbows and been silent witness to many verbal salvos. Perhaps because Henchy's has been a resort of artists and writers, Paddy O'Reilly had put up framed facsimiles of poems by such poets as Seamus Heaney and John Montague.

Henchy's has always enjoyed a good custom, and this evening it thrived. Nonetheless, I found a slot at the corner of the bar near the front of the house, got a whiskey in hand, lit my pipe, and was soothed by the hum of cheerful disputation around me. I recalled that the last time I'd been in Henchy's, I'd stood in the same spot and enjoyed a memorable encounter that I recorded in my journal then. That evening, I hadn't been long there before a small, red-faced, bearded Barry Fitzgerald sort beside me remarked that I was not a regular and wondered how long I would be in Cork. He disclosed that he was from Fermoy and that his name was Cotter: "Originally MacOitir—that is, MacOtter—so I make it my business to give a piece of my mind to any otter hunter I should encounter." (There are still packs of otter hounds in Ireland.) I didn't record my response, probably not "Hear! hear!" but likely something inane, and Cotter continued to fulminate against cruel and predatory behavior.

"I studied meteorology at the University of Florida for a year, and the women of Tallahassee were immense," he confided. "The rednecks from nearby Alabama used to prey on them." Cotter said he was also shocked by the bigotry of Alabamians. That led him to segue to the savage treatment of Indians by the white settlers of the American West, adding that some of the most fearsome brutality the Indians endured was inflicted by Irishmen of the U.S. Cavalry.

I remarked that he doubtless knew General Philip Sheridan's pithy pronouncement on the goodness of Indians. Mournfully Cotter replied that he did. While Cotter had been expatiating, a man on an adjacent bench who'd been listening arose impressively, like a submarine surfacing, and closed in on us. A large man with small tortoiseshell glasses on a face like a loaf, he towered over Cotter, holding a pint of lager, clearly not his first, which he drank down, but he was not yet stocious, as the Irish used to say. When the bane of the otter hunters declared, "On the whole, I find humankind a pretty sorry lot," our new companion opined solemnly, "I quite agree." A moment of silence ensued as we contemplated this wisdom and our empty glasses. Then we ordered refills.

This evening, I observed Paddy O'Reilly and thought I'd never seen a more adept dispenser of drink. I watched as alone, on a busy night, he filled four pints at the same time, made change, and managed a conversation here and there. My comment about his deftness with the beer pulls brought the response that he "had grown up in a pub since [he] was five." In turn, he extracted from me that I had been a university teacher in the States. When he asked about the students I'd had, I remarked that a number of them were Asians or Asian Americans and that I found the Chinese particularly dedicated and industrious.

"Ah, the Chinese!" said O'Reilly, who then recalled a Chinese family he'd known in Dublin who produced an astonishing quantity of food from their tiny backyard plot. But we returned to education, and he spoke with modest pride of his then thirteen-year-old daughter. "She's a fine student, and she plays hockey and the violin," he said. "She's already thinking of Oxford or Harvard."

"Why shouldn't she?" I said. "The world is her oyster."

Journey's End: Kinsale

. ❀ .

THERE'S A PLACE IN THE TOWN OF KINSALE CALLED WORLD'S
End, and it's fitting that there should be. The old Gaelic world—the world
of the brehon lawgivers, of chieftains and princes with bards at their tables, the monastic world of scholars and scribes into which the old Gaels
had fitted perfectly—essentially ended with a battle here. Later, perhaps,
the landing here of the deposed King of England, Ireland, and Scotland
may be thought of as a tragic echo of the earlier event.

The Battle of Kinsale, fought on Christmas Eve 1601, was the first of
these events, and it was much on my mind as I made my way from the dull
industrial suburbs of Cork toward Kinsale, about fourteen miles distant. I
could see on my map that from Cork Airport, about four miles from the
city, there was a road parallel to the main N27, but somehow I missed it.
After about four hellish miles with speeding cars and big lorries brushing
by me, at Riverstick I found my way over to the parallel road. It had almost no traffic and led through sparsely settled country. The going was
good, and I swung along in high spirits. Coming to a bosky place, I
thought to pause for lunch, but a patch of litter and a plastic bag like a
nasty pennant on a branch put me off, and I moved on. (In an inspired
stroke, in March 2002, the Irish government imposed a thirteen-cent tax on

every plastic shopping bag, to be paid by the shopper and contributed to an environmental fund.)

After finding another pleasing spot to lunch, I came to a place with signs indicating where the Irish army had encamped on high ground before the fateful battle. Somewhat farther on, I was startled by a glimpse of the sea, shining like an immense mirror. I wasn't high on a peak in Darien, nor like Keats's stout Cortez was I gazing on the Pacific Ocean, but on the Atlantic. Yet I felt no less exalted: I had reached Kinsale, which would be journey's end.

DURING THE REIGN of Queen Elizabeth I, the English made further incursions into Ireland, dispossessing Catholic landholders, particularly in the Southwest, effecting the so-called plantation of Munster. The English also continued to maintain garrisons in the North, and in implementing their domination, they came into conflict with the Great Hugh O'Neill, 2nd Earl of Tyrone. He was also The O'Neill, the last formally inaugurated chief of his clan, with a princely pedigree that stretched back for centuries. O'Neill was a crafty politician and a capable soldier. His resistance to English rule (although he occasionally seemed to acquiesce), with that of his allies, was called the Nine Years War or, sometimes, Tyrone's Rebellion. As one means of protecting his own position, O'Neill eloped with Mabel, sister of Sir Henry Bagenal, an English magnate in southeast Ulster and a marshal of the English army. Yet when Bagenal moved to relieve a garrison on Ulster's Blackwater, O'Neill ambushed Bagenal's force. Bagenal was killed with some eight hundred of his men at the Battle of the Yellow Ford in 1598, the worst defeat of English arms in Ireland during the sixteenth century.

Resistance to the English plantation of Munster spread. In a notable instance, Kilcolman Castle, near Doneraile, Cork, the residence of the poet and English functionary Edmund Spenser, was burned in 1598. Seeing the chance of turning the tide against the English and Protestant encroachment in Ireland, O'Neill appealed to the Catholic sovereign Philip III of Spain for military assistance. Although a pious Catholic, Philip was doubtless glad to strike a blow against the English Queen, whose navy had defeated his father's armada in 1588. He dispatched Don

Juan de Aguila with a force of something less than four thousand men, who landed at Kinsale on October 2, 1601. Hugh O'Neill, with his ally and son-in-law Red Hugh O'Donnell, Earl of Tyrconnell and chief of his clan, were in Ulster, about as far from Kinsale and the devoutly hoped for Spanish force as they could be. Nonetheless, having learned of the Spaniards' arrival, O'Neill, O'Donnell, and other chiefs gathered their adherents and started south on their long march.

The Spanish, under their experienced commander, occupied the walled town, whose populace was largely English colonists, and several outlying fortresses. Meanwhile, the English Lord Deputy of Ireland, Charles Blount, Lord Mountjoy, hastened to deal with these alarming developments. (He had replaced Robert Devereux, 2nd Earl of Essex, the queen's erstwhile pet, who had parleyed with but failed to subjugate O'Neill and, disgraced, returned to London and that very year paid with his head for a misguided conspiracy to seize power.) Mountjoy, who reached Kinsale on October 16, 1601, established his principal camp at a high point just to the east of the town and proceeded to invest the Spanish positions.

Mountjoy was reinforced by the arrival of such confederates as Sir George Carew, provincial president of Munster (the English administrator), and Richard Burke, Earl of Clanricard, one of those Catholic nobles who found it expedient to support the Protestant English to ensure their own positions. Ordnance for Mountjoy came by sea from Dublin, and in time the Earl of Thomond arrived with other guns, one thousand foot soldiers, and one hundred cavalry from England. Mountjoy's bombardment of the Spanish in the walled town was relentless, and in hard fighting his troops dislodged the Spanish from the outlying fortresses they occupied. The Spanish, however, did not merely shelter behind Kinsale's walls but made bold sallies outside, engaging in fierce skirmishes and at least once spiking the guns of one or more English batteries.

As the siege went into a third month, there was considerable loss of life, and both sides were feeling serious privations. As a harsh winter came on, the Spanish and English commanders parleyed to discuss terms for a Spanish surrender, but no accord was reached. The Spanish general was counting on the arrival of O'Neill and O'Donnell's forces. On receiving reports of the approaching Irish host, Don Juan de Aguila sent one or more messages to Lords O'Neill and O'Donnell (at least one of which was intercepted and brought to Mountjoy), entreating their succor soon, reporting that his resources had been seriously strained by the English siege but saying, too, that the enemy was also weakened. He proposed that the Irish and the Spanish concert their attack at an agreed time, the Irish to fall upon one section of the English positions while the Spanish issued from the town and made an onslaught on another.

O'Neill and O'Donnell, who arrived near Kinsale in early December and made their camp at a high point called Coolcarron, north and slightly west of the town, reacted differently to de Aguila's message. O'Neill was fifty-one years old, shrewd, pragmatic, and masterful at delaying tactics. He cautioned patience until famine became an Irish ally, for by now their forces had cut off Mountjoy's men from foraging in the countryside and obtaining food and water for their horses and themselves from the land. O'Donnell, twenty-nine years old, was impetuous. He had been a warrior since his early teens (imprisoned for four years in Dublin Castle, he had made an extraordinary escape), and he argued in council that they should act on the Spaniards' plea for quick relief. O'Neill and the other chiefs eventually agreed.

WE HAVE TWO principal records of the battle, which took place near dawn on Christmas Eve, after a night of thunder and lightning. One is that by Mountjoy's secretary, Fynes Moryson. Another, called *The Annals of the Four Masters*, was compiled by a Franciscan friar in a monastery in Donegal, with the help of three lay scholars. I am indebted to David Willis McCullough's editing of these accounts, in his excellent *Wars of the Irish Kings*. While each version tends to celebrate the prowess of the English and the Irish sides, nonetheless, there is remarkable agreement on many points. Fynes Moryson writes that on the night of December 23, "One of the chiefe Commanders in Tyrone's Army . . . by a letter wished [Mountjoy] that the English army should that night bee well upon their guard, for Tyrone meant to give upon one Campe, and the Spaniards upon the other." In *The Annals*, the Four Masters write, "Some assert that a certain Irishman had sent word and information to the Lord Justice [Mountjoy], that the Irish and Spaniards were to attack him that night" and advising that the queen's army be positioned in "the gaps of danger." Many societies have their Judases, but the informer has been a feature of Irish life. Perhaps one affected the Battle of Kinsale.

The principal camps of the English and the Irish were on high ground, and the smoke from their campfires was visible to each other's soldiers. Below and between them lay boggy ground. There were low hills between what would be the battleground and the place where the besieged Spanish waited. Well before dawn on Christmas Eve, the Irish forces began their advance, and quickly Lord Mountjoy was alerted. The Irish were in three contingents. The vanguard was led by a Tyrrell, likely from Westmeath, one of the "Old English," in Ireland for centuries, who had remained Catholic; with his own men he had also two hundred Spaniards who had landed from a ship at Castle Haven. O'Neill and his troops were in the middle. O'Donnell and his cohorts made up the rear guard. In the darkness, O'Donnell's force lost its way and became separated. Chaos ensued.

O'Neill moved westerly to get onto better ground but, on encountering a strong English force, turned toward the bog. When dawn came, the English pressed forward. Accustomed to guerrilla warfare, skirmishes, and ambushes, the Irish were ineffective confronting regular formations in the open field. Fynes Moryson writes: "Then the Marshiall [sic] finding a way through a Ford, to the ground where the Rebels stood . . . he passed over with the Earle of Clanrickard, Sir Richard Greames . . . and their horse, and offered to charge one of the Rebels Battailes of one thousand eight hundred men: but finding them stand firme, our horse wheeled about." However, the English brought up more men, using their cavalry to great effect. When the English, with horse and foot, made a passage by a stream through the bog and drove at the Irish, many of the Irish broke and ran.

The Four Masters write that the English "fell upon O'Neill's people, and proceeded to kill, slaughter, subdue, and thin them." O'Donnell's men, moving forward behind their cavalry, which encountered an English onslaught, were scattered as their horsemen fell back to regroup. According to *The Annals*, on reaching O'Neill's men, who were now fleeing, O'Donnell cried out for them to stand and fight and urged his own men to do likewise, but, the Four Masters write, the Irish battalions were routed in succession.

In Fynes Moryson's account of the battle, he writes, "The Irish Rebels left one thousand two hundred bodies dead in the field, besides those that were killed in two miles chase: we tooke nine of their Ensignes, all their Drummes and Powder, and got more than two thousand Armes."

During the three hours the battle raged, the Spaniards never emerged from behind the walls of Kinsale, supposedly still awaiting a signal from the Irish to join the attack on the English and unable to hear the din of the battlefield because of the intervening hills. After the battle, hearing celebratory volleys from Lord Mountjoy's camp, the Spanish made a sortie but were beaten back. At the end of December, Don Juan de Aguila met to parley with Lord Mountjoy, and according to Moryson, deploring the perfidy of the Irish and accounting the English Lord Deputy an honorable foe, the Spanish general offered to surrender the town if he and his force would be permitted to depart on honorable terms. So it was arranged; the Spanish returned to Spain.

AFTER THE DEBACLE the Irish made their way north to the respective territories of the various chieftains enlisted in the Irish cause. The consequences of the Battle of Kinsale for the Irish were dire and incalculable. Red Hugh O'Donnell, acting on the advice of Hugh O'Neill, took ship for Spain, again to implore His Most Catholic Majesty Philip III to provide men and arms to thwart the English Protestant occupation of Ireland. A year later, barely thirty years of age, he was dead. Rumor had it that he was poisoned by an English agent. As for the rebellious Great Hugh O'Neill, harassed, poor, desperate to preserve his patrimony, he submitted to his old nemesis, Lord Deputy Mountjoy—at the former abbey of Mellifont, become the home of Sir Garret Moore—in late March 1603, unaware that Queen Elizabeth had just died. The coalition of chieftains that had threatened England's ascendancy in Ireland was no more. Thus ended the Nine Years War.

ON SEPTEMBER 14, 1607, Hugh O'Neill, Earl of Tyrone, and Rory O'Donnell, Red Hugh's brother and successor as Earl of Tyrconnell and chief of his clan (who had also yielded to Mountjoy but continued to conspire with the Spanish), together with Cúconnacht Maguire, Lord of Fermanagh, boarded ship at Rathmullan, Donegal, for the Continent, never to return, dying in exile. They were accused of treason, and their lands were confiscated. Their departure, immortalized in Irish history and legend as the Flight of the Earls, was the coda to the fateful chapter written at Kinsale. Had the Irish been victorious there, English domination of Ireland, which had been immensely costly, might have been halted and aspects of the old Gaelic way of life perpetuated. I know of no more eloquent appreciation of what had ended in Ireland than that of the French historian Roger Chauviré, in his succinct, perceptive *History of Ireland:*

> Gaelic society must have exercised an immense attraction, since for centuries it was able to assimilate its conquerors, the Danes, the Normans and even the English. And it was not so surprising that feudal lords and aristocrats were able to take their place without friction in a society which was in itself so aristocratic in spirit. . . . [The Irish peasant] knew that he was one of *Clann na nGael,* the children of the Gaels. He did not admit the superiority of his conquerors. . . . His own tradition was essentially aristocratic and patriarchal, content with inequality and indeed based on it, in which the humble man took pride by proxy in the greatness of his princes, as long as they were legitimate. What had happened to them now, the O'Neills, the O'Donnells, O'Connors, MacCarthys, O'Briens? They were serving under foreign standards, and their castles were empty or had been usurped. Who was there to honour and to care for the poets, the trustees of those ancient memories in which a whole people had shared since the earliest ages, and which from the highest prince to the lowliest of the *spálpini* [laborers] made them to be one?

Traces of that doomed society lingered on; a few great Irish Catholic families survived by wile or compromise, honoring old ways; we have the poetry and songs of some wandering bards, like Carolan, who survived into the eighteenth century; and sparks of rebellion against the colonizing English were never quenched in Irish hearts.

KINSALE WAS TO be the site of one more epochal event in Irish history: on March 12, 1689, James II of England, deposed by his people and succeeded by William of Orange, landed at Kinsale to lead the loyal Irish and some French allies against the Dutch and English army of King William III, in hopes of reclaiming his kingdoms. Ignominiously vanquished at the Battle of the Boyne on July 1, 1690, James made a precipitous withdrawal to Kinsale. On July 12, 1690, the hapless ex-monarch reembarked for France. He lived out his days in exile, the last Stuart King of England, Scotland, and Ireland. His son and grandson, James Francis Edward, the Old Pretender, and Charles Edward, the Young Pretender, were equally ill-fated in attempts at a Stuart Restoration.

KINSALE'S PLACE in history, as well as its location on the southern coast of Ireland, made it a logical place for me to end my journey, but the town has other attractions. Kinsale is situated on a spectacular, well-protected harbor at the mouth of the river Bandon. What had been the old walled town of the besieged Don Juan de Aguila can still be perceived as two long streets, now named Upper and Lower O'Connell Streets, which parallel the waterfront. Other streets run steeply up Compass Hill, which is prettily terraced with old houses. The motley colors of some of them and the soft climate of this favored coast give Kinsale a somewhat Mediterranean air.

I walked down to Pearse Street and along the waterfront of the inner harbor, where a few small boats were moored to buoys close in. Then turning, I walked through Emmet Place (amused that several streets were named for Irish patriots in a town so long a bastion of British power) to Pier Road, which runs southerly along the middle harbor. Quays line one side of the road, and sailboats and working craft were moored to them. Walking on, I came to a vast marina and stood for a while, admiring sailboats great and small, clustered as thickly as a shoal of mackerel, and some impressive yachts. Hundred of halyards slapping against their masts made music to gladden a sailor's heart. Kinsale is one of Europe's major yachting centers, and all the services connected with that pursuit must, to some extent, have replaced the fishing industry that flourished here, particularly in the nineteenth century, when several hundred boats sailed out of Kinsale. When the great run of mackerel appeared in the spring, a vast armada of boats appeared from all over the British Isles to reap the harvest.

About forty-five miles as the crow flies, to the southwest of Kinsale and some seven miles offshore, is Fastnet Rock, destination in the famous Fastnet Race, one of yachting's most challenging. When the weather is foul, the sea here can be treacherous, and the Fastnet Race has claimed lives and boats.

Much closer to Kinsale—indeed, within sight of the promontory called the Old Head of Kinsale—one of the most fateful of maritime tragedies occurred. On May 7, 1915, on a day of calm seas, without warning, a German submarine fired a torpedo that sank the British passenger liner *Lusitania,* with the loss of 1,195 lives. Because 128 of the dead were Americans, who had boarded ship in New York, American opinion turned against Germany in the First World War. To President Woodrow Wilson's strong protest against the sinking of an unarmed passenger vessel without warning, Germany responded by declaring that the *Lusitania* was carrying munitions for the Allied powers. However, the loss of so many civilians, many of them women and children, outraged much of the world, and it was a factor in the United States' eventually declaring war against Germany.

When I reached the area called World's End and the modern Trident Hotel, artfully integrated into old stone buildings, I was standing where the Royal Naval Dockyard once had been. Kinsale had been taken for William of Orange by John Churchill, then Earl of Marlborough. Since then its splendid, almost landlocked harbor—protected by forts I was eager to visit—was to make it a strategic asset of Britain's naval might for centuries.

THERE WAS MUCH to see and enjoy in Kinsale, but it was time I headed to a B&B high above the town. In Market Square, I paused to look at the fine stone building known as the Court House, which was formerly the Market House. Built in 1600 and enlarged at the beginning of the eighteenth century, with its three Dutch gables, the building reflects the Queen Anne style. In addition to serving as the town market, the handsome edifice, with its octagonal cupola, has also been the seat of the town government. Here the Corporation of Kinsale, under its chief officer, titled the Sovereign, met to administer the town's affairs. The building now contains a municipal museum.

Starting uphill from the Court House, I came to the Church of Ireland's parish church of St. Multose. One of Ireland's numberless saints, Saint Eltin, or Saint Multo (Mo Eilte Ógh in Irish), anglicized as Saint Multose, built a church on this site in the sixth century, perhaps succeeded by another before the basic structure of the present church was erected, possibly about 1195. It has been enlarged and mutilated several times. Nonetheless, St. Multose, which has survived as a place of continuous Christian worship for eight hundred years, repays a visit.

Here Prince Rupert, gallant royalist cavalry commander in England's Civil War and nephew of the executed King Charles I, proclaimed Charles II King of England, Scotland, and Ireland more than a decade before the actual restoration of that Stuart monarch in England. Interesting monuments, windows, regimental colors, and other mementos are to be seen in St. Multose. One that enlightened me is a wooden plaque celebrating the achievement of the Kinsale shipbuilder Thomas Chudleigh. He fabricated a boat which, disassembled, was transported overland to the Lower Lake of Killarney. There the Cromwellian General Ludlow employed it as a floating battery for the bombardment of Ross Castle, forcing the surrender of that strong fortress, in which Lord Muskerry had been holding out with fifteen hundred men. I'd visited Ross Castle and knew of the cannonade from the lake and its consequences but not the means by which it had been effected.

From St. Multose, I trudged up what seemed, at the end of a long day, a steep hill. My rucksack had not grown any lighter since I'd set off from Malin Head. I had been obliged to keep posting off books, maps, and journals I'd bought, to avoid adding to the weight. At the hilltop, I came to Riverside, a bright new house with a panoramic view. The extremely pretty blond owner, who welcomed me, showed me to a neat and simply furnished room that faced the front garden and the road I'd traveled. After scrubbing up and resting, I got into my dining-out kit and knocked at the door to the kitchen. It was opened by my host, Orla Griffin, around whose legs frisked an adorable child, naked as a cherub. Behind her was a tall, lithe young man, as good looking as his wife, who scooped up the child. I said I'd probably be back late, was told "no problem," and was shown how to admit myself.

LIGHT OF HEART and of back, I strolled down the long hill to town, keen to sample its delights. For many years, Kinsale has traded on a reputation as

Ireland's gourmet capital. It earned that cachet when very few Irish towns boasted restaurants whose chefs had trained abroad or with those who had, and before the emphasis on choice local ingredients and refined, classical methods of cooking had been promulgated by Myrtle Allen at her restaurant and school at Ballymaloe House, Shanagarry, Cork. Today one can dine extremely well, sometimes superbly, at any number of restaurants and country-house hotels scattered around the country. This evening I stopped first at the Blue Haven, on Pearse Street. One of the earliest of Kinsale's establishments to become renowned, I'd heard that the small hotel and restaurant had changed hands over the years. The ground floor of the Blue Haven is smartly appointed, plushly comfortable, but after glancing into the large, dimly lit, almost deserted dining room, I decided to have a preprandial drink at the bar and scout about.

Sauntering onward in the dusk, I peered into several restaurants on Upper and Lower O'Connell Streets before anchoring at Max's Wine Bar, on Main Street. This was a happy landfall, as a sailor might put it. Max's is tiny, candlelit, unadorned; though it was quiet, the diners conversing amiably emanated a marked contentment, as I soon did. My dinner, nicely served by a young woman who would probably be reading economics at some university this fall, was just what I wanted: first-class oysters; the fish of the day, John Dory; perfect spuds; several glasses of a decent white wine; and coffee. My notes show the tab was I£29.40.

Like every Irish town, Kinsale has its public houses, and since its fame as a yachting center, visual appeal, and amenities attract many visitors, there are ample pubs to gratify them. I moseyed around, enjoyed the fresh air off the sea and my pipe, looked at the windows of shops strung up and down the narrow streets, then stopped at a pub called An Seanachai, which I'd passed on my promenade earlier, when the place was sparsely occupied. Now patrons were bulging onto the sidewalk. The pub's name, not uncommon for public houses, means "the storyteller," one of a traditional class that endured almost to the end of the last century (now and again a survivor is saluted), from whom the common people, country people, learned the history of their race. Rather, one might better say they absorbed the myths, legends, deeds, and folklore of their forebears. The strains of song and music occasionally floated over the din of voices and beckoned me in to An Seanachai.

The clientele was loquacious and polyglot, loud but orderly. I inched my way through the throng to the bar and stood behind two good-looking girls, one Irish, one Dutch, not yet twenty years old, and watched them as they were importuned—they would have said "hit on"—by a German, an Italian, and a Dutchman, whom they fobbed off with practiced repartee. Then, with a large whiskey dispensed by one of two Siva-armed barmaids, I threaded my way toward the center of the inner room, where a guitarist sat on a stool and sang.

Near the musician were perhaps four couples and maybe a foursome of middle age who were listening to him. The rest of the crowd, in their twenties or thirties, babbling joyfully, seemed oblivious of the singing and playing of Sean Thompson. His repertoire of Irish songs, old and new, seemed limitless. After a break he sang a song that I had heard a number of times on my trek, pianist-composer Phil Coulter's affecting "The Town That I Loved So Well," about the agony that Derry has endured in our time. He did it well, then he asked, as he had before, for requests. No one made one, until I asked for "The Fields of Athenry," perhaps prompted by his last number. In a pub in Killarney a few years before, I had heard a young woman get up from a table and sing, a cappella, "The Fields of Athenry," and it so stilled the room that you could have heard a shamrock fall. The words and music are by Pete St. John, but the song was made famous by the performer Paddy Reilly. Like many great Irish ballads, it is imbued with a deep melancholy that conveys a piercing longing and despair, for a lost love, freedom, and the native land. "The Fields of Athenry" has become a modern anthem. This night, Sean Thompson did the composer proud. I won't say a hush fell over the room; to many of the foreign crowd, the lyrics—recalling the famine and Britain's transportation and imprisonment of Irishmen for petty offenses—would have had little or no nationalist resonance; yet for a few moments the packed room was muted as Thompson sang:

> By a lonely prison wall
> I heard a young girl calling
> Michael they have taken you away
> For you stole Trevelyn's corn
> So the young might see the morn.
> Now a prison ship lies waiting in the bay.

Low lie the fields of Athenry,
Where once we watched the small free birds fly.
Our love was on the wing, we had dreams and songs to sing.
It's so lonely 'round the Fields of Athenry.

It seemed a very long way uphill to Riverside House, and I decided that next day I'd try to find lodging in the center of town. I slept as if poleaxed, then breakfasted happily in a sunny room. When I bid good-bye to my host, she surprised me. Maybe because I was not English, she remarked in a conversational way, "Aren't the English awful? So superior! They act as if they still ruled the country." If I made any response except possibly a vague head shake, I didn't record it later. I was stunned to be made aware again how long it takes for ancient wounds to heal, but remembered I was in the Rebel County.

HAPPILY, I WAS able to get into the Old Bank House, on Pearse Street, the styishly appointed guesthouse of Michael and Marie Riese. For some time, Michael, an expatriate German, had one of Kinsale's most renowned restaurants, but these days he seems content to run an establishment where breakfast is the only meal. Leaving my rucksack, I went off to explore several of Kinsale's most historic relics.

Walking a short block uphill again, past the little cottages on Chairman's Lane, I came to Desmond Castle. A stout tower house with additions, it was built in the late fourteenth or early fifteenth century, evidently by an Earl of Desmond, a Fitzgerald, one of those Norman families so thoroughly gaelicized that they were said to be *Hibernicis ipsis hiberniores,* "more Irish than the Irish." Various Fitzgerald devices are embedded in the fabric of the building, which was originally a customs house. When the Spaniards were besieged in Kinsale, they used it for a magazine. The castle is now a museum, maintained by Dúchas. Part of it is a wine museum, commemorating Ireland's long connection with the Continent in matters vinous and spirituous. Perusing documents, letters, pictures, and artefacts, I delighted in such trivia as the fact that John Galwey—first cousin of Richard Hennessy, who founded the cognac house—had once been exclusive purveyor of brandy to the czar; that the Lawton family, still extant in Bordeaux, had been wine suppliers to George Washington and

Thomas Jefferson; that Anthony Barton, owner of Châteaux Leoville-Barton and Langoa-Barton, whom I had once visited, is a descendant of Thomas Barton of Fermanagh, who had settled in Bordeaux in 1725, and that Anthony Barton was born in Straffan House in Ireland.

Desmond Castle is also known as the French Prison, because Frenchmen captured in the Napoleonic Wars were incarcerated there. In one section of the castle, there are several large cells where Tussaud-like mannequins, clad in rags, in settings of grim verisimilitude, represent American sailors captured from privateers by the British during the American War of Independence. A wall placard displays a copy of a letter published in a local paper in 1782: "They have been closely confined for about six months, without any prospect of exchange; many of them are almost naked; many of them are sickly and dying; all of them are in the greatest distress and without any bed other than the hard board." All that was missing from these tableaux was the stink.

THE AIR OFF the sea felt rejuvenating after the prison scene, and I hiked past World's End to the bridge across the mouth of the Bandon and the sprawing promontory called Ringrone. One finger of it is a high peninsula jutting into Kinsale's great harbor, demarcating the Middle Harbour from the Outer Harbour. I lunched at the Dock, on the Middle Harbour side, at what is the peninsula's isthmus, reading James Thuillier's informative *History of Kinsale*, from which I learned much. Then I ascended by a narrow path to the height where the ruins of James Fort command an extraordinary prospect. The fortress was erected between 1602 and 1604 on the site of Castle Parke by the English engineer Paul Ive, or Ivyes, being completed in the reign of King James I of England and VI of Scotland. An early governor was Sir William Penn, father of William Penn, the Quaker founder of Pennsylvania who served as an Admiralty clerk here.

I stood first on the substantial outer earthwork around the great ditch that encircles the outer fortress walls, of which little remains, trying to reconstruct in my mind's eye the mighty fortress when it was intact. It was built in the shape of a five-pointed star, with bastions at the points, projecting from the wide connecting walls, permitting enfilading fire at an attacking enemy, and James Fort may reveal the first use of such bastions in Ireland. Within those walls there was another high stone wall surrounding the inner fort, which consisted of barracks and a massive keep with twin towers. The fractured skeleton I viewed still gave some idea of the strength of James Fort.

Below the fortress, originally connected by a covered way, there are the remains of an older blockhouse close to the harbor level; its battery could blast, at almost point-blank range, ships attempting the relatively narrow passage from the Outer Harbour into the Middle, to attack town or shipping. The higher fortress had cannon on its harbor-facing bastions. Despite its strengths, in 1649 James Fort surrendered after Cromwellian gunners placed a piece on Compass Hill, above the town of Kinsale, and fired into the fortress. In 1689, in the Williamite War, James Fort fell again, to troops under two of Marlborough's commanders, who attacked across the isthmus, from Ringrone, aided when an explosion of gunpowder killed many of the garrison.

Over time clearly much of James Fort has been despoiled for other uses. Nevertheless, I was glad to have come here for the panorama, superlative, even on a day when sky and water appeared to meld into a sheet of tinfoil. To the north was the town of Kinsale, nestled against its hillside, the tower of St. Multose a gnomon pointing heavenward. To the west the river Bandon wended its bendy way past verdant banks from the town named for the river. Below lay the splendid harbor wrapped around the peninsula; in the Middle Harbour the marinas, with their multicolored sailboats, made pretty mosaics. Across the harbor, on its east side, a pod of fishing boats was moored near the old enclave called Scilly. Farther east the immense Charles Fort guarded the Outer Harbour.

Back in town, I browsed in a bookstore, shopped for small gifts, napped, and read. That evening I dined agreeably at the unpretentious White House, on the street called the Glen, indulging again in oysters fresh enough to spring off the plate. For a nightcap, I stopped at the pub named Lord Kingsale, after the title borne by the Anglo-Norman de Courcy family, Myles de Courcy having been created 1st Baron Kingsale in 1223.

BREAKFAST AT Old Bank House was to set me up for the last day of my journey, and it did, served by Suzanne, a friendly apprentice from Germany. Afterward I bought a few books and posted them home from the *oifig an phoist* next door, then collected the makings of a picnic from the grocery across the street and set off for Charles Fort. What a day I'd been favored with: the sun was a golden torch; the air was like silk. I'm sure I whistled as I walked.

I followed a road that winds along the shoreline of the harbor, by the hamlet of Scilly, along the eastern shore of the Middle Harbour, then past the narrow section opposite James Fort, where at certain times a chain boom supported by barrels was stretched to halt or slow an invading ship right under the guns of blockhouse and fortress. Farther east, at the place called Ringcurran, there had stood the fortress taken by Don Juan de Aguila, then captured by Lord Mountjoy. On that site in 1677, the lord lieutenant, the Duke of Ormond (raised to that rank at the restoration of King Charles II in 1660), caused a mighty fortress to be built, to defend the important harbor and town of Kinsale.

Charles Fort was designed by Sir William Robinson, who also reconstructed the older James Fort, and it is an immense structure, irregularly hexagonal in shape, with three prominent bastions facing the landward side and two giant bastions anchoring the seaward walls, which are perforated with the embrasures of gun emplacements. Small lookout turrets are placed strategically. Within were barracks, officers' quarters, the governor's residence, hospital, magazine, stables, cookhouse, storehouses, and a parade ground. A wide, deep ditch, or moat, surrounds the walls, and the fortification on its landward side, though somewhat overgrown, exhibits the complex design of such military engineers as Louis XIV's great Marshal de Vauban, with counterscarp, covered way, and glacis, meant to deflect cannonballs and to thwart and expose attacking forces.

Charles Fort appeared to be impregnable from the sea, at least to the naval guns of the seventeenth and eighteenth centuries, when the English feared that the Spanish or French might strike at any point on the isles the English held. But as I could see from the high ground above, to the east and south an enemy could look down upon the fortress from the landward side. There, in 1690, Marlborough's gunners placed their batteries and fired away. After thirteen days the fortress wall between two bastions was breached; Colonel Scott, who commanded the Irish garrison, called for a truce and surrendered Charles Fort. The Irish officers were treated honorably, retaining their swords.

Thereafter, with the great harbor of vital interest to England's navy and Kinsale a point of English power in Cork and Southwest Ireland, from the Williamite victory in 1690 until the establishment of the Irish Free State, in 1922, Charles Fort was garrisoned by British soldiers. When the British withdrew, Irish republican irregulars burned the fort in one of those senseless acts of revenge for centuries of colonization that have left Ireland bereft of many monuments to its tragic history. Ironically, when I was here, the complex was closed for restoration by Dúchas. I could only look down on the gutted, roofless buildings within the fort. Without, it appeared virtually intact.

I walked down through the moat along the high southern wall to the seafront just below the soaring Charles bastion. Sitting on the breakwater, I picnicked, watched a white Alsatian dive into the pellucid water to retrieve waterlogged sticks tossed by his mistress, and thought about the life and death to which this fortress had been witness.

As for life, Charles Fort had contributed much to Kinsale's. The needs of the garrison—which seems to have been battalion strength—for food, drink, clothing, and other necessaries filled the coffers of townspeople. The officers had a club in town and played lively social roles with the Anglo-Irish gentry roundabout. There were balls and parades, soldiers marched out and back to church, and all the usual military ceremonies were observed.

As for death, not only war took casualties at Charles Fort. John Thuillier has written of an astonishing wedding day here. It seems that Wilful, daughter of Charles Fort's Governor Warrender, was strolling on the battlements with her bridegroom, Sir Trevor Ashurst, when she spied some flowers among the rocks below, near what is now called the White Lady turret and the lighthouse. She asked her husband for them, and he dispatched the sentry to gather the flowers, saying he would stand watch. While the sentry dutifully complied and the bride retired to the governor's residence, Sir Trevor fell asleep, perhaps affected by the wine on his wedding day. Coming upon the somnolent Sir Trevor, asleep at the sentry's post, Governor Warrender, a martinet, had him shot where he was. Utterly distraught at hearing of her husband's death, the bride rushed to a parapet and hurled herself to her death.

Despite its martial history, the world about Charles Fort seemed sublimely tranquil this day. Outward bound, a few sailboats caught an offshore breeze, and spinnakers blooming, they glided on the blue breast of the sea like the swans of Lohengrin. As it grew cooler by the water, I walked up the moat to a higher point near the East, or Cockpit, Bastion, settled on the velvety grass above the ditch's counterscarp, and made some notes. Then I lay back, ruminating, pleasantly warmed by the descending sun, its blaze turning the sea into a sheet of hammered brass.

THIS WAS JOURNEY'S END. I thought of R. C. Sherriff's play with that title. It opened in London in 1929, the same year as *The Silver Tassie* by Sean O'Casey. Both were antiwar plays. Sherriff's, written by a young Oxford man who had been in the trenches of Flanders, is about the shattering experience of an heroic young English captain of quintessential noblesse oblige and the stiffest of lips and called for a totally realistic production. O'Casey's is about a working-class Dubliner, like himself, an athlete and an idol who comes home from the carnage of Flanders broken in body and soul. But while its first and third acts are naturalistic, the second act is a daring expressionistic nightmare. W. B. Yeats rejected it for the Abbey Theatre (which, he acknowledged, O'Casey had saved from possible financial closure by three successful plays), saying that O'Casey knew nothing about the battlefields of the Great War and that playwrights should not be writing plays of opinion about news or political matters. A master of invective, O'Casey, who had called Sherriff's play (his first), "backboneless & ribless" and "a play of false effrontery," wrote a vitriolic reply to Yeats, but the rejection confirmed him in choosing exile in England while, like Joyce, continuing to write about Ireland. (Ultimately O'Casey, who admired Yeats enormously as both poet and playwright, was reconciled with him.) This train of thought, stimulated by my journey's end, made me reflect on O'Casey, to whom I had become close. He liked the word *paradox* (he has fun with it in *The Shadow of a Gunman*) and told me that Ireland was a paradoxical country. Since he was the most paradoxical man I've ever known, I kept thinking about that on my journey.

Sean O'Casey was born an Irish Protestant and baptized as John Casey, but the man who became an agnostic dedicated two volumes of his (six-volume) autobiography to professors at the Catholic seminary and college of Maynooth. As a young fellow he was pipe major of the marching band of Dublin's St. Lawrence O'Toole Catholic church and later in life lampooned Ireland's Catholic heirarchy in several plays (one causing a brouhaha in the theater, another banned). Onetime secretary of the revolutionary Irish Citizen Army, he came to mock martyrs for nationalism. He was an ardent communist in conviction, but not a party member, who could scarcely have a conversation without invoking God. He was a proletarian, a common laborer until his forties, who was taken up by members of London's high society and loved it. A merciless correspondent with opponents, when meeting an epistolary enemy, he could be affectionate as the family pet. I loved him, I disagreed with him (at our first meeting my praise of Orwell could have been fatal), and he made me think.

I had found Ireland as paradoxical as O'Casey said. A people, millions of whose forebears had settled in other countries, were proving hostile to asylum seekers being accommodated by the government. The Irish, who have benefited incalculably from the largesse of the European Union, initially rejected by referendum the Nice Agreement to admit a number of other nations, making Ireland the sole EU member to do so. (After intense government pressure, a second referendum was affirmative. However, the government also rejected EU criticisms of its fiscal policies.) Many people showered with the benefits of precipitous industrial expansion seemed indifferent to the grave environmental problems that come with it. The government's planning authority, An Bord Pleanála, is charged with making final rulings on constructions and developments that may have environmental consequences and is addressing the challenge. (While I was on my journey, An Bord Pleanála rejected the plans of the President of Ireland, Mary McAleese, and her husband to build a country house on a lake in Country Roscommon "as highly obtrusive and visually damaging" to the area's rustic character and with possible adverse ecological impact. Subsequently the McAleeses altered their site and plan, and won approval.) Some Irish paradoxes are perhaps whimsical. G. K. Chesterton wrote:

> For the great Gaels of Ireland
> Are the men that God made mad,
> For all their wars are merry,
> And all their songs are sad.

Neat and paradoxical, witty and not quite true. Anyone who has been in a traditional singing pub will have heard many merry songs, and the green fields of Ireland have been watered by blood spilled in wars that were not merry. But recalling those lines made me think of Ireland's poets, whose work measures the beating of Ireland's heart. Padraic Pearse, one of the leaders of the 1916 Rising, which ultimately led to Ireland's independence, who had written that "bloodshed is a cleansing and a sanctifying thing," was a poet who paid with his life for his ideas about the price of Irish nationhood. He was one of three poets among the fifteen leaders of the Rising who were executed in Dublin (the others were Thomas MacDonagh and Joseph Plunkett). The extraordinary leaders of the American Revolution were not poets, nor were the key figures of the Russian Revolution.

Frequently I had been reading in the Irish newspapers columnists and letter writers concerned that Ireland's industrial boom, its high-tech prosperity, was infecting the Irish with materialism, was sapping the Irish soul. (If so, the recent fizzle of the information technology explosion and resultant rise in unemployment may act as a cruel corrective.) I had seen satellite dishes on modest country houses and people glued to their TV screens. But I'd met many who could still speak magically, using a language not their own, and had a shrewd, quirky way of thinking. The country was rich with musicians, writers, artists, and filmmakers. Never more so. I'd found an Irishness that seemed unquenchable. There was still the problem of the North. Diehards, old hatreds—but there had been progress, and there was hope.

Looking past the lofty ramparts of Charles Fort over the glittering sea toward the tip of the Old Head of Kinsale, watching the soaring gulls, wondering what a poet could make of this place, I remembered that among the writers living in Kinsale were the poets Derek Mahon and Desmond O'Grady. I brooded about all the persons I had not met, all the things undone, on this journey. There was a pull to linger. However, the sand was running from my hourglass, the wallet was thin, a loving wife and family were at home, far away. Time to go, now. While I can't say I'd walk this Irish way again, there is an Antrim Way, a Wicklow Way, a Kerry Way. The dreaming castles, the ruined abbeys, the salmon rivers, the horses, the pubs, the theaters, films, music, my friends, the Irish, will be here. So will I.

Acknowledgments

IN MAKING MY TREK THROUGH IRELAND, I WAS GREATLY ASSISTED BY the exceptional kindness of several persons to whom I am particularly grateful: George M. Murphy, Dr. David and Nora Nowlan, John and Barbara Quested, and Dr. James Sheehan.

I am also indebted to various organizations and their members for invaluable help: at the Irish Tourist Board (Bord Fáilte), Orla Carey, Joe Lynam, Catherine McKevitt, Ruth Moran, Damian O'Brien, and Ellen Redmond; at the Northern Ireland Tourist Board, Maebeth Fenton and Jan Nugent; at Aer Lingus, Rosemary Curran, Eileen O'Halloran, and Suzanne Thompson; at Dúchas, The Heritage Service, Ann Grady and David Sweetman; at the Tyrone Guthrie Centre, Sheila Pratschke and staff; The Queen's Lancashire Regiment's officers and other ranks; at the Industrial Development Board, Ireland, Finn Gallen; at the Industrial Development Board, Northern Ireland, Valerie Lyttle; at An Garda Siochána, Superintendent Kieran McGann; at Bord Pleanala, Diarmuid Collins.

Besides all the others named in this book to whom I am grateful for their hospitality, information, and introductions, I wish to thank Patrick Casey, Terry and Rita George, Patrick Granville, Dick Hogan, Mary Leland, Tom and Rosaleen Maher, and Eileen Roantree.

I have been inspired by poet Seamus Heaney and gratefully acknowledge the use of a line from his collection *Seeing Things* as an epitaph and for the lines from *Sweeney Astray*.

After hanging up my boots, as I distilled my journals into this book, I benefited greatly from the encouragement, counsel, and perception of my editor, Robert D. Loomis, who saved me from stumbles I had managed to avoid during a joyous journey. Then, while my pages moved toward realization as a book, I enjoyed the care, judgment, and forbearance of production editor Sybil Pincus.

Bibliography

Aalen, F.H.A., Kevin Whelan, and Matthew Stout. *Atlas of Irish Rural Landscape*. Cork: Cork University Press, 1997.

Boswell, James. *Life of Samuel Johnson, LLD*. Vols. 1–4. Edited by George Birbeck Hill and L. F. Powell. Oxford: The Clarendon Press, 1934.

Bowen, Elizabeth. *Bowen's Court*. New York: Knopf, 1942.

Boylan, Henry. *A Dictionary of Irish Biography*. Dublin: Gill and Macmillan, 1978.

Butler, David J. *Cahir*. Cahir: Cahir Tourism, Heritage Association, 1999.

Campbell, Stephen. *The Great Irish Famine: Words and Images from The Famine Museum, Strokestown Park, County Roscommon*. Strokestown: Famine Museum, 2000.

Carey, John, ed. *Eyewitness to History*. Cambridge, Mass.: Harvard University Press, 1987.

Chancellor, E. Beresford. *Regency Rakes*. London: Pallan, 1925.

Chauviré, Roger. *History of Ireland*. Translated by the Earl of Wicklow. Dublin: Clanmore and Reynolds, 1952.

Coghlan, Ronan. *A Pocket Dictionary to Irish Myth and Legend*. Belfast: Appletree Press, 1985.

Colum, Padraic, ed. *A Treasury of Irish Folklore*. New York: Wings Books/Random House, 1992.

———. *Broad-sheet Ballads*. Dublin: Maunsell & Company, 1913.

Connolly, S. J., ed. *The Oxford Companion to Irish History*. Oxford: Oxford University Press, 1998.

Dangerfield, George. *The Damnable Question*. Boston: Atlantic/Little, Brown, 1976.

Delany, Ruth. *By Shannon's Shore*. Dublin: Gill and Macmillan, 1987.

De Paor, Máire and Liam. *Early Christian Ireland*. London: Thames and Hudson, 1958.

Department of Foreign Affairs, Government of Ireland. *Facts about Ireland*. Dublin: 1999.

Donnelly, James S. *The Great Irish Potato Famine*. Phoenix Mill, Gloucestershire: Sutton Publishing, 2001.

Dudley, Ruth Edwards. *An Atlas of Irish History*. London: Methuen, 1973.

Evans, E. Estyn. *The Personality of Ireland*. Belfast: Blackstaff Press, 1981.

Foster, R. F. *The Irish Story*. London: Allen Lane/Penguin Press, 2001.

———. *The Oxford History of Ireland*. Oxford: Oxford University Press, 1989.

Girouard, Mark. "Birr Castle, Co. Offaly." *Country Life*, Feb. 25, March 4, March 11, 1965.

Guinness, Desmond, and William Ryan. *Irish Houses & Castles*. New York: Viking, 1971.

Hall, Betty Dillon, ed. *Millennium Year Book and Diary*. Cork: Cork Corporation, 2000.

Harbison, Peter. *The High Crosses of Ireland*. Vols. 1–3. Bonn: R. Habelt, 1992.

Heaney, Seamus. *Seeing Things*. London: Faber and Faber, 1991.

———. *Sweeney Astray*. London: Faber and Faber, 1983.

Hoagland, Kathleen. *1000 Years of Irish Poetry*. New York: Devin-Adair, 1953.

Jackson, Robert Wyse. *The Scoundrel of Cashel*. Cork: Mercier Press, 1974.

Kee, Robert. *The Most Distressful Country*. London: Penguin, 1972.

Kennedy, Ludovic. *Pursuit: The Chase and Sinking of the Bismarck*. Annapolis: Naval Institute Press, 2000.

Kiely, Benedict. *Ireland from the Air*. London: Weidenfeld and Nicolson, 1985.

Kinsella, Thomas, trans. *The Tain* (*Táin bo cuailnge*). Dublin: Dolmen Edition, 1969.

The Knight of Glin. "Castles in the Eire." Review of *Great Houses of Ireland,* by Hugh Montgomery-Massingberd and Christopher Simon-Sykes, in *Country Life,* Dec. 9, 1999.

Lord Killanin. *My Ireland*. London: Windward/W. H. Smith, 1987.

Lord Killanin and Michael Duignan. *The Shell Guide to Ireland*. London: The Ebury Press, 1962.

Krause, David. *Sean O'Casey: The Man and His Work*. London: Macgibbon & Kee, 1960.

Lacy, Brian. *The Siege of Derry*. Dublin: Eason & Son, 1989.

Leask, Harold G. *Irish Castles*. Dundalk: Dundalgan Press, 1964.

Leland, Mary. *The Lie of the Land*. Cork: Cork University Press, 1999.

———. *Cork/Corcaigh*. Cork: Cork Corporation, 1999.

Lydon, James, and Margaret MacCurtain, eds. *The Gill History of Ireland*. 11 vols. Dublin: Gill and Macmillan, 1972–1975.

Manning, Conleth. *Cahir Castle*. Dublin: Dúchas, The Heritage Service, 1999.

———. *Clonmacnoise*. 2d ed. Dublin: Dúchas, The Heritage Service, 1998.

———. *Rock of Cashel*. Dublin: Dúchas, The Heritage Service, 2000.

MacSharry, Ray, and Padraic White. *The Making of the Celtic Tiger*. Cork: Mercier Press, 2000.

McBride, Ian. *The Siege of Derry in Ulster Protestant Mythology*. Dublin: Four Courts Press, 1997.

McCullough, David Willis. *Wars of the Irish Kings*. New York: Three Rivers Press/Crown, 2002.

Milligan, C. D. *History of the Siege of Londonderry*. Belfast: H. R. Carter, 1951.

Mosley, Sir Oswald. *My Life*. New Rochelle, N.Y.: Arlington House, 1968.

Murray, Peter. *Masterpieces from the Crawford Municipal Art Gallery*. Cork: 1992.

Newby, Eric. *Round Ireland in Low Gear*. New York: Viking, 1987.

O'Brien, Conor Cruise. *On the Edge of the Millennium*. New York: The Free Press, Martin Kesler, Simon & Schuster, 1995.

O'Brien, Jacqueline, and Peter Harbison. *Ancient Ireland*. New York: Oxford University Press, 1996.

O'Brien, Máire, and Conor Cruise. *A Concise History of Ireland*. New York: Beekman House/Crown, 1972.

O'Casey, Sean. Autobiography, 6 vols.: *I Knock at the Door,* (1939); *Pictures in the Hallway* (1942); *Drums Under the Window* (1946); *Irish Fallen Fare Thee Well* (1949); *Rose and Crown* (1952); *Sunset and Evening Star* (1954). London and New York: Macmillan, 1939–1954.

————. *The Letters of Sean O'Casey*. 4 vols. Edited by David Krause. Vols. 1 and 2, New York: Macmillan, 1975, 1980; vols. 3 and 4, Washington, D.C.: Catholic University of America Press, 1989, 1992.

O'Connor, Frank, ed. *A Book of Ireland*. London: William Collins, 1959.

O'Faolain, Sean. *The Irish*. New York: Devin-Adair, 1949.

O'Keefe, Daniel D. *The First Book of Irish Ballads*. Cork: Mercier Press, 1963.

O'Lochlainn, Colm. *Irish Street Ballads*. Dublin: Three Candles, 1952.

————. *Irish Folk Music and Song*. Dublin: Three Candles, 1952.

O'Riordáin, Seán P. *Antiquities of the Irish Countryside*. 3d ed. London: Methuen, 1953.

O'Sullivan, Donal. *Carolan: The Life and Times of an Irish Harper*. 2 vols. London: Routledge and Kegan Paul, 1958.

Pakenham, Thomas. *The Year of Liberty: The Great Irish Rebellion of 1798*. Rev. ed. London: Weidenfeld and Nicolson, 1997.

Pouchin Mould, D.D.C. *Ireland of the Saints*. London: B. T. Batsford, 1953.

Praeger, Robert Lloyd. *The Way That I Went*. Dublin: Allan & Figgis, 1980.

The Queen's Lancashire Regiment. *The Regimental Handbook*. Preston: 1997.

Quennell, Peter. *Samuel Johnson: His Friends and Enemies*. New York: American Heritage Press/McGraw-Hill, 1973.

Rice, H. J. *Thanks for the Memory*. Athlone: The Inland Waterways Association of Ireland, 1974.

Robinson, John Robert. *The Last Earls of Barrymore*. London: Sampson Low, Marston & Company, 1894.

The Royal Inniskilling Fusiliers Regimental Museum. *A History of the Royal Inniskilling Fusiliers*. Enniskillen, ca. 1990.

Russell, Diármuid, ed. *The Portable Irish Reader*. New York: Viking, 1946.

Smith, Daragh. *A Guide to Irish Mythology*. Dublin: Irish Academic Press, 2001.

Somerville-Large, Peter. *Irish Eccentrics*. London: Hamish Hamilton, 1975.

Sweetman, David. *The Medieval Castles of Ireland*. Cork: The Collins Press, 1999.

Thuillier, John. *History of Kinsale*. 4th ed. Kinsale: Brennan, 1994.

Tinniswood, Adrian. *County Fermanagh: Castle Coole, Florence Court, The Crom Estate*. London: The National Trust, 1998.

Welch, Robert. *The Oxford Companion to Irish Literature*. Oxford: Oxford University Press, 1996.

Wheeler, Henry, Dave Pollock, and Jane Fenlon. *Cahir Castle*. Edited by Conleth Manning and Aighleann O'Shaughnessy. Dublin: Dúchas, The Heritage Service, 1999.

Woodham-Smith, Cecil. *The Great Hunger*. London: Hamish Hamilton, 1962.

Yeats, W. B., ed. *Fairy & Folktales of Ireland*. New York: Macmillan, 1983.

Index

Page numbers in italics refer to illustrations.

ABOUT THE AUTHOR

ROBERT EMMETT GINNA studied the history of art at
Harvard after serving as a naval officer in the Second
World War. After a brief period as a museum curator, he
became an editor of four magazines, a contributor to
many others, and editor in chief of Little, Brown and
Company. Intermittently, he has been a writer, producer,
and director of films for television and a producer and
writer of theatrical feature films. Since 1988, he has taught
writing and film courses at Harvard. Over the years, he
has spent much time in Ireland and is a dual citizen of the
United States and Ireland.

ABOUT THE TYPE

This book is set in Fournier, a typeface named for Pierre Simon Fournier, the youngest son of a French printing family. He started out engraving woodblocks and large capitals, then moved on to fonts of type. In 1736 he began his own foundry and made several important contributions in the field of type design; he is said to have cut 147 alphabets of his own creation. Fournier is probably best remembered as the designer of St. Augustine Ordinaire, a face that served as the model for Monotype's Fournier, which was released in 1925.